GOVERNMENT BY COMMUNITY

I Margaret

Government by Community

IOAN BOWEN REES

with an introduction by
Professor Max Beloff

CHARLES KNIGHT & CO. LTD.
LONDON
1971

Charles Knight & Co. Ltd.
11/12 Bury Street, London EC3A 5AP
Dowgate Works, Douglas Road, Tonbridge

Copyright © 1971
Ioan Bowen Rees

First edition 1971

SBN 85314 083 9

Printed by BKT City Print Limited, London.
A member of the Brown Knight & Truscott Group.

Contents

List of Maps

Preface

IN ORDER to retain some topicality, this book has had to be written against the clock. Because of this, I have been unable to discuss what I was writing with colleagues and friends who are much more expert than I am in various fields. I apologise to them all for not having written a book more worthy of someone with access to their company. I also apologise to my wife and children for the prickliness which deadlines engender and for neglecting our pleasures as well as my chores. My wife has not even been able to exercise her privilege of censoring everything I write. The book has suffered as a result but at least I can (and do) lay it at her feet as all my own work.

My employers, the Pembrokeshire County Council, are in no way responsible for anything I have written. I must nevertheless say how grateful I am to them — and to my colleagues in their service — for the knowledge and experience which have come to me through them — and also for that political tolerance and good humour which generally prevail in Pembrokeshire.

One thing which has struck me in putting this book together is the high standard of that section of the Press which deals with government — not only in specialised journals like the *Local Government Chronicle, The Justice of the Peace and Local Government Review* and *Town and Country Planning,* but also in weeklies like *New Society, The Spectator* and the *New Statesman,* dailies like *Neue Zürcher Zeitung, The Times* and the *Western Mail,* and Welsh-language periodicals (operating to a different time scale) like the monthly review *Barn* and the weekly newspaper *Y Cymro.* However much one may quarrel with journalists — and every Welshman worth his salt quarrels with the *Western Mail* twice weekly — there is an astonishing amount of meat in their columns. I am grateful to the Editor of *Barn* for permission to reproduce the letter in Appendix 1 and to the authors of a letter to *The Times* for permission to reproduce the letter in Appendix 2. I am also grateful to the Royal Institute of Public Administration for permission to reproduce passages from my essay, Local Government in Switzerland (*Public Administration,* Winter 1969), in Chapters 6 and 7. One of the adjudicators who awarded the Institute's Haldane Medal to that essay was Professor Beloff and I cannot say how grateful I am to him for his encouragement and for consenting to contribute a professional introduction to an apprentice work. I must also thank Mr. H. W. Bailey-King O.B.E. of Charles Knight for venturing to invite me to write this book.

My gratitude to the Press — and to other less ephemeral sources — can to some extent be measured by the references at the end of each chapter. These are included, not to give an appearance of the definitive, but because it is particularly important for an author who lacks time and detachment to cite his authorities. I am, however, more concerned about a lack of passion in the following pages than about any lack of objectivity. Local government can only be rescued by people who believe in it to the point of being prepared to sacrifice, possibly professional reputation, probably party unity and certainly the quiet life.

IOAN BOWEN REES

Maenteilo,
Llandeilo Llwydarth,
Sir Benfro

Introduction

*by Max Beloff**

It is a pleasure as well as a privilege to introduce Mr. Bowen Rees' admirable book to what one must hope will be a wide and varied readership. The literature of local government is often worthy but rarely exciting; *Government by Community* is exciting not only because it directly challenges the very basis of the thought behind recent official reports and inquiries into the subject, but also because it brings to bear upon it an unusual combination of political philosophy and practical experience.

To find a product of the Oxford history school who has retained from it the ability to connect historical with political argument and the good sense to ask why we study political theory and in particular Tocqueville's *Democracy* and then fail to apply it to contemporary issues, is to have one's faith renewed; it leads one to ask why, if this kind of thing can be done in the County Offices of Pembrokeshire, those who have remained in academe so rarely contribute to our debates at this level. Perhaps the answer is that they have remained in academe; perhaps the answer is that those whose voices are heard have increasingly not been trained in the humanities but in the "social sciences".

For Mr. Bowen Rees' principal argument in these pages, which is that our problems in local and regional government will only be solved when we see them as part of a much wider problem, and that it is only by dismantling the overgrown and overblown machinery of Whitehall that we can renew the vigour of local communities and the pristine vigour and capacity for self-government of the British people, is only made

*Gladstone Professor of Government and Public Administration in the University of Oxford and Fellow of All Souls College.

possible because his approach is essentially humane rather than administrative or economic. It is not just a question of how to provide the best services most cheaply, but also of the consequences in human terms of doing this in one way rather than another. If it is done in the wrong way, the frustrations and antipathies created, the disaffection from the political system as a whole that may be engendered and the deterioration in human relationships that may result are all in the long run inimical to efficiency as well. Good government, central as well as local, depends as much on the calibre and attitudes of those who can be got to serve government and on the degree of understanding and involvement of the governed as it does upon any organisational blue-print.

The apathy towards local government manifested in the low polls in local elections is, argues Mr. Bowen Rees, not to be seen as something necessary and given, but as a consequence of increasing centralisation and of the lack of powers and of financial means in the organs of local government themselves. Furthermore, the spread of party politics into local government where the elected members simply voice the distant behests of central party machines, themselves maintained in power by an unjust electoral system, and their joint manipulation of the publicly-owned or controlled television and radio, also helps to make public-spirited people feel that to work in local government, particularly on the elected side, is bound to be frustrating. So we use apathy in the localities to justify further centralisation which itself creates further apathy or alternatively the unconstructive anger of extremist groups.

An argument along those lines which underlies both Mr. Bowen Rees' criticism of the fashionable nostrums of the Redcliffe-Maud and similar reports and his positive proposals can only be sustained by bringing together modes of thought and aspects of knowledge and experience that are not normally found in combination. As a local government official, Mr. Bowen Rees can demolish from inside knowledge and understanding of the relevant material many of the claims so confidently put out about the minimum requirements in size for a particular unit to be able to fulfil its alloted functions adequately, and to show that what passes for an efficiency test is often simply the subjective impressions of officials of central departments, themselves naturally biased in favour of the increased centralisation from which they derive their powers. The education service understandably provides Mr. Bowen Rees with a splendid example; since it is there above all that official estimates about efficiency are determined by "input" rather than "output", not by how well children are taught or motivated to further study, but by the quantities of equipment and above all of "experts" that particular authorities can deploy. Mr. Bowen Rees is, one would rather guess, a partisan on the whole of "comprehensive" schools; but this does not prevent him from pointing out that the attempt by the Department of Education and Science, itself in the grip of dogmatists of the comprehensive approach, and of its local satraps the Directors of Education to impose their will upon the responsible local authorities has been as bad for education as it is insulting to local democracy. Yet the outcry when a new Secretary of State seemed to be rather timidly putting back some responsibility onto the localities shows how deeply ingrained the preference for extreme centralisation has now become, particularly among the professional organisations like the National Union of Teachers whose pressure is all in favour of centralisation which gives their own national officers the maximum degree of bargaining power and public prestige.

But Mr. Bowen Rees goes further and asks whether the degree of central control, or even of control by the top tier of local government, is as necessary as is often taken for granted. Why have Directors of Education, etc., at all? Whatever one thinks of private education, no-one denies that there are many good independent schools which are subject to no external controls other than infrequent inspections. The reason why Mr. Bowen Rees can ask this kind of question and others of a similarly penetrating kind relating to the potentialities of relatively small communities is his deep knowledge of and sympathy with a country which is in respect of democratic practice at the other extreme from this one, namely, Switzerland.

Much nonsense is nowadays written about or taught under the label "comparative government"; students at Universities pervaded by the spirit of American "political science" are encouraged to classify and analyse and compare and contrast governments and governmental institutions of a wide variety of countries, none of which are known to them and for none of which (except possibly their own) they have any genuine feeling. The absurd formalism by which it is suggested that things can be compared without knowing them individually — as though beauty queens could be chosen by blindfolded wielders of tape-measures — has discredited comparative government in its true sense, which means the deepening of one's own understanding of the familiar by having something unfamiliar with which to contrast it. If the Swiss can do it, why can't we? There may be good reasons here or there why we can't; the important thing is to ask the question.

Once again, Mr. Bowen Rees is not just concerned with units of government and their size and powers; he can see that part of the richness and vitality of Swiss life and part of the abilities of the Swiss to do what we have lost the art of doing — something for oneself or one's neighbour without calling in Whitehall — is due to the unusual reliance on the locality rather than the centre, and within the locality on the elected rather than the appointed official, and ultimately, in the referendum, on the citizen himself. The variety and high quality of the Swiss newspaper press compared with our own ailing Fleet Street giants is good evidence of which Mr. Bowen Rees makes excellent use.

But it has not been necessary, though it has been useful and illuminating, for Mr. Bowen Rees to go outside these islands to find proof of the inadequacies of the current approach to local and regional government; his native Wales whose constituent units and whose problems bear no relation at all to what we find in the great English conurbations show how absurd it is to try to impose a uniformity of local government organisation over the entire United Kingdom. The fact that Mr. Bowen Rees is an obvious enthusiast for the Welsh language and culture will tend to make some people wary of his proposals for Wales itself; yet this element of nationalism in his thinking and the ability to bring in the national-cultural argument does not make him blind to other and more general-ised ideas. On the contrary, he can see all the more clearly what would be left to argue for in the English "provinces", even where the linguistic-cultural argument did not apply, and the degree to which there also, localism might be a revivifying influence.

Nor need localism mean parochialism in the pejorative sense of that term; on the contrary, what divides men most in our society into small and mutually suspicious and hostile group-ings is not the parochialism of geographical locality but the parochialism of the various professional specialisms, the organisations that sustain them and the Whitehall departments whose arrangements at headquarters and in the field help to sustain them in all their exclusiveness.

Mr. Bowen Rees seems to take it for granted that Britain is going to "enter Europe"; whether he is right or not may be more evident when this book sees the light of day. But he is a good enough European to see that Europe can only be con-structed in a way that keeps European civilisation alive if there is federalism in the form of greater devolution, as well as of the delegation of powers to a new centre. Indeed it is notable that centrifugal forces in Europe have become more evident *pari passu* with the growth of the new European institutions. And given the pattern which they are likely to follow, he is surely right in saying that it is not the United Kingdom as such that should become a member of the EEC but England, Scotland and Wales (and perhaps Northern Ireland) in their own right.

Britain at the moment is divided in many different ways; one of the principal divisions is between those who think that everything is so well-run that there is no need to do anything but apply more of the same well-tried recipes, or to appoint trusted members of the Establishment to give the same reassuring answers to any conceivable doubts, and those, especially among the young, who feel everything is so appalling that the only solutions are to end the "system" by violence or to contract out of it altogether by one of the now familiar escape mechanisms. Hopeless complacency on the one hand and complacent hopelessness on the other . . . what a prospect!

Mr. Bowen Rees falls into neither category. He is well aware that we are not, as is usually thought, well-governed, but on the contrary very badly governed for the best of good reasons. How otherwise could a body of men like the Roskill Commission think that the way to meet the volume of air-traffic caused by a wish to come to this country should be met by destroying precisely the things that still attract people to it; its natural and historic heritage? How could a country which is well-informed about the increasing world-pressure of population upon food-supplies sacrifice acres and acres of good agricultural land — irreplaceable when lost — to concrete runways; or a country where housing is one of the gravest of social problems destroy homes and their amenities because of its inability to think of a better solution to traffic congestion than tearing up cities for motor-way boxes.

We will certainly not improve matters by concentrating power at the centre, or endowing central departments with more planning and research units; we shall only be giving more power to the kind of mechanistic thinking that is responsible for all these nonsenses. Mr. Bowen Rees suggests another way — to give back to the communities the power to regulate their own lives and to make the best of their own resources, to get planning back onto a scale which citizens can understand. It may be utopian; the passion for central-isation may have gone too far. One cannot tell. But Mr. Bowen Rees' book should be compulsory reading for all those entering upon a career in either central or local government; it is likely to do them more good than all the economic textbooks and manuals of management they are ever likely to see.

1. A Rare and Fragile Thing

"La liberté est une chose rare et fragile ... Une société très civilisée ne tolère qu'avec peine les essais de la liberté communale; elle se révolte à la vue de ses nombreux écarts, et désespère du succès avant d'avoir atteint le résultat final de l'expérience. Parmi toutes les libertés, celle des communes, qui s'établit si difficilement, est aussi la plus exposée aux invasions du pouvoir."

ALEXIS DE TOCQUEVILLE

("Liberty is a rare and fragile thing ... A very civilised society finds it hard to tolerate attempts at freedom in a local community; it is disgusted by its numerous blunders and is apt to despair of success before the experiment is finished. Of all forms of liberty, that of a local community, which is so hard to establish, is the most prone to the encroachments of authority.")

Trans. *George Lawrence*

"THE personalities of Leeds public life," wrote Beatrice Webb of her first investigating tour into local government, "are neither interesting or attractive. Leeds and its inhabitants strike me as equally unlovely ... The saving grace, which has kept Leeds municipal government free from the grosser forms of corruption, has been the childish vanity which makes the ordinary Leeds shopkeeper desire to hear himself called 'Alderman', still more 'my Lord Mayor.'"[1] Manchester was little better: "hard-heeled shopkeepers divided in their mind between their desire to keep the rates down and their ambition to magnify the importance of Manchester as against other cities."[2] This is the image of local government which has stuck — and it does not help to read of a more enthusiastic episode recorded in Mrs. Webb's diary, 'We have had a happy and successful time here writing the chapters on the Commissioners of Sewers".[3] To an Englishman, local government is sewers and drains, cliques and caucuses, haughtiness with a

1

dropped h. Yet one of the greatest political thinkers of Europe could write in his study of democracy in America, "C'est dans la commune que réside la force des peuples libres."[4] Is it not our trouble in the United Kingdom that we have been conditioned to looking at local government – and practically every other facet of society – from the top down?

Actually, there are two fundamentally different ways of looking at local government, from the top down and from the bottom up. Those who look from the top down consider that the whole authority of the state is concentrated at the centre. To them, the centre is the only legitimate source of power: it is from the central government that local authorities receive their powers: indeed the central government actually creates the local authorities, dividing up the state into more or less uniform divisions in the process. The central government does this for the more efficient and economic provision of its services. It involves the leading citizens of every locality in the business of government, not so much in order to hear their views, as in order to embrace them and make them identify themselves with the system. This school of thought might be called the classical school of local government. It is more interested in efficiency than in democracy, in uniform standards than in local responsibility; it regards the citizen more as consumer of services than participant in government. even at its best, it is apt to be patronising.

The opposite is true of the other school, the romantic school, as it might be called or, in some countries, the historical school. This school sees the state itself as a conglomeration of localities, each of which has, it is true, surrendered much of its authority to the centre, but each of which retains some authority in its own right as well as a basic identity of its very own. The romantic school places the emphasis on local authorities as nurseries of democratic citizenship, revels in diversity and local initiative, is impatient of central control and wishes to involve the citizen in government, not so much to bring him into contact with the state as to foster his self-reliance.

Of course, in practice, the situation is much more complicated than this, with elements from each school combined in varying proportions in the same system, even in the same thinker, and with the emphasis changing from era to era. The fact that so many of us look "down" from the centre and "up" from the localities, suggests that it is the centralist school which predominates in most countries today. In the United Kingdom, certainly, the philosophy of this school has predominated since 1832 at least: according to the Report of the Royal Commission on Local Government in Scotland, "the national considerations must shape the local, not the other way around".[5] The other school has nevertheless made itself felt at times. There is an interesting example in a speech made by the Liberal Chief Whip soon after the passing of the Local Government Act, 1894, the Act which created urban district, rural district and parish councils. "What are the advantages for which we look in the extension of local government?" he asked himself, and went on: "First comes the value of the communal and civic training . . . parish and town meetings are to liberty what primary schools are to science. Secondly, it enables the people to secure and maintain their hold on the land . . . Thirdly, it supplies the means for all the members of a community to discuss the affairs of their parish or their town . . . and for giving effect to their deliberately expressed wish or resolution"[6] — *their* wish, be it noted. That Chief Whip was Tom Ellis, the golden boy of the nationalistic Welsh Liberals of his period. In Wales, "encouraged by the ambitious dreams of (the same) T. E. Ellis," the early councils thought of themselves as miniature local Westminsters and debated such national issues as leasehold reform, Sunday closing and sweated labour.[7] Ellis died prematurely in 1899, however: the pressure of local issues and central directives soon brought the Welsh county councils to heel and by 1963 a highly conventional Local Government Commission for Wales could write, without any feeling of impropriety, "the wishes of the inhabitants are, we repeat, important. The *paramount* consideration is their well-being."[8] Even in the field of local government, the centre knows best what is good for us locals.

Most of the pressure for larger units of local government which is now so strong has come from the centralist school. The pressure has been building up since the '30s and '40s at least. It probably began with the publication of W. A. Robson's *The Development of Local Government* in 1931, and it became general with the issue of the second, enlarged, edition of that work in 1948. Robson's is one of the very few readable books ever written about local government, and he is capable of such sentences as "All too often the rural and urban district councils, stamped by their very names with the frigid welcome which attended their birth, have remained the stunted, misshapen and impotent creatures their progenitors conceived".[9] Robson's fervour and originality, his fundamental belief in local government, his plain speaking, were refreshing indeed at a time when local government was rapidly losing to the centre such functions as trunk roads, hospitals, public assistance, gas and electricity, when the Labour Party seemed to be turning its back on the municipal socialism of the Webbs as well as upon the Welsh and Scottish nationalism of its pioneers and upon the regionalism of G. D. H. Cole, and when, in the conurbations, many of the boundaries imposed in 1894, often quite arbitrarily, were already being obliterated by the spread of bricks and mortar and by daily tides of commuters.

Paradoxically, Robson is far from being a classicist pure and simple. One of his main themes was the need to create municipal units large enough to withstand any further loss of function and to regain lost ground. When the Town Clerk of Eastbourne explained to the Onslow Commission that he looked upon towns as "commercial concerns", Robson could attack this "low commercial outlook" as unlikely "to prove a source of inspiration for the building of a great city."[10]

As happens so often, the muscular challenge and "highly controversial" ideas of this "courageous" pioneer soon became ossified in the hands of disciples in search of a neat solution. Hundreds of lesser men have followed Robson in advocating what he called "Plimsoll lines in local government," i.e. a minimum population for a particular function (and H. G. Wells had lectured on "the need for some scientific adjustment of units of administration to functions or services" and suggested "some ideal areas for all purposes based on the function of locomotion" as early as 1903).[11] Few have given the same weight to Robson's observation (in the very chapter in which he deals with Plimsoll lines) that "it does not require very much insight to appreciate the inadequacy of arithmetic as a criterion of fitness to receive independent status," that "in the present state of knowledge, quantitative factors, although relevant and helpful, are by no means conclusive". "If we cannot create . . . a civic community at will, neither," according to Robson, "can we destroy it: at any rate not without producing disastrous conflict and causing irreparable loss to the body politic. We cannot always erase municipal frontiers merely because they appear arbitrary on the map . . . social tissue may have grown up within these illogical administrative divisions . . ."[12]

Still, it was Robson who popularised the Webbs' Denunciation of "the confusion and inefficiency, the waste and overlapping extravagance, which necessarily result from the present imperfect machinery," showed up the financial weakness of small districts and argued that local government should follow the general commercial trend towards large units. The germ of much that appears in the reports of the Royal Commissions on Local Government in England and in Scotland and also in the Welsh Office White Paper, *Local Government in Wales,* (which should be read together with the Local Government Commission for Wales Report of 1963) can be found in his work.

At present there are, outside London, 78 County Boroughs in England, 4 County Boroughs in Wales and 4 Cities in Scotland. These are responsible for the whole range of local government functions. Outside them, in the Counties, (45 in England, 13 in Wales and 31 in Scotland) the functions are divided. In England and Wales, the County Councils are primarily responsible for education below University level, for most highways apart from the trunk roads taken over by the Government, for those health services like maternity clinics, district nursing and immunisation which belong neither to the hospitals nor to the general practitioner, for the welfare of the elderly, the handicapped, deprived children and families at risk, for town and country planning, for the fire service, for protecting consumers from short measure, false description and impure food and for the more important libraries and museums. This leaves the ordinary (non-county) Boroughs, the Urban Districts and the Rural Districts, (1086 in England and 164 in Wales) with little of substance to administer in their own right apart from providing council houses and community centres, ensuring that all houses – and, indeed, the streets and the environment generally – are fit to live in, refuse collection and sewerage: they also collect the rates for all levels of county government. Their remaining functions can be drawn out into an impressive list in a text book but do not amount to very much in the way of expenditure or of democratic interest: more important by far are the functions which some of the larger Boroughs and Districts have delegated to them by the Counties – the Borough of Rhondda, for example, has its own education and health services and some freedom of action within the limits of county policy. The 31 Scottish Counties include 21 Large Burghs, which are independent of their County Councils apart from education, and 176 Small Burghs, which correspond to Urban Districts: there is no Scottish equivalent of the Rural District Council. Scottish District Councils, like the 7,500 or so English and Welsh Parish Councils and Meetings, are permitted few functions apart from providing parks, village halls, bus shelters and the like, although some develop into authorities of substance and forums of influence. In London, functions are shared between the Greater London Council, which has overall control of planning and traffic and 32 Boroughs plus the City of London, which deal with the more personal services themselves and share the remainder with the G.L.C. in a rather complicated system. All over the United Kingdom, police, water supply and some other functions are becoming the responsibility of joint authorities over which there is, in practice, little local control.

Map 1. Redcliffe-Maud's Division of England

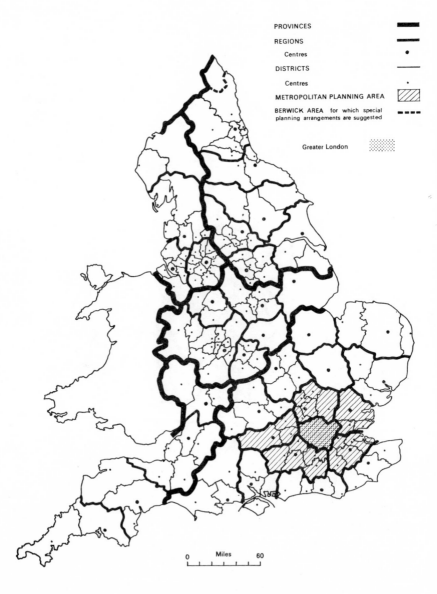

PROVINCES
REGIONS
　Centres
DISTRICTS
　Centres
METROPOLITAN PLANNING AREA
BERWICK AREA for which special
planning arrangements are suggested

Greater London

0　Miles　60

Map 2.　Derek Senior's Division of England

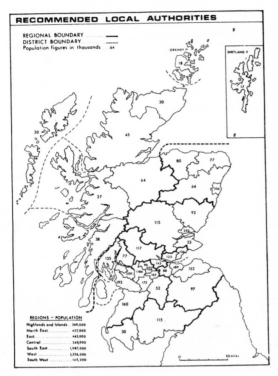

RECOMMENDED LOCAL AUTHORITIES

REGIONAL BOUNDARY
DISTRICT BOUNDARY
Population figures in thousands ... 64

REGIONS – POPULATION
Highlands and Islands . 369,000
North East 427,000
East 443,000
Central 260,000
South East 1,087,000
West 2,536,000
South West 145,000

Map 3. Wheatley's Division of Scotland

In England, Scotland and Wales there are now 1,620 Local Authorities excluding Parishes and Scottish Districts. The English Royal Commission proposed that England outside London should be divided into 61 areas, 58 of them administered by a Unitary Authority with the whole range of functions, 3 of them to be administered by a Metropolitan Authority roughly similar to the G.L.C. with district authorities (20 in all) responsible for education, the social services and housing. (The Labour Government accepted the case for Unitary Authorities where possible but proposed another two Metropolitan Areas.) The Scottish Royal Commission proposed to divide Scotland into 7 regions and 37 districts, with the regional authorities responsible for most services, including even the building, if not the improvement, of houses, but the districts administering development control and design planning. The Welsh Office White Papers on Local Government proposed three Unitary Authorities in South-East Wales and 4 Counties divided into districts in the remainder of the country. If the Royal Commissions and the Civil Service have their way, therefore, the number of local authorities is likely to be reduced from 1,620 to about 160. The Labour Government certainly did not intend to create many more and though the Conservatives favour a two-tier system for England as well as for Wales and Scotland, they too seem likely to reduce the number to about 270 — this is the number advocated by Derek Senior who, in the minority report of the English Commission, advocated 35 regions and 148 districts. Proposals so drastic suggest a national emergency rather than the adaptation of the existing system to take account of social and economic change.

There is much to admire in the Royal Commission Reports, Redcliffe-Maud's four red volumes on England, Wheatley's two blue volumes on Scotland, and a Welshman should be jealous that we have had nothing comparable for Wales. To be able to handle these attractively produced and comprehensive volumes, on so despised a subject as his, must have softened the heart of many a local government officer. To realise that volumes written so well, with such unity and sometimes with a fine turn of phrase, were produced by committees faced with a strict time schedule, is to feel very humble; and it is not for nothing that the Chairman of the English Commission is known not only as an eminent scholar and former permanent secretary at the Ministry of Education but as a defender of local government (against Beveridge's wish to abolish it) and brilliant after-dinner speaker. After four or five decades of softening up and two of uncertainty, cringing under swords held by commissions which appeared Damocletian enough at the time, no wonder that many local government men feel that the small unit and the historic county can now be surrendered with honour.

In spite of all this, Royal Commissions do not have a reputation for finality. Traditionally, all they produce is, in Lytton Strachey's phrase, "a very fat Blue Book on a very high shelf." "A list of committees and royal commissions whose work lies mouldering in Whitehall files would," says Professor Chapman, "present a daunting balance of wasted time and public money,"[13] though that seasoned commissioner Lady Wootton takes a somewhat less cynical line about the results of Commissions, this is hardly surprising if, "normally the majority of a commission will be chosen from persons likely to produce conclusions acceptable to the appointing government or at least to the contemporary Establishment, while an appearance of impartiality is preserved by the inclusion of a minority of persons ... who are likely to hold heterodox opinions."[14] The tenor of J. P. Mackintosh's remarks on the English Commission is indeed that it was packed in favour of the city region solution by a Minister who, as Member of Parliament for Coventry, was impressed by the vigour of Coventry City Council and because Whitehall already favoured this solution. "It is possible," says Mackintosh, "that later when (Mr. Crossman's) receptive mind grasped the significance of Scottish and Welsh nationalism and when he realised the difficulties the regional planning councils were encountering, he might have wanted to unpack the Royal Commission and repack it with those who were more impressed with the case for larger regional units, but by then the Commission had started work".[15] So much for the sanctity and authority of Royal Commissions!

As Mackintosh points out, there was a third factor which tended to produce a City Region Royal Commission: the fact that the terms of reference of the Commission led them to concentrate their attention on examining the best way of reforming the *existing* functions of local government. This must have diverted the Commissions away from the type of regionalism advocated by Mackintosh, the type of regionalism which sees the United Kingdom in terms of about a dozen large provinces. This type of regionalism would in itself tend to lead to a different type of local government structure from that advocated by the Royal Commissions, not necessarily the same one within each region. And, regionalism apart, once the local government functions and financial system to which we are accustomed are in the melting pot, once central government itself is in the melting pot, the whole problem changes. That is one important reason why the Royal Commissions should not be allowed to have their own way. There are other reasons even within their own terms of reference, there is room to question the extent to which they relied so much upon subjective evidence from the civil service, paid so little attention to the much smaller scale of local government on the Continent and in America and gave so little weight to the mounting evidence that people feel cut off from society as a whole, let alone from participation in government. Fundamentally, however, a local government man should quarrel with the Commissions because of their assumption that local government is something to be organised from the top down, never from the bottom up, that communities exist only by courtesy of the centre. If there were eminent practitioners and champions of local government in their midst, spiritually they appear to have been no more free to challenge this assumption than a Dubcek or a Husak is free to challenge the overlordship of the Soviet Union. There was never any question of the reorganisation of local government being effected by the central government and the local authorities in partnership. As Professor J. A. G. Griffith puts it, "the two sides are not equal . . . any discussion of the relationship must assume that the Government will reject any reform which makes more difficult the execution of the Government's policies."[16] Indeed, local government has, for so long, consciously or unconsciously, regarded itself as an extension of central government that one doubts whether such a partnership was possible. Not a few chief officers of local authorities regard themselves primarily as agents of a central department, or agents at least of that general enlightenment represented, to them, by the central establishment: some find the greatest satisfaction in thwarting the untutored wishes of their nominal masters and in censoring their correspondence; some committee chairmen are little more than, at best, public relations officers or, at worst, ventriloquist's dolls, to such officers. As for the members themselves, wherever party politics hold sway, for all their outward municipal importance, their tendency is to subordinate local interests to those of a centrally orientated party. Not even the local authority associations have had the imagination to set up shop outside London preoccupied until recently with fighting one another in the name of unitary or two-tiered government, rather than with the question of keeping government local, even the valuable side of their work, their continuous dialogue with the ministries, inclines them to think in terms of "the country as a whole" and of that nebulous abstraction "the national interest". There do remain hundreds of members and officers who believe Pembrokeshire, say, to be capable of thinking today what Cardiff or London will think tomorrow but most local government leaders are essentially managers rather than policy makers; they feel themselves weakest where the civil service is strongest. Experienced in winning arguments but losing verdicts against the centre, they prefer to fight about the details of a policy or about its implementation rather than about the fundamental principles at stake.

If there is anything basically wrong with Redcliffe-Maud and with Wheatley, and let us concede that there is much that is plausible, practicable and even admirable about their reports, it is the way in which they always look from the top down. It is implicit in these reports that the technological revolution cannot "go on revolving and yielding optimum statistics if its wheels are clogged with idealism," to quote some ironic remarks of Thomas Jones, C.H., the political diarist and former Deputy Secretary of the Cabinet, about the closing of pits during the Depression — "two hundred mining disasters the villagers call the process, taking the short parochial view".[17] Here then is the "short parochial view" of a local government officer brought up in the least populous county but one in Wales, one who could not if he tried "write in the guise of an Englishman."[18] If what he writes does less than justice to the English conurbations or even to some parts of

Wales, it will scarcely redress the balance of published opinion in favour of more rural areas — and if it did, there are a thousand academics and civil servants to put him in his place. In any case, is not the universal present in my parish as well as in your town? But the reader need have no fear that the author entertains illusions about the depths to which discussion can plummet in a parish or the lengths to which democrats can carry intrigue. One of his earliest memories is of his mother,[19] a far from demonstrative person, returning almost in tears from meetings of an urban district council which kept rejecting as extravagant, her proposals for introducing council housing, for a community centre, for street names in Welsh — the language spoken upon those streets — even for a covered refuse lorry. During a quarter of a century's service, my mother was never fully reconciled to the cussedness which can be encountered in local government — and never accepted that academics and professional men and chief officers are at times at least as peevish as, at times, councillors and electors. But she also encountered good humour and kindness and good sense in local government. Local government is human — this is its great virtue — and humans must accept the chaff with the wheat. And as it happens, long before her term of office came to an end, my mother's first aims had all been achieved and had been achieved, not by direction from above, but by local persistence.

Notes to Chapter One

1. Barbara Drake and Margaret I. Cole (Ed.), Beatrice Webb, *Our Partnership*, London, 1948, p.157.
2. *Ibid.* p.162.
3. *Ibid.* p.172.
4. 'The strength of free peoples resides in the local community', J. P. Mayer and Max Lerner (Ed.), Alexis de Tocqueville, *Democracy in America I*, Fontana, 1966, p.74.
5. Royal Commission on Local Government in Scotland 1966-69, Report, H.M.S.O., 1969, para.243.
6. Thomas E. Ellis, *Speeches and Addresses*, Wrexham, 1912, pp.167-70.
7. A. H. Dodd, *A History of Caernarvonshire 1284-1900*, Caernarvonshire Historical Society, 1968, p.412.
8. Local Government Commission for Wales, Report and Proposals, H.M.S.O. 1963, para.30.
9. William A. Robson, *The Development of Local Government*, 2nd ed. 1948, p.228.

10. Robson, p.231.
11. Reported by Beatrice Webb, *Our Partnership*, p.175.
12. Robson, p.229.
13. Brian Chapman, *British Government Observed, Some European Reflections,* London, 1963, p.32.
14. *In a World I Never Made,* London, 1967, p.256.
15. *The Devolution of Power,* London, 1968, p.53.
16. *Central Departments and Local Authorities,* London, 1966, p.506.
17. "What's Wrong With South Wales?" (1935) collected in *Leeks and Daffodils,* Newtown, 1952, pp.100 and 105.
18. The phrase is Conor Cruse O'Brien's about his countryman Burke.
19. No contribution to Anglo-Welsh literature is complete without a mother. See Gwyn Thomas's play *The Keep,* the anti-hero of which is a Deputy Town Clerk.

2. The Will o' the Wisp of Size

"The efficient size is . . . a will o' the wisp"
THE RT. HON. R. H. S. CROSSMAN

ACCORDING to their terms of reference, both Royal Commissions on Local Government were required to have regard to two factors in considering "the structure of Local Government . . . (in England, outside Greater London, and in Scotland, respectively) in relation to its existing functions." The first was "the size and character of areas in which these (functions) can be most effectively exercised"; the second was "the need to sustain a viable system of local democracy,"[1] In spite of some professions to the contrary, each Commission placed much the greater emphasis on the effective exercise of functions. They always appeared to be searching for a minimum size for efficiency rather than a maximum size for democracy. Indeed the Scottish Commission stated quite bluntly, "local government . . . exists to supply public services. If it does this well it justifies its existence: if badly, its raison d'être is at once in doubt. Those who in the evidence have placed self-expression, self-determination and other virtues on a higher plane than effectiveness, and possibly in opposition to it, are failing in our judgement to take a realistic view of the place and purpose of local government within society";[2] and again, "effectiveness is the key concept in local government. It is with a view to greater effectiveness that local government should be made more powerful. And local democracy and local involvement should be sought less as ends in themselves than as the means of achieving effective services".[3]

17

In the climate of thought which prevails in the United Kingdom, such remarks should surprise nobody. Neither is it surprising that each Royal Commission should have recommended much larger units of government in order to attain efficiency. Almost unanimously, the ministries had pleaded for 30 to 40 first tier or all-purpose authorities in England. Their evidence abounds with such phrases as "below somewhere round about the 200,000 mark we do begin to run into difficulties"[4] and "half-a-million is a good round figure".[5]

Little challenge came to the civil service conception of the minimum from the Local Authority Associations. Even on behalf of the second tier, the Associations of Rural District and of Urban District councils were reluctant to defend areas with fewer than, respectively, 30,000[6] and 20,000 people.[7] It was left to the Parish Councils Association, through Professor Keith-Lucas, to defend a town of 12,000 to 15,000 people as "a unit strong enough and big enough to carry substantially more functions (than a parish)",[8] to individual authorities to stress the importance of democratic control and civic identity.

Even in the sparsely populated areas of Wales and of Scotland, where amalgamation brings serious problems of communication and yet leaves activities dispersed, and where there is no population explosion to blow away the significance of county boundaries, the doctrine of the minimum is still the canon.[9] Wales was outside the jurisdiction of the Royal Commissions, but the Welsh Office proposed in 1966 to reduce the number of counties in Wales from 13 to 5 (average population 426,000 as opposed to 159,000) and the number of districts from 164 to 36 (59,119 as opposed to 13,101).[10]

Yet the Minister who had appointed the English Commission — no less a figure than Richard Crossman — had, in addressing the County Councils Association in 1965, expressed doubt about "the view of those who think there is a solution to be found in equalisation of numbers, and argue that the way to solve this problem is to lay down a number — 100,000, 150,000, 155,000 or 220,000 — and keep to it . . . the efficient size is . . . a will of the wisp".[11] And though the Redcliffe-

Maud Commission did conclude that a minimum population was necessary and that the evidence pointed to a minimum of 250,000,[12] almost in spite of themselves both Royal Commissions, not to mention Derek Senior in his dissenting report, came very much nearer to vindicating Mr. Crossman than one might realise from reading their conclusions alone.

The English Commission stress that determining the necessary minimum is "a question of great difficulty".[13] The general impression they gained even from the Greater London Group study of the South-East (which suggested that education, health and social service functions could be effectively performed with a minimum of 200,000) was "the difficulty of establishing a demonstrable relationship between size and performance."[14] Again, on their own admission "the overriding impression which emerges" from three specially commissioned investigations into the relationship of size and performance, as well as from the Commission's own study of the staffing of local government is that "size cannot statistically be proved to have a very important effect on performance".[15] Neither was much help forthcoming from commissioned studies of London* and of Birmingham.[16] Obviously an authority like Birmingham can appoint an exceptionally wide range of specialists to its own staff and provide numerous specialised institutions within its own boundaries, but Birmingham also has problems of flexibility and co-ordination, to say nothing of problems on an exceptionally large scale. G. W. Howell made such a reputation as Town Clerk of Wolverhampton that, after ten years in the position, he gained the Town Clerkship of Manchester: at Wolverhampton, administering a population of about 130,000, he was able to run the corporation as a whole; at Manchester, on his own admission, he was unable to keep all departments under control.[17] Management techniques have developed since Howell's time but it was not altogether surprising to learn this year that the senior officers principally concerned with research in three major departments of an

---

* The Central Housing Advisory Committee Report on town development states that regional authorities "with the resources of the Greater London Council" are required. But what region's resources can possible rival London's?

authority with a population of one million, met recently for the first time at an external course. Authorities big and small have their advantages and their drawbacks: no conceivable authority could rival Greater London, not only in resources but in problems. Computers are indispensable in a large unit but are not always a satisfactory substitute for natural vision and for what Leopold Kohr describes as "the general operational translucency of a small scale".[18] One suspects that it is better to be a deprived child in a sparsely populated Mid-Wales County with one unqualified Child Care Officer, than in a teeming London Borough with 31 highly specialised ones.

By the time they reach paragraph 218 of their report, the Commission can speak of the absence of a statistical relationship between size and performance as "a general finding", concede that this finding became apparent in an appraisal made of comparable studies undertaken earlier in this country and the United States and go on, "our examination of various studies of the effect of scale on efficiency in particular manufacturing industries in Britain and the United States also suggested that the bearing of scale on performance was hard to demonstrate statistically".[19]

One study which the Commission may have had in mind is that of Harvey Shapiro, who, in an exercise entitled Economics of Scale and Local Government Finance, compared the 1957 per capita expenditure of the counties of 48 states of the United States of America.[20] In ten of the states, the highest expenditure per head occurred in counties with a population of over 250,000, while in no state did counties of this size have the lowest expenditure. In the population range 50,000 – 100,000, the position was reversed, with fifteen states having the lowest expenditure in that range and none the highest. It was only when one reached the ranges with less than 10,000 and, very markedly, less than 5,000 people that the trend went against the smaller unit.

The next two paragraphs of the English report speak of the great problems of relating size to performance and of finding a satisfactory measure of performance, though the Commission never go so far as to make the obvious point that what is efficiency to a county treasurer often appears Scrooge-like to a children's officer, that what is a minimum acceptable standard to a director of education sometimes seems to be gross extravagance in the eyes of his ratepayers. After the failure of their objective studies to establish that efficiency increases with performance, one might reasonably have expected the Commission to treat the two remaining reports on size and performance with great circumspection. On the contrary, the whole edifice of their thought on minimum population rests on these reports, two studies by central departments which the Commission state were "particularly helpful since they enabled (them) to *supplement* what were essentially statistical exercises with the subjective impressions of those who have direct *disinterested* knowledge of the quality of local authority performance in two major services"[21] (education and children). The words "supplement" and "disinterested" are hardly justified in this context. Far from supplementing the statistical exercises, these subjective reports contradict them. The objective research published by the Commission failed to establish that size has an important effect on performance: the subjective studies purport to show that it has — and they are put forward by possibly the least disinterested bodies in the whole discussion, two departments of a service which, well in advance of the studies, was already convinced of the superiority of large authorities. Could anyone have failed to predict, give or take a few thousands, that the studies would show that the least efficient education and children's authorities tended to have populations below the 200,000 mark? By now, one of the most sinister aspects of such studies by government departments and the like is the facility with which they can produce an air of great authority by quoting from one another and referring to a general drift of evidence (when what they mean is a general drift of opinion) in what is virtually the same service or at least the same milieu.[22] In considering no less than 48 government reports relevant to local government, all but one published between 1956 and 1968, the Royal Commissions' research staff themselves found that "the general drift of the recommendations of most reports has been towards larger units of administration".[23] The lowest minimum which accords with the general drift is the 30,000 recommended by the Bourdillon Committee on libraries. At the other extreme are the ad hoc redevelopment agencies on an urban-regional scale suggested by Buchanan. Such reports tell us more, perhaps, about the respective values, interests and propensities for co-operation of librarians, engineers and other professional groups than about the right local government structure for democratic communities concerned with life as a whole.

The Department of Education and Science *Enquiry Into Efficiency of Local Education Authorities,* sub-titled *Report on Returns submitted by H. M. Inspectorate,* is included in Appendix II of Volume III of the English report. Fundamentally it consists of a table in which the English education authorities within various population ranges, are graded, on an overall assessment, "very good", "good", "acceptable", "slightly below acceptable", or "weak", and further tables showing the scores attained by grading them under the sixteen headings below and weighting these scores in accordance with the figures in the right-hand column:—

1.	Adequacy of senior administrative staff	
	(a) Number	7
	(b) Quality	9
2.	Adequacy of specialist advisory staff	
	(a) Range	6
	(b) Quality	8
3.	Encouragement of modern educational methods	6
4.	Willingness to experiment	7
5.	Arrangements for in-service training of teachers	8
6.	Staffing policies	7
7.	Relations with other authorities	
	(a) "Free trade" in pupils and students	3
	(b) Consultation over common problems	4
8.	Relations with the public	
	(a) Sympathetic handling of complaints	5
	(b) Efforts to explain policies	5
9.	Efficiency in regard to educational building	7

10.	Expenditure on books and equipment	8
11.	Arrangements for assistance to pupils and discretionary awards to students	5
12.	Arrangements for the appointment of managing and governing bodies and their effectiveness	5

Overall grading for the authority   Total   100

It will be noted that quality of teaching, examination results, university and college places secured and adequacy in the eyes of parents and employers do not feature in this list: as it happens, it is the smallest counties of Wales which top the league for university places gained per head of school population,[24] not, one suspects, because of any exceptional merit on the part of the local administrators but because of the traditional values of the local people, and their facility in two languages from an early age.[25] Is it conceivable that the schools of, say, rural Norfolk will, in the foreseeable future, be able to compete with those of Cardiganshire in educational output, however distinguished a Director of Education Norfolk may have in Dr. Ralphs, however advanced the Hunstanton Secondary School may be in design and however many advisers and headquarters staff Norfolk, with a population of 440,000 may be able to employ? Even amongst units of the same size there is little correlation between forms of administration and good schools.[26] In both the United States and in Switzerland, educational units are small and educational administration extremely decentralised. In the United States, however, the schools tend to be progressive in the sense of "encouraging modern educational methods", while in many Swiss cantons they tend to be conservative. Almost any type of education is possible under almost any size or type of administration. Again, a system which is "progressive" in the sense of promoting parental influence is likely, for that very reason, to be "conservative" in its methods and its curriculum, like the Protestant schools of the Netherlands.[27] In the long run, it may be safer even for the "progressive" educationalist to

put the education of parents (as school managers and councillors in dozens of small units) before the education of the
children so as to avoid the backlash which the rule of saints
so often provokes. This is a question of basic political philosophy, however, not of educational expertise. Educationalists
rightly have an immense opportunity to influence local government schools through the universities, the training colleges,
the educational journals and bodies like the Schools Council.
Their opinion on the general structure of local government
deserves no special priority: this is a bigger question altogether.
Today, the educationalist may be able to identify central
government with professional freedom. Tomorrow, the profession and the Department may be at loggerheads, while the
leaders of the profession itself may become as fossilised as
the B.M.A. or the Law Society appear to be to the younger
professions today.

It is typical of the subordination of politics to administration in contemporary official thought that no allowance is
made in the Department of Education's gradings for deliberate,
legitimate political decisions not to comply with the Department's standards — for example, a decision to employ fewer
specialist advisers than the Department advocates, so as to be
able to spend the money on road improvements for the sake
of attracting industry and providing employment for school
leavers. Is it not probable too that many of the differences in
marking between good and weak authorities concern the
trimmings of a good educational system rather than its substance, the jam rather than the bread and butter?

One of the few concrete points that the Local Government
Commission for Wales could have made against the council of
one of the smaller Welsh counties was their failure to provide
a drama organiser. The Commission did not mention — if they
knew — that the presence of a number of gifted amateurs in
the county had produced a level of dramatic activity both in
the schools and in the community which probably surpassed
that of another county which employed an organiser. This is
not to say that the appointment of organisers to promote
drama as a general medium of teaching is not desirable. But

even the presence of the admirable Midlands Arts Centre for Young People at Cannon Hill, Birmingham, is related not only to what Birmingham can afford but to what Birmingham needs: a survey had revealed that the vast majority of children in the area had never attended a live dramatic or musical performance of any kind, something which is hardly credible in rural Wales, in most areas of which, for better or for worse, almost every child competes at, let alone attends, the local eliminating round of the youth National Eisteddfod organised by Urdd Gobaith Cymru, a grant-aided but voluntary body.[28]

All this is not to say, of course, that the subjective impressions of experienced men should not be given some weight in an investigation: there is very little else to go on in the comparison of local authority performance. Neither can it be denied that there is much ability, experience and idealism amongst Her Majesty's Inspectors of Schools, though there are authorities which have seen painstaking objective estimates of the increase of school population disregarded as the result of a subjective whim on the part of an inspector. To place great weight upon a study based solely upon the opinion of men of much the same background, belonging to the same hierarchical service, a service which has long cherished the ideal of the big unit and the unified service, is nevertheless astonishing. We shall probably never know exactly how the department set about their study, or how much conscious collusion may lie behind it: we do know that each Inspector's report was submitted to the department through one of nine divisional inspectors and that the overall assessment of all authorities was considered by the Chief Inspector who organised the survey and who found that there was "good comparability between regions in the allocation of grades".[29] And even if we discount collusion, conscious and unconscious, we shall never know how much variation there may have been between each Inspector's standard — "subjective" in this kind of context can mean almost anything from utterly prejudiced to obsessively non-commital. Few bodies would dare to put up a pseudo-scientific study of this type for cross-examination at a public inquiry but the Royal Commission themselves did not, on the face of it, subject it to close scrutiny. They were only too eager to clutch at any straw pointing to a minimum population, and even then their own minimum population figure of 250,000 is much lower than that which, according to both departmental studies, produces the most efficient type of authority. "The commission appear," concludes K. P. Poole, "to have shut their eyes and plumped for 250,000 in hope or desperation".[30]

So much for the English Royal Commission's views on minimum population. Faced with the same kind of evidence the Scottish Commission were much more canny, too canny by far to ask for a study of Scottish Education Authorities comparable to that carried out by the Inspectorate in England. "Many education authorities in Scotland are too small to come into the reckoning at all," they say, begging the whole question, "they simply cannot provide the whole range of services that are now generally considered necessary. If these are excluded, the remaining education authorities form far too small a group from which to draw reliable statistical conclusions. Extraneous factors which have nothing to do with size would make interpretation of the results a hopelessly difficult task".[31] Neither did the Scottish Commission think that objective research into the effects of scale on the discharge of local government functions was worth the effort. So formidable are the variable factors in such an investigation that they "could not imagine positive conclusions emerging" within the time at their disposal.[32] Housing needs, for example, varied widely in kind and in number amongst authorities ranging in population size from under 350 to nearly one million, but the variation was not necessarily in proportion to population size: performance was affected by local standards and by the availability and quality of sites. In any case, the experience of their English counterparts had shown that it was "impossible to find a satisfactory measure of performance".[33]

The only statistical study commissioned by the Scottish Commission was a study by Mr. C. S. Page, Senior Lecturer in Public Administration at the University of Strathclyde, into administrative costs in different sizes of authority. The most important finding of this study, according to the Commission, was that, in small burghs, administrative costs form a very high proportion of total expenditure, that authorities of this kind could expand their service expenditure considerably without a proportionate increase in administrative costs and that there would thus be a saving if their services were to be provided over wider areas.[34] In view of the population range of the small burghs of Scotland (the 24 included in Mr. Page's sample ranged from 9,800 to 24,300) this seems to be a sensible enough conclusion. Even so one doubts, judging by the printed report, whether sufficient allowance was made, not only, in the larger bodies, for administrative work carried out by service staff (this the Commission acknowledge) but, in the smallest places, for service work carried out by administrative staff: in Wales at any rate, the Clerk of a small district or borough is often something of a housing manager, social worker, planning officer and industrial development officer as well, and the whole tone of a town may be the better for having, on the spot, a resident official of some status. What is really striking about Page's report is, however, the way in which, in authorities with over 25,000 people or so, administrative costs as a percentage of public expenditure bear little relation to size, and that, in the counties, (eight of which in the sample had a population under 29,000) "the increase in scale economies is slight".[35] The low average percentage of administrative costs in the counties studies (2.4%) also emphasises that there is little point in isolating one aspect of an authority's work. It is the picture as a whole in a particular area that matters and there is no getting round the variables.

Not surprisingly, the Scottish Commission, unlike the English, recommend no particular minimum size for an authority as such. They confine their remarks to minimum size for particular functions or groups of functions and even here they are concerned, not so much with any relationship of size and efficiency, as with attempting to translate "staffing requirements at the supervisory and specialist level" into terms of population size.[36] Even this comparatively hard headed approach eventually runs into the sands of subjectivity, however. Not all witnesses on this point approached their task in the same way: some "laid greater emphasis on specialist services," others, "on the administration and the need to secure chief officers of the highest quality". There was also a considerable variation in the minimum population size for an education authority advocated by the experts — "from about 150,000 to 250,000" (a 40% variation) was considered "appropriate"; the "ideal size" ranged from "about 250,000 to upwards of half-a-million".[37]

These figures are substantially smaller than those advocated by the corresponding English experts and, as a result, Wheatley sought administrative units for education with a minimum population at least 50,000 smaller than Redcliffe-Maud.[38] Is this not due to the fact that Scotland has always been used to dealing with everything on a smaller scale than England and that attempts to hit upon the ideal size are, not only subjective, but relative to the country or region in question, so that it is a nonsense to seek to apply the same minimum to Wales as to England, to Cumberland as to Essex? The Scottish Commission's final conclusion on the size of education authorities also tends to discredit all these attempts to establish maxima and minima. "The evidence suggests that this range is very wide", say the Commission: at the lower end an authority with less than 200,000 people would face difficulties; on the other hand, while very large authorities offer no educational or administrative advantages, there is "no convincing evidence of disadvantages that could not be overcome by a suitable form of organisation if such authorities were thought correct for other reasons".[39] Could it not be argued with equal force that there are no disadvantages in small authorities that could not be "overcome by a suitable form of organisation if such authorities were thought correct for other reasons"?

Shortly after the Royal Commissions reported, the Bonham-Carter Report on the District General Hospital was published. This report, like the report of the Scottish Royal Commission, approaches the question of catchment areas on the basis of the specialists available. In "the country as a whole", assuming that consultants in each of the major specialities should work in pairs, the Bonham-Carter Committee found that, unless most district general hospitals serve populations of at least 200,000, there will be, in the foreseeable future, insufficient consultants to go round.[40] Instead of being dogmatic about minimum population, however, the Committee concede that, where the population is sparsely distributed, there will have to be some hospitals serving "less than 150,000 people and in a very few places even less than 100,000" and that special arrangements may have to be made to help them.[41] The Scottish Royal Commission, on the contrary, made no attempt to consider how less populous areas could be helped to have the same specialist services as densely populated areas without loss of identity. Like so many official bodies, they put the demands of the service before the demands of the local community. It is possible that some local communities with a long history of separate political identity are in danger of being sacrificed as a result, not of long term trends, but of purely ephemeral figures as to the number of specialists available for a particular service. The number of qualified people now available in services such as Town and Country Planning and Social Work is certainly inadequate. By the time that plans for training such people have materialised, however, there may be enough to go round: in 1968, the Town Planning Institute had 3,240 students on its roll, as opposed to 715 in 1948. The Robbins report established that there would be a rapid increase in the proportion of school leavers of the standard required for higher education and so far the estimates in the report have proved to be very conservative: the proportion entering all forms of higher education increased from 6.3% of the age-group in 1956 to 12.1% in 1966.[42] Jeremy Bray speaks of a series of tidal waves of highly qualified men building up and sweeping in: "in the 1980s the 60-year olds will see eight highly qualified young people where only one stood in their youth".[43] At present there is little attempt to influence young people to acquire the skills in greatest demand, while forecasting is becoming increasingly difficult as technological requirements change, so that a better supply of one kind of trained person often causes a deficiency in another more vital field. The growing popularity of in-training and second careers and the gathering momentum of educational change could nevertheless ease the position in local government before long. In the meantime, should not the Commissions have suggested some kind of transitional arrangement to enable local communities to keep their basic identity? If the local community is important, why do we never consider building up the weaker communities so that they can preserve their autonomy?

One cherished myth which the research staff of the English Royal Commission demolished (somewhat reluctantly judging by the wording of their report) is the myth that staffing shortage in counties and county boroughs is related to small size. Not only did the researchers conclude that "it has not appeared to be the case that large authorities are better able than small to attract and retain good quality staff",[44] there was "some slight indication that, for whatever reason, large authorities have more vacancies than small".[45] Neither did environment (as measured by rateable value per head) or employment prospects outside local government appear to have much influence on recruiting.[46] Could it be that a preference for serving his own people in his own town or county or region is still a potent influence on a man's choice of authority − this is certainly the case in Wales, where many officers could command higher salaries if they were prepared to move to England. The researchers do not consider this possibility. Perturbed by their findings, they prefer to stress the defects of their own methods.[47] The Mallaby Committee likewise found that the returns to their questionnaires gave no indication that small authorities have more difficulty in recruitment than large[48] − and they too fell back on their own subjective opinion that they must have:[49] it takes more than a statistician to destroy the myth of economic man.

It is Derek Senior who, taking the fullest advantage of the fact that an individual can reason and a committee cannot, brings some common sense into the discussion of minimum population. Senior's scepticism about the possibility of establishing objectively what size of authority is demanded by overall cost effectiveness is all the weightier for his admission that, if this could be done, it would be "difficult to resist the case for a structure which subordinated all other considerations to the demands of overall cost effectiveness"[50] and that "if local government's capacity to give value for money . . . is in any way governed by the size of its units in population terms, we must find out how and prescribe accordingly".[51] Manifestly, Senior belongs to the classical school. He has, nevertheless, to admit that few of the considerations involved in restructuring local government can be assessed in quantitative terms,[52] that efficiency has several aspects and that, where there is no simple profit test as in commerce, efficiency must be distinguished from effectiveness: for example, to make all your decisions within a certain time limit, is efficient but if some of those decisions are inconsistent with your basic policy, the process cannot be said to be effective.[53] Senior might have added here that, in considering local government reform, the efficient solution for one unit might be completely different from the efficient, let alone the effective, solution for another. What is "effective" in government depends, in the last resort, on the point of view adopted. From the Pembrokeshire point of view, the effective solution to the problem of hospital development in South-West Wales is to concentrate district general hospital facilities at Haverfordwest: from the point of view of Carmarthenshire, such facilities should be concentrated at Carmarthen: a comprehensive cost benefit study carried out from the point of view of, say, the Welsh Hospital Board, would, however revealing, still leave decisions to be made in the light of value judgments. Should travel be equalised for everyone, or should hospitals be placed where the population is concentrated? Is competent service on the spot better, in an emergency, than outstanding service thirty miles away? Does the possibility of attracting marginally better doctors offset the possibility of substantially less visiting? What weight should one give to the views of parents, of doctors and of accountants respectively? If the last word is to be granted to the medical profession, which type of doctor should adjudicate, general practitioner, medical administrator or consultant? If consultant, which type of consultant?

So piercingly sceptical an authority as J. A. G. Griffith can assert that the case for devolution "must be argued and made out over a multiplicity of circumstances and then adopted where it does improve a service and rejected where it does not:" of provisions of the Town and Country Planning Act, 1968, whereby more planning decisions would be taken locally, he can say "it is not apparent ... that all these changes will make for better decisions". Decisions can and should be made more systematically than is usually the case but a good decision from the point of view of an affluent ornithologist may well be a bad decision from the point of view of an unemployed builder's labourer. Some experts favour the ornithologist, some the unemployed. Some politicians defer to the international oil companies, some to the local timber merchant. Some conservationists favour house building in small villages so as to conserve the rural community itself: others seek only to conserve nature and seek an absolute ban on building in the country. Some planners wish to re-deploy London across South-East England: others are afraid to tamper with a going concern of such complexity. From one political point of view, devolution has led to atrocious government in Orange Northern Ireland but might well have led to admirable government in social democratic Wales. From another standpoint, the reverse is the case. In the last resort, for all his management techniques, no administrator can avoid weighting his opinion with his or his employers' values and attitudes. No amount of sentimentality about impeccably informed and independent public servants weighing conflicts and deciding how the "public interest" will best be served can conceal this. Sentiment about the public service is better than sentiment about nothing but it is no substitute for politics. Devolution means letting the local political standpoint prevail (so long as it is constitutional) and accepting it for better or for worse: it is an extension of free political activity and there is no such thing as freedom without risk.

To Senior, quality of service is "inherently unquantifiable" while "improvements in techniques of measurement do not, as the advocates of large units are inclined to assume, offer any hope of removing this obstacle; at best, they would distort judgment by concentrating attention exclusively on such aspects of quality as did prove measurable"[56]. Senior makes short shrift of the Commission's own research studies: "the one thing these researches have put beyond doubt is that no positive correlation whatever between population, size and performance can be statistically established even in the present local government system"[57]. Indeed, the findings of research study no.3 "suggest the opposite of what has been the common view about the effect of an increase in the population of a local authority on its efficiency. They even provide some evidence that dis-economies of scale operate with an increase".[58] Again the only significant finding of research study no.4 is "the unexpected one that large education authorities do not exploit their potential advantage, on which their advocates place so much stress, of being able to afford a higher proportion of specialist advisers. Even the cost of educational administration and inspection seems to increase proportionately with population":[59] again, one marvels at the weight which the majority of the English Commission were prepared to place upon the subjective views of H. M. Inspectors. Research study no.5 indicates that size of population, unlike such other factors as the type of area, has little influence on measurable aspects of the health, welfare and children's services, except insofar as it is related to the density at which people live. The fact must therefore be faced that "no objective basis exists on which to attribute any material significance to population size as a factor in any way influencing the performance of existing major authorities," while subjective impressions or *a priori* reasoning "cannot pretend to the overriding significance that might have been claimed for a statistically demonstrable correlation".[60]

To Senior, the widely varying population figures suggested by witnesses as desirable minima for this or that service are subject to a variety of qualifications. In the first place they have nothing to do with the cost effectiveness of the local government service as a whole, with all other factors taken into account: yet the majority accepted them as basic. [61] Secondly, they deal only with "what seems functionally desirable for a particular service at a particular stage in its development as seen from the managerial or administrative standpoint by a Government department or professional association that is primarily concerned with the quality of the input in that particular service . . . unpredictable and short-term fluctuations in minimum unit size may justifiably determine the restructuring of single purpose instruments of central government, but they cannot reasonably take precedence over the pattern of community structure in determining the scale of an organ of representative government with a general responsibility for the well being of its people."[62] We have seen how the concern of H. M. Inspectors of Schools with input rather than output made their report particularly unfair from the point of view of the small counties of Wales but this is typical of all official reports on local government: in most local government services, input is, in fact, almost the only factor one can attempt to measure. Often enough, all input itself amounts to is the quality of the staff so that the tempting assumption that the best-paid are in fact the best and that the worse paid must be weak in itself constitutes an argument for larger authorities. But this assumption is dangerous, not only in absolute terms but also in relation to the difficulty of the problems to be faced by large and small authorities respectively: in relation to the magnitude of his problems, the superior Clerk of a large city might prove much less competent than the inferior Clerk of a small district.

The tendency to equate higher salaries with greater effectiveness is not the only danger inherent in the Civil Service obsession with input, particularly when this obsession is combined with fanatical departmentalism. Unless basic general objectives are defined and unless performance is measured against such objectives, there is no limit to the amount of input for which the professional advisers of a particular service will press – few advisers can conceive of the expansion of their own service as anything other than a desirable end in itself: that is why they are where they are — and that is probably what it would be in a perfect world. There is no evidence that the Civil Service criticism of local government, department by department, was in fact related to any basic general objectives in accordance with the practice of programme budgeting which is now said to be gaining ground in central as well as in local government. Each local government service seems to have been measured in a vacuum, against the standards of an ideal world, instead of in that real world in which local government services compare well with the local services provided by the Government itself and by nationalised industries operating over immense regions — and in which, as Rudolf Klein puts it, "politics are essentially about the reconciliation of conflicting interests — not about the achievement of a perhaps unattainable and illusory perfect solution."[63]

Thirdly, and this is perhaps the most important point of all made by Senior, the choice of functional requirements upon which to base evidence on population minimum is often arbitrary. Some cases require facilities which can economically be provided for a population of, say, 50,000, while others need a population of 500,000. Where the line should be drawn between facilities which each unit should provide and facilities which must be shared is a question to which "functional considerations supply no answer."[64] The tendency among people accustomed to running a hierarchical bureaucracy is to draw the line as high up in the range as possible without inflating the unit's headquarters staff to unmanageable proportions, but when account is taken of the need for effectiveness from the standpoint of the people served, for the service to be community-based, accessible and promptly responsive to changing needs, the choice of a much lower point in the range is likely to be indicated. In parts of the country where this results in a considerable shortening of excessively long lines of communication within the unit, there is likely also to be a gain in administrative efficiency.[65]

Latter on in his report, Senior disposes of the Department of Education and Science study by suggesting that it is, in effect, an assessment of chief education officers, who are almost exclusively recruited from the teaching profession; [66] teachers with a good chance of becoming heads of large secondary schools do not find it worth while in terms of salary to accept appointments as directors of education of small authorities, while able officers tend to gravitate to the counties, where chief officers are more remote from inter-ference by members – and it is the counties which predomi-nate in the higher population ranges. Having nevertheless accepted that, below the 200,000 mark, the exclusive employ-ment of specialist advisers becomes increasingly uneconomic, Senior then faces the question of those areas where a minimum population cannot be reached without creating a unit so extensive that the advisers will spend most of their time travelling, a question which the majority too might have had to face had they been dealing with Wales as well as with England. Even if such advisers could be employed without spending most of their time travelling – and there will be many more schools per head to visit in a sparsely populated area – "would the marginal disadvantage from the chief officer's standpoint of not having the full-time use of that adviser's services outweigh the very substantial advantage to councillors and citizens alike, of having a local government unit with a comparatively accessible centre"?[67] "The simple truth of the matter," concludes Senior, "is that there are educational and other disadvantages inherent in sparsity of population. They can be remedied only by increasing the population of the areas affected, they cannot be remedied by joining sparsely popu-lated districts together".[68] Thus, even if there was a certain minimum population necessary for efficient administration, it would have been proved only that local government cannot be fully efficient and democratic in the many parts of the country where the minimum could not be attained within a coherent area. "Technical education was almost non-exis-tent,"[69] says the Local Government Commission for Wales of Merioneth, but this was the result of low, sparse population and of the absence of industry, not of the size of the local government unit: a North Wales unit would have regarded it as grossly uneconomic to place a technical college within the county: the central government itself is all too prone to sanction the closing of hospitals, schools and railways in such areas and to deny them better roads, while central bodies often lack the will to succeed outside the main centres of population. One of the facts of life in counties like Merioneth is that a minority have to travel long distances to obtain certain services. Why add another handicap by depriving them of control of what they can provide and of the change to capitalise on one of their advantages: a capacity for community effort? Another of the facts of life in such areas in the inherent tendency to be a decade or so behind the cities in adopting some fashions and in succumbing to some problems. Sometimes for better, sometimes for worse, that time-lag will always be a feature of their life, whatever the form of government – it is wrong to equate it with inefficiency.

It is typical of our times that the question of travelling time by specialist advisers should have precedence in these reports (even in Senior's) over the question of the travelling time of elected representatives. As Dr. G. W. Jones asks, if the Royal Commission attached high importance to "the direct contact between a member and his constituents" why weaken this by reducing drastically the number of councillors (from about 40,000 to 5,000) and creating constituencies in which one part-time unpaid member, preferably young and therefore with plenty of career and family problems on his plate already, will represent upwards of 10,000 people?[70] Are we going back, in the country, to rule by the parson and the squire, in the city to rule by the full-time trade unionist and the retired business man, with gerontocracy placed even more firmly in the saddle than at present? (The average age of councillors – excluding Aldermen – is even now 55). In the country, the recruitment of candidates is already a problem and so is public transport. It is perfectly true that travel by car, if not by rail, is very much easier now than it was in 1888 or 1894, but, by comparison, is not the time saved over a certain distance more than counterbalanced, in public life today, by the number of times the journey has to be made? In 1888, a

typical county councillor only had to travel to his county
town four or five times a year.[71] Today an active member
may well have to attend 60 meetings of County Council
committees, to say nothing of meetings of the numerous other
bodies to which he is likely to belong as a result of his membership of the council and his interest in public life.[72] Neither
Royal Commission saw fit to consider whether the committee
is not in fact an even faster breeder than the motor car. The
world may be smaller, but its population is much greater. The
very mobility of that population brings more, not fewer,
problems for government, let alone more need for participation. In 1888, it was something to have acquired a vote. By
1988, more and more citizens will expect a personal hearing
from the authorities.

Both the Scottish and the English Royal Commissions put
forward two entirely separate lines of argument in favour of
larger units. The first relates to the environment – to "the
pattern of life and work", to the delineation of areas which
lend themselves to planning as separate units. This is a problem
which we shall have to consider later. As for the second line of
argument, which maintains that many local authorities are
"too small in size and revenue and in consequence too short of
highly qualified manpower and technical equipment to be
able to do their work as well as it could and should be done," [73]
both Royal Commission Reports are, even within their own
terms of reference, highly unconvincing. We are left with
what Senior describes as relevant contributions "thrown into
the pot for what they are worth".[74] It did not, of course,
require Royal Commissions to establish that, where it is possible to concentrate a service without injustice, the pooled resources of several areas can, up to a point, be used to greater
effect than the resources of one alone, so that, potentially, the
unifield area can do more than each area could by itself – or do
what it does at less cost per head. Even at the parish level,
however, this does not settle the constitutional argument of
whether a proposed unified authority would be as fair and
responsive, as flexible and lively, from the point of view of all
its parts, as a federated authority or separate authorities.

Neither do analogies with commercial enterprises take into account the non-competitive nature of local government: the fact that it is under the wing of the government of a very much larger unit; that the larger local government units themselves, to say nothing of professional associations, pressure groups and ministries, are more than willing to share knowledge and expertise with small units; that, with the exception of rural depopulation, about which, as the constitution now stands, local government can do little, the big problems are in the big places, and that different areas may justifiably have different priorities and different standards. It is, nevertheless, a great pity that neither Royal Commission saw fit to commission a comprehensive cost-benefit study of the advantages to two or three particular local government units of amalgamating into one unit. Such a study would have had to include many unquantifiable items on each side of the calculation, but it would have been useful to have had a tentative idea of the actual economies of scale, if any, likely to be achieved by unifying administrations, a tentative idea of how much extra, if any, it costs either the ratepayers or the United Kingdom taxpayer to maintain small autonomous local government units.

That the results of a cost-benefit study might not have supported the evidence of the ministries is suggested by two studies considered in a recent EFTA report on growth centres. Each of these studies analyses the relationship of cost per head of infrastructure with town size. One study, carried out on the basis of existing conditions in Switzerland, found that the minimum cost per head was at a population size of about 10,000.[75] There were considerable variations around the average, probably as a result of such factors as the industrial structure of the town, its past growth, its physical setting, its prosperity and, above all, its proximity to a larger town which it could exploit; making every allowance for the exploitation of large towns by small, however, the optimum population size in Switzerland is astonishingly low, while the curve rises very steeply above that figure: if the optimum point is taken to be 100, the index is 212 for a population of 100,000. The second study considered in the EFTA Report is more academic and based on the infrastructure considered necessary by an Italian team, rather than upon what is actually provided in Italy – to a large extent it assumes a free-standing town. Even in this study, however, the minimum cost is at a population of between 20 and 50,000.[76] The author of the relevant section of the EFTA Report itself considers the minimum to be at about 30,000–35,000 and states that, though institutions like hospitals need larger populations than this if they are to be provided economically, the Italian evidence suggests that the higher cost per head of network provisions, which begins to rise at quite a low population, will offset such diseconomies with "the big indivisibles".[77] And though management costs are not included in either study, he concludes that "there seems little reason to think that the costs of managing a town will significantly alter the shape of the cost curve"[78] and that "with a population of, say, 30,000, even sophisticated indivisible infrastructure could be provided without exorbitant costs per capita"[79] – this indivisible infrastructure, we must remember, includes hospitals and industrial training centres. It should be emphasised, of course, that the studies considered in the EFTA Report apply only to towns and are based on actual conditions in Switzerland and on what is considered necessary in Italy, respectively. The actual experience of Switzerland is, however, the experience of an exceptionally prosperous country where building standards and costs are extremely high. Moreover, these studies – particularly the Italian – form, with certain modifications, the basis of the minimum population figure which was recommended to the EFTA Working Party by their consultant as a figure to be borne in mind in actual practice in establishing growth centres, though he does stress that 30,000 in "very much a minimum" since "industry would be ... more attracted to a larger centre,"[80] and institutions like hospitals and schools are becoming increasingly specialised and "indivisible."[81] Is it perhaps significant that the authors of the two studies in question were dealing with the infrastructure as a whole as opposed to such part of it as might be allocated to local government? United Kingdom local government units are small, not merely in area or population, but in the range of services for which they are responsible, so that the very terms of reference of the Royal Commissions may have led them to under-rate the potential of the small unit.

Be that as it may, even within their own terms of reference, the minimum population figures advocated by the Royal Commissions are unconvincing. Their objective research studies failed to confirm the subjective opinions of the civil service and neither the Commissions not, in most cases, their predecessors were prepared to put their case to the test by investigating actual authorities in depth, listing their defects in detail and giving them the opportunity to reply. The abolition of the main institutions of counties, cities and towns with a history as long or longer than that of England, Scotland and Wales is nevertheless too serious an operation to justify any reticence for the sake of hurt feelings. It is astonishing that, after so much reporting and research, we still have little idea of how much it costs the people of, say, Newport to have the privilege of being a county borough, or how much they lose by way of services for the sake of controlling those they have.

This is not to say that there is nothing at all in the civil service view and in the views of the many bodies which supported them. What is appalling is that general views should be converted into specific minimum figures, applied with little discrimination to particular situations, and accepted so uncritically. After all, it is a common human failing for an able man to wish to enlarge his empire, a perfectly normal aim for an administrator to attempt to simplify his, a natural result of specialisation that specialists seek to draw the less and less about which they learn more and more, from a wider and wider area. It is also understandable that professions should wish to organise themselves monolithically, without regard to boundaries (except, of course, the boundaries between professions), exert the maximum influence upon their employers and escape as far as possible from lay control:

this is much easier in large hierarchical units than in small democratic ones and in our generation it is the consumer, not the capitalist, who suffers as a result. Even within local government, it is the natural empire-builder who tends to attain prominence, while the local authority associations, far from being natural champions of the small authority, are dominated by large authorities, many of which stand to gain from fixing a high minimum population — on the question of local government reform in Wales, the CCA in no way represented the majority of the Welsh County Councils: it would be fairer to say that it represented Glamorgan.[82] The administrative and advisory structures of organisations generally are admittedly becoming more and more important with the development of technology but it is easy for administrators at all levels of government, including the local, to exaggerate this process — so easy for the educational administrator to forget that there exist very good private schools with no county offices at all to which to turn for guidance, so easy for a Home Office Inspector to think that the lack of a Senior Probation Officer to supervise two or three (senior but not Senior) officers of great experience and compassion is the end of the world, so easy for all we administrators to forget that administrators are there to be inconvenienced. "If the professionals are in charge," says J. P. Mackintosh of so humanitarian a service as health," there is a gradual but definite tendency for the convenience and criteria of those running the service to come first and the customers and patients to come second."[83] Truly said but the fundamental problem is deeper and is easier to distinguish on the exaggerated scale of international politics. Even on that scale, we seem to have forgotten Hitler, let alone Napoleon, "the conquerer for conquest's sake, the conqueror who would not state his aims because he never knew if he could not go beyond them." [84] But it was to democracies that De Tocqueville was referring when he said that able and ambitious men "will labour constantly to increase the scope of social power, for they all hope sooner or later to control it themselves." "It is a waste of time," he went on, "to demonstrate to such men that extreme centralisation may be harmful to the state, for they are centralising for their own interests."[85]

Notes to Chapter 2

1.   Royal Commission on Local Government in England (RCLGE) 1966-1969, Report (Cmnd.4040) (iii); Royal Commission on Local Government in Scotland (RCLGS) 1966-1969, Report (Cmnd.4150) (iii).
2.   RCLGS para.138.
3.   *Ibid.*, para.161.
4.   RCLGE, Minutes of Evidence, II (Ministry of Health), H.M.S.O. 1967, para.112.
5.   *Ibid.*, V (Dept. of Education and Science), para.442.
6.   RCLGE, Written Evidence of the Local Authority Associations, H.M.S.O., 1967, para.254.
7.   RCLGE, Minutes, X (UDCA), para.1068.
8.   *Ibid.*, VI (NAPC), para.127.
9.   Local Government Commission for Wales, Report and Proposals, H.M.S.O. 1963, para.550.
10.   *Local Government in Wales* (Cmnd. 3340), H.M.S.O., Cardiff 1967, Appendix I. The averages are a little misleading in that the range of population even after amalgamation would have been considerable. Revised proposals provide for a sixth county and a further White Paper for unitary authorities in the South-East.
11.   Address to the annual meeting of the County Councils Association,1965.
12.   RCLGE I, para.9(vii).
13.   *Ibid.*
14.   *Ibid.*, para.186.
15.   *Ibid.*, para.217.
16.   Research Studies 2, 8 and 10, of which the last, Administration in a Large Authority: a Comparison with Other County Boroughs, by the Institute of Local Government Studies (University of Birmingham), is the most pertinent.
17.   G. W. Jones, *Borough Politics, A Study of the Wolverhampton Town Council, 1888-1964,* London, 1969, p.275.
18.   Leopold Kohr, "Wales Free: The Politics of Permanence", *Resurgence,* July/August 1970, p.7 (cf. Senior para.103).
19.   RCLGE I para.218.
20.   *Land Economics,* May 1963.
21.   RCLGE I para.221.
22.   E.g. see RCLGE III, Research Appendices, Appendix 10, para.6.
23.   *Ibid.*, Appendix 9, para.3.
24.   A first leader in *The Guardian* (9 February, 1970) urged the Government to give the children of Holland (Lincs.), where only 36 per 1,000 children gain university admission, the same opportunity as those of Cardiganshire, 103 per 1,000 of whom do so — Cardiganshire (53,000) has only half the population of Holland.
25.   Such is the conclusion of a recent University of London study.
26.   Heinz Kloss, *Formen der Schulverwaltung in der Schweiz,* Zürich, 1964, p.155.
27.   *Ibid.*, p.156.
28.   Shortly after writing this, I was obliged as a parent to listen to 28 children under eight successively reciting the same poem, and 17 under eight singing the same song, with the higher age groups concentrating ominously at the back of the hall. It is this phenomenon, as opposed to any superior lung-

power, which accounts for the prominence of the Welsh in international opera.

29. RCLGE III, Appendix Eleven, para.6.
30. Prospects for Compromise—I, in Geoffrey Smith (Ed.), *Redcliffe-Maud's Brave New England*, London, 1969, p.50.
31. RCLGS para.362.
32. *Ibid.*, para.91.
33. RCLGS, Appendices, p.115.
34. RCLGS, Appendices, Appendix 27, para.7.
35. Administrative Costs of Local Authorities, RCLGS Research Studies I, Edinburgh, 1969, para.10.4 and Appendix III.
36. RCLGS, para.576 and para.367.
37. *Ibid.*, para.368.
38. Para.566 cf. RCLGE I, para.9.
39. *Ibid.*, para.371.
40. Department of Health and Social Security, Central Health Services Council, *The Functions of the District General Hospital*, H.M.S.O. 1969, paras.20-26.
41. *Ibid.*, para.27.
42. Committee on Higher Education, Report, London, 1963, Table 30.
43. *Decision in Government*, London, 1970, pp.28-32.
44. RCLGE III, Appendix 10, para.48. Cf. RCLGS para.90, which reveals that staff shortages in Scotland are on the whole more serious in the four cities, though generally uneven: the Commission fall back on "uneconomic use."
45. *Ibid.*
46. *Ibid.*, paras.51 and 52.
47. *Ibid.*, para.56.
48. Committee on the Staffing of Local Government, Report, London, 1967, paras.44 and 216.
49. *Ibid.*, para.216.
50. RCLGE, Volume II, Memorandum of Dissent by Mr. D. Senior, (Senior) para.255.
51. *Ibid.*, para.261.
52. *Ibid.*, para.256.
53. *Ibid.*, para.259/60.
54. Central-Local Relations and The Maud Commission, 133 *Justice of the Peace and Local Government Review*, p.799.
55. *Ibid.*, p.799.
56. Senior, para.262.
57. *Ibid.*, para.264.
58. *Ibid.*, para.265. The quotation is from the study itself — S. P. Gupta and J. P. Hutton, *Economies of Scale in Local Government Services*, H.M.S.O., 1968, p.6.
59. Senior, para.266.
60. *Ibid.*, para.268.
61. *Ibid.*, para.269.
62. *Ibid.*, para.270.
63. Quoted in Dilys Hill, *Participating in Local Affairs*, London 1970, p.196.
64. Senior, para.272.
65. *Ibid.*, para.273.
66. *Ibid.*, para.338.
67. *Ibid.*, para.342.
68. *Ibid.*, para.343.
69. Local Government Commission for Wales Report, para.223.
70. "Questions for the Commission," in *Redcliffe-Maud's Brave New England*, p.33. In this devastating essay, Dr. Jones also asks why there was no consideration of the role of political parties, the Commission having been specifically enjoined to deal with the sustenance of local democracy.
71. I base this on the earliest Minutes of the Pembrokeshire County Council.

72.   This emerged when the Pembrokeshire County Council were engaged in reforming their committee structure in the light of Maud on Management; a reduction in the number of committees tends, however, to require even more attendances at the County Offices on the part of Chairmen and Vice-Chairmen.

73.   RCLGE I para.6.

74.   Senior, para.271.

75.   *Regional Policy in EFTA: An Examination of the Growth Centre Idea,* Report of an EFTA Economic Development Committee Working Party, Edinburgh, 1968, p.89.

76.   *Ibid.,* pp.89-90.

77.   *Ibid.,* p.91.

78.   *Ibid.,* p.92.

79.   *Ibid.,* p.97.

80.   *Ibid.,* p.98.

81.   *Ibid.,* p.101.

82.   Ioan Bowen Rees, Llywodraeth Leol: Yr Adwaith i'r Papur Gwyn, *Barn,* Ionawr, 1968, p.63.

83.   *The Devolution of Power,* London, 1968, p.90.

84.   Pieter Geyl, *Encounters in History,* Fontana Library, London and Glasgow, 1967, p.332.

85.   Alexis de Tocqueville, *Democracy in America, II,* Fontana ed.1968, p.924. It is only fair to add the next sentence: "the only public men in democracies who favour decentralisation are, almost invariably, either very disinterested or extremely mediocre; the former are scarce and the latter powerless." Local government officers presumably come into the latter category!

3. *Apoplexy at the Centre*

"The immense (and generally approved) centralization of English government."
NEVIL JOHNSON

I

EVEN the most conventional critics of local government have listed amongst its most serious defects, lack of power, meagre financial resources, unwieldy management and lack of public interest, as well as small size and inappropriate area. Confined as they were to considering the existing functions of local government and, in effect, its existing financial structure, the Royal Commissions were doomed from the start to consider reforms so partial that only by placing a wholly unwarranted emphasis on defects of area and population size could they give the appearance of having achieved the kind of radical reform which they were expected to produce.

During the past thirty-five years, local government has lost to the central government or to the nationalised industries, 1,545 hospitals, over 8,000 miles of highway, numerous gas and electricity undertakings, and one of the most typical local functions of all, public assistance to persons in need.[1] With the general expansion of government activity after the Second World War, new services in the field of town and country planning and of welfare made up to some extent for this loss. In the wake of the continuing spate of central legislation, all sorts of odds and ends from helping to set up regional arts councils to certifying the fitness of a shop's fire precautions have helped to give infinite variety and interest to the work of a local administrator. If sheer activity and expenditure is any criterion, local government is, for all its loss of functions, more important today than it has ever been. In relation to central government, however, it is, even on the surface, less important, while if one probes beneath the surface and considers the extent to which local authorities are free to act at their discretion, in fact as well as in law, one begins to wonder whether we are justified in describing the system as local government at all.

The additional freedom given to local authorities by the General Grant which, in 1958, replaced percentage grants for particular services is more apparent than real. It is based on the average expenditure of all authorities on particular services so that each department of an authority is quick to insist on its "national" proportion of the General Grant. Indeed, when, in 1969, in deference to the government call for a squeeze, the Cheshire County Council made cuts in their further education estimates, they were accused by an Under-Secretary of State for Education and Science of "spending education grant aid (*sic*) on other purposes." The Under-Secretary, Mr. Denis Howell, went on to say that "while the county was entitled to do this under the general grant arrangements, the morality of it must be left to the electors and ratepayers of Cheshire"; [2] to him the cuts were "unbalanced, harsh and deplorable". It must be admitted that, when a major issue arises, many think that the Departments are right to press local authorities, and remiss in not taking greater advantage of their ample statutory power to direct and to withhold grant. "At present . . . all (the Secretary of State for Education and Science) can do is exhort by circular," commented the Editor of *The Guardian* on the "comprehensive" bill; "he, like the ratepayers, ought to have a voice, proportionate to his contribution". [3] Even to some of us who support the comprehensive system (with our children as well as with our pens) such remarks are sinister in the extreme. One did not know whether to laugh or to weep when the *New Statesman,* as soon as Mr. Crossman had become editor, had this to say about the new Government's policy of local option: "the Tory government is not handing over our children's future to some idealised form of PTA: it is committing their destiny and their birthright to the municipal martinets of the nation's county halls — to the butchers and bakers, without any serious interest in education but with a strongly developed partisan instinct, who all too often make up the membership of the country's LEAs."[4] To a real Socialist like G. D. H. Cole, poverty was only the symptom — "slavery" was the disease.[5] Is not the Eleven Plus too only a symptom of a certain servility, a certain authoritarianism and fear of democracy which is endemic in English life — so much so that the *Statesman* cannot defend the comprehensive system itself without seeking to debar butchers and bakers (and by the same token engine drivers[6] and miners) from the "A Stream" of government? Who could have imagined that, in 1970, a socialist journal would have had so much in common with those county magistrates who, in 1838, threatened to strike because a grocer had been appointed to sit on the bench with them!

To the Webbs themselves, the history of English Local Government between 1836 and 1922 saw the gradual replacement of ad hoc oligarchies with commercial standards by an all-purpose Consumer's Democracy attracting to it, "both as elected representatives and as officials, ever more and more of the ablest and best trained intellects, who find, in its service, whether paid or unpaid, an inspiration and a scope actually superior, in their own estimation, to that offered by the pursuit of pecuniary profit."[7] It has not taken half a century for the wheel to come close to the full circle. Local government has been losing out to ad hoc authorities with commercial — or, in some cases, narrowly professional — standards and local councillors are continually being told that they are getting in the way of an essentially technical process, best run from the centre. There may be some hope that new provincial authorities could bring functions back into (comparatively) local government but one recalls with trepidation that the Department of Economic Affairs told the Royal Commission "we do not see a function for that type of area which is properly discharged by an elected authority"[8] — and that,

with the introduction of colour on BBC 2, an exclusively
metropolitan programme, well in advance of BBC 1 and the
Welsh and Scottish programmes,[9] and with the demise of
regional radio in England, broadcasting is becoming ever more
powerful as an agent of unconscious, painless and at times
even pleasurable centralisation.

The Royal Commissions (particularly the Scottish), the
Maud Committee on Management in Local Government and
the Fulton Committee on the Civil Service have all stressed
the need for decentralisation and, in their White Paper
Reform of Local Government in England, the Labour Government professed to accept this need.[10] If anything, however,
the trend towards centralisation is gathering even greater force.
As the County Councils Association put it in an admirable
Brief to Members of Parliament, "it is monstrous that within
only a matter of days (of the publication of the White Paper),
the Government should publish in quick succession the Local
Authorities Social Services Bill (providing for detailed Government control of the reorganisation and management of local
authority social services) and Green Paper proposals to
establish area health authorities which, in effect, would be
the local agents of the Department of Health and Social
Security".[11] The Social Services Bill even requires that the
person appointed Director of Social Services by a local authority should be approved by the Minister, but on the whole this
is the kind of thing which local government has come to expect.
What is most disturbing is the decision to deprive local authorities of the personal health services and keep the new unified
health service outside local government altogether. For all
their pride in privacy and independence, the medical profession, who bear much of the responsibility for this, are
even more centralist than the Civil Service.

In addition to the severe statutory and financial restrictions
upon local originality, local government has to put up with a
degree of central supervision and instruction that is simply
obsessional. During the 22 working days up to the end of
December, 1969, the clerk to the council of a certain small
county received no less than 135 communications of substance

from the central government proper and a further 95 from quasi-governmental bodies such as the Industrial Training Boards and the Countryside Commission. Many of these communications were useful enough and one or two invaluable. Most of them were nevertheless the product of that presumption of incompetence which is the traditional central government attitude towards everything local. Even local names appear to amuse some metropolitan minds, and to annoy others: some years ago the Director of Education for a Welsh county received three successive letters from the central Department asking him to refrain from using in official correspondence the name given by his council to a certain school and to use only the English form ("X County Secondary School"). Had the county been a Swiss canton not an eyebrow would have been raised if the Director's letters to the Department had been written entirely in Welsh.

In most European countries, the authority responsible for minor highways for vehicles, let alone footpaths, is usually the equivalent of our parish council. In the United Kingdom, however, under Section 1(3)(*a*) of the Highways Act, 1959, the basic responsibility for the most modest rural right of way on foot lies with the County Council. In 1968, the Government nevertheless deemed it necessary to express the hope that (*inter alia*) "in placing signposts (on footpaths) in agricultural area highway authorities will bear in mind the need to avoid the obstruction of farming operations and arrange for temporary adjustments of signs when necessary."[12]

An example of the elegance with which a Central Department can state the obvious is provided in a recent six-closely-packed-foolscap-page circular inviting authorities to review their meals-on-wheels arrangements,[13] paragraph 7 of which reads: "Even though meals-on-wheels may not be able to approach the catering standards attainable in meals served on the premises, nevertheless, three principal requirements must be met if the meals-on-wheels are to be palatable and nutritious. First, the processes from preparation to service must be carried out not only on the same day but also in the shortest practicable period. Secondly, the processes should be un-interrupted. Thirdly, the hours during which meals are de-livered must be kept within limits acceptable to the recipients, and the time allowed for each delivery to a home must be sufficient for meals to be attractively presented and served." The Department are not content with generalisation. By the time we reach paragraph 10, we learn that: "The third require-ment — limited delivery time — has unavoidable effects on the whole organisation. It should be the aim to serve the first meal not earlier than noon and the last not later than 2.00 p.m. Since the travelling time between the recipients' houses, and the time taken to enter and leave the homes and serve the meal, can hardly be less than 3 minutes per meal even in favourable circumstances, it is unlikely that more than 40 meals can be properly and acceptably served by one vehicle and crew. The number may well be less, depending on distances and traffic conditions, and poor equipment or unskilful packing may further reduce it."

If Bagehot's distinction between the "dignified" and the "efficient" parts of a constitution (in his time, the monarchy and the cabinet) were to be applied to the local administration of the United Kingdom, it could be argued that local councils as such now belong to the dignified section, their chief officers, acting as agents of the appropriate ministry, to the efficient. Not that Bagehot disparages the dignified parts — without them the efficient parts would lack authority. Even as dignitaries, however, local councillors are tending to lose their role. It is to The Member of Parliament, not to the local councillor, that most people complain about what is tech-nically a local responsibility. "An ancient and ever-altering constitution," says Bagehot, "is like an old man who still wears with attached fondness clothes in the fashion of his youth: what you see of him is the same; what you do not see is wholly altered".[14] In the case of local government, even what we see is treated with irreverence in comparison with the dignified parts of the central constitution. Up to a point, this may be due to the more equal spread of education; but have

the public not also sensed "the extent to which", according
to Mr. Crossman himself, "the institutions and the behaviour
of voluntary totalitarianism have been retained since 1945". [15]
According to Mr. Crossman, "the rapid concentration of
power" in finance, industry, newspapers and television, as
well as in government, has occurred "almost unnoticed by an
indifferent electorate". One fears, however, that the electorate are well aware of the situation and have trimmed their sails
accordingly. What they have not noticed, and have not been
allowed to notice, is that there is an alternative.

II

Neither Royal Commission saw fit to balance the enquiry
by H. M. Inspectorate of Schools into the efficiency of local
education authorities with an enquiry, under twelve heads, by
officers of local authorities into the efficiency of a central
department! Up to a point, the central-local presumption of
incompetence is mutual. Professor Griffith's picture of a small
authority's relations with a central department being affected
by "the relative inexpertness and lack of qualifications of their
officers"[16] will evoke a hollow laugh from many a local
government officer. Academically, at first degree level at any
rate, most entrants into the administrative class of the civil
service are probably superior to their local government
equivalents, but experience is a great leveller, and Brian
Chapman's description of senior British Civil Servants as
"sheltered spinsters compared with French prefects and their
equivalents in other European countries who have the advantage of real experience of a wide range of services in the
field"[17] bears repetition in this context. Not that one wishes
to add to that indiscriminate contempt for civil servants —
"bureaucrats" — which is somehow considered less improper
than indiscriminate contempt for racial groups. It is not individual civil servants as such who are stiff and distant — some
are as different from the norm as it is possible to imagine —
while the Welsh Office is often distinctly Welsh in style if not

in substance. It is the civil service tradition which creates inhibitions and prevents the central-local relationship from becoming a true dialogue or a partnership, together with that political authoritarianism which is by now perhaps even more characteristic of the Labour Party than of the Tories.

If local government usually loses the verdict in a tussle with the centre, this is not often because it has lost the argument, but because the centre makes the rules, many of them as it goes along. An authority which spends defies the squeeze: an authority which makes cuts has unsatisfactory standards. To spend more per head on a service than the national average means that you are uneconomically small: to spend less means that you cannot afford a full service. The quality of local government officers does not vary with the size of the authority to the degree which is sometimes suggested. Some years ago, a county treasurer of Merioneth (population 37,000) became deputy county treasurer of Lancashire (population 2 million), while the Clerk of Merioneth has just been appointed Circuit Administrator for Wales by the Lord Chancellor, advised, no doubt, by his civil servants. Recently a senior solicitor on the staff of Birmingham City Council (population 1½ million) became Deputy Town Clerk of Swansea (population 170,000). No county officer would be so foolish as to write off the clerk of a small Urban or Rural District merely because he had no formal professional qualification.

If local government sometimes fails to do as well as one would wish, it does not follow that there are defects in the local government system as such. According to Brian Chapman, "European observers would . . . probably comment not unfavourably upon the public services provided by the best British local authorities . . . They have, however, undoubtedly suffered from the evasiveness and irresponsibility of some of the central ministries with which they have to deal and their internal organization could probably be improved."[18] And if Chapman admits, as he must, that some local authorities bear a direct responsibility for aesthetic and social blight, he goes on, "one has to work with the material available, and if we do not have city fathers with the energy, capacity and imagination of those in some Dutch and German municipalities this is a more general shortcoming in British society as a whole, and not specifically a failure in the local government system".

Neither does the fact that local government has defects in an absolute sense mean that it is defective by comparison with central government. One of the major criticisms of local government administration is its excessive departmentalism and lack of central co-ordination and it is certainly not for a deputy clerk to try to play this down. Compared with the situation in central government, however, co-ordination in local government appears to be a bed of roses: at times, the local administrator has the impression that there is no central government, only a series of independent contractors, some oblivious of one another, others in competition. In spite of the general consensus of opinion that the social work of a local authority ought to be closely co-ordinated, when the West Bromwich County Borough Council decided some years ago to place their health, welfare and children's departments under the loose overall supervision of their medical officer of health, it is the Home Office, which dealt with the children's service (while health and welfare came under the Ministry of Health), which intervened to insist on the statutory autonomy of the children's department. And though an Act has now been passed to compel local authorities to amalgamate their social services, these are still supervised centrally by two ministries (three in Wales), and there has been no indication yet (August 1970) which of them will give way. A certain local authority recently received, by the same post, one communication from the government declining to authorise, because of the economic crisis, an urgently needed sewerage scheme (upon the lack of which the appropriate local government commission had no doubt commented unfavourably) – and another regretting that the authority was not prepared to contribute more towards the provision of a sub-regional swimming pool, this in an area particularly well endowed with recreational facilities.

We now have it on the authority of an outstandingly

gifted former Junior Minister, Dr. Jeremy Bray, that the government's methods of economic management, their statistics and their attempts at forecasting and planning are not nearly good enough and that "models, strategies, and operating decisions are more familiar in some city halls than they are in the liveliest parts of Whitehall".[19] According to Dr. Bray, the only overall planning operation that is working — under great strain — is the management of total demand. Yet "the way the chips fall in a particular area from a series of separate national programmes in education, housing, transport, employment, industrial development, taxation and subsidy does not by any means necessarily represent a coherent and balanced course of local community development. The absurdities, so obvious at a local level, get lost in the national view and produce great frustration locally."[20] Thus many millions of pounds can be poured into capital intensive industry in development areas without substantially increasing employment — sometimes the grant decreases it by subsidising automation (the Esso refinery at Milford Haven can be operated by seven men[21]) — while the development of roads, technical education and light industry is neglected, and railways may be closed or in jeopardy. A decision on the economy as a whole which is right for one industry or region may be wrong for another industry or region, so that help is often given to those who need none and the handicapped are handicapped yet again. According to another writer, the Roskill Commission, having "conducted the most elaborate planning inquiry in history," has found that there is "neither a national airport policy nor a regional planning policy to which it can relate its findings."[22] Such comments cannot have caused much surprise to anyone in local government. So departmentalised is the Government that it is impossible to contemplate trying to secure an improvement in transport facilities to solve say, a question of hospital location, while as between a nationalised industry like British Railways and a department of government like the Ministry of Transport, there are differences, rooted in statute, not merely of organisation but of basic philosophy. Where British Railways propose to withdraw freight services from a line, the Minister of Transport has no power to intervene and does not consider it proper to exhort: neither, in Wales, does the Secretary of State. It is clear too from Mr. Mervyn Jones' evidence to the Crowther Commission that it was because the Gas Council in London was compelling him to flout the policy of the Government itself towards Wales as a Development Area that he resigned from the Chairmanship of the Wales Gas Board at the end of 1969 and took up the chairmanship of the Wales Tourist Board instead. "A London-based view of any nationalised – particularly service – industry," says Mr. Mervyn Jones, "must today involve a contraction of its activities in Wales and the outer parts of the United Kingdom and a concentration on the prospering over-active Midlands, London and South of England. The trend is clear. The rich get richer with lower gas prices. The poor get poorer with higher ones . . . area chairmen must acquiesce to London in thought and deed."[23]

Then there is the sheer multiplicity of bodies which trying to govern 50 million people from one centre entails. Government today is necessarily so slow and complicated that there must be devolution of some kind, functional devolution if not regional devolution, self-government for British Railways if not self-government for Wales. Brian Chapman made much the same point after returning from studying French local government "with the totally unexpected conclusion that Britain was a more centralised country than France".[24] When his department at the University of Manchester held a special meeting of the regional and local heads of the field services of the various ministries, he found that these hardly knew each other: the university was acting as a convenor of governmental services![25] The system thus exhibits the worst vices of both the federal and the unitary systems. It is federal in that each service operates with "scant regard for the operations and needs of other services". It is unitary in that the regional offices of each Ministry regard themselves simply as extensions of Whitehall. They are too federal for a unified approach, too unitary not to be subservient towards Whitehall. We have, therefore, "a parameter of maximum inefficiency of vertical integration and subordination together with horizontal separation and separatism",[26] with the departments behaving "as if they were independent satrapies pursuing their own aims and pressing their own definitions of public policy against all-comers, and not infrequently manipulated by the very pressure groups they are supposed to control."[27]

One advantage of having a Welsh Office is that, in the fields transferred to that office, local government officers only have to travel to Cardiff to meet their opposite numbers in the Civil Service. Members of a Whitehall Department nevertheless attend such meetings from time to time. The charitable explanation is that co-ordination cannot begin too early. At times, however, one cannot help thinking that the Whitehall men are the mild English equivalent of Moscow in a more compliant Prague. In a recent article, Rhys David speaks of "the deadening influence which other departments whose job in Wales the Welsh Office does, can exert over it," — "even within the same programme detailed Treasury control prevents the switching of resources."[28]

Administrative devolution on the pattern of the Welsh and Scottish Offices is manifestly not enough: the divisions in Whitehall still show through. "Something needs to be done to secure greater consistency between one department and another in policy and administrative practice towards local authorities," say the Scottish Royal Commission, "the fact that there is a single Scottish Minister . . . does not of itself achieve this result."[29] Consider this list of centrally-appointed bodies intimately concerned with the economy of central Wales: the Mid-Wales New Town Development Corporation, the Rural Development Board appointed by the Minister of Agriculture, the Countryside Commission with its Welsh Committee, the Development Commission, the Forestry Commission, the Nature Conservancy, the Sports Council for Wales, the Wales Tourist Board, the Water Resources Board with its Welsh Committee, the Central Electricity Generating Board and other nationalised industries (most of whose regions cut across Wales), to say nothing of the government departments themselves and the nominated Welsh Council appointed by the Welsh Office; no wonder that the Welsh Council in their report on land use strategy in Cardiganshire, Montgomeryshire and Radnorshire complain about the multiplicity of agencies involved;[30] and that the first permanent secretary at the Welsh Office, soon after his resignation to take up the post of Principal of University College, Aberystwyth, came out strongly in favour of an elected Welsh Council because the existing system "does not provide for sufficient accountability of the executive to the electorate."[31]

III

The relevance of the preceding pages is that one cannot consider the reform of local government apart from the reform of central government or cure any paralysis at the extremities without also trying to cure the apoplexy at the centre. Any review of local government which does not also probe deeply into the defects of central government is itself likely to be defective. Any solution for the problems of the former can only be partial and unbalanced unless it solves the problems of the latter too. If there are serious shortcomings in the local government system, the first question which should be asked is not, "what is wrong with the local council?" but "what is wrong with the supervising ministry in question?" — a question seldom put by the various Commissions charged with reform. Strictly speaking, Crowther should have preceded Redcliffe-Maud or at least the two should have been inter-related. It is all very well for the English Royal Commission to say that the province is not the right area for local government functions and that the question of decentralising central functions to provincial councils must be left to Crowther — the fundamental question to be answered is which functions should be local and which central, or, in some cases, where the line should be drawn between the local and the central aspects of a particular function. The answers to these questions may well vary with the distance of the centre and its susceptibility to democratic control. Further education under Whitehall is one thing; further education under an elected council for Wales is another. A separate County Council for Merioneth responsible for full-time further education is one thing; a Merioneth County Council relieved of further education by an elected Welsh Council is another. As the *Local Government Chronicle* put in recently, "there are big risks involved in taking decisions on the main structure of service-running authorities before the very important question of devolution from the centre, which must basically affect the operational structure, has been properly considered ... the debate must go on".[32] Unfortunately, part of the attraction of the city region solution for Whitehall is that it would make devolution of further powers like the hospital service more difficult.[33]

At the moment local and central government in the United Kingdom are inextricably intertwined. Central departments regularly take the credit for local achievements: permission to a local authority to spend its own money on a project put forward on its own initiative is often announced in terms calculated to give the impression that the Government itself has decided to provide, say, a new school at Y, or to spend so many thousand pounds on welfare projects in the county of X. At the same time, generally well informed members of the public can be heard criticising local authorities for the faults of the central government: a frequent example is the criticism of county councils for failure to control the afforestation of beautiful countryside in the National Parks, much of it carried out by the central government itself in the shape of the Forestry Commission, and all of it the result of the central government's failure to make afforestation subject to planning permission, or even to say that it would consider the approval of "blanket" Tree Preservation Orders on deciduous woods over a wide area. In amenity and open-air pursuit circles, the Caernarvonshire County Council is regularly castigated for not having yet published its Definitive Map of Public Rights of Way. Yet if access to some hills in the county is still difficult, and if some rock-climbing crags are at times overcrowded, there is already enough accessible territory in Snowdonia to keep any reasonable walker or climber happy for life: the Definitive Map could not reasonably be given a high priority in a county which has much more than its fair share of un-employment and depopulation.[34] What is really disturbing in the National Parks is the extent to which the central govern-ment itself has permitted major disfigurements of the land-scape, in cases called up for central decision, or on appeal from a contrary decision by the county council. The amenity bodies could well lose more in the fire of ad hoc National Park Boards appointed by the government than in the frying pan of the county councils.

Central departments too, usually through the medium of Commissions and the like, are quite capable of criticising local government for their own shortcomings. The small authority which is "too poor to be able to provide", say, a sheltered workshop for the handicapped may well have had loan sanction refused for such a project. The rural authority which "lacks the expertise and resources to develop its health and welfare services" might well have provided more clinics but for the intervention of a district auditor who considered that any clinic should serve a larger minimum population than most of the centres of that county could reasonably include in their catchment areas; if such a county is short of qualified staff, this is probably due to a national shortage to which the lack of foresight of the central department has contributed; and there is no end to the local government defects which arise from the limited financial resources which central government is prepared to allocate to the localities.

IV

In the course of the debate which followed publication of the White Paper, *Local Government in Wales,* Mr. Alan Williams, M.P., then a Junior Minister, asserted: "nearly every local authority in Wales, many of which now argue their proud case for being exempt from boundary changes, has lived with one hand in an English pocket".[35] This is typical of the prevailing official attitude to local government finance. Local government has only two major sources of revenue — the rate on the value of property and government grants. The central government, on the other hand, has at its disposal every other tax which the Exchequer has had the ingenuity to devise, from income tax to selective employment tax, from petrol tax to the tax on beer and tobacco. The rate on property is a regressive tax in the sense that, in respect of the same kind of house, it hits a poor man proportionately much harder than a rich one. Neither is the rate-yield buoyant: unlike income tax, it does not rise automatically with the increase in the national income. Again industry and freight transport premises are only partially rated, while agricultural land and buildings and caravans (as opposed to their sites) are completely exempt, while the itinerant labour force, often highly paid, and the tourist, often highly affluent, cannot make a direct contribution towards the facilities provided for them. In practice, therefore, there is a limit to the rate that can be levied and J. P. Mackintosh M.P. goes so far as to say that "it is possible that successive governments have retained this method of raising local revenue precisely because its inflexibility and unpopularity imposes a severe limit on how much the local authorities can spend".[36] Over 40% of local government expenditure now comes in grants but the complicated way in which grants are calculated makes it difficult to establish in advance how much a particular authority will receive, while planning ahead is further inhibited by uncertainty as to whether loan consent will be forthcoming from the appropriate central department. As the Wheatley Commission put it, "the financial resources of authorities do not match their responsibilities".[37]

Alan Williams' reference to Welsh authorities having their hands in "an English pocket" has a certain schoolboy truth about it in the sense that the British Treasury (if not, in its entirety, the Royal Mint) happens to be in London, England. Indeed one often hears Members of Parliament for the less affluent Welsh constituencies chiding devolutionists on the grounds that "£9 out of every £10 spent by your county council" (or whatever the figure may be) comes from the Government in London, as if the Chancellor was the ultimate fountainhead of the wealth of these countries, rather than the non-productive middleman he is. (My favourite non-sequitur of this vintage is that of a hard-pressed Labour candidate during the last election campaign: "I will not have this county run by a lot of teachers who support self-government for Wales but have their salaries paid by the Government in London," which makes an interesting comparison with the *Statesman* editorial quoted on page 49.) The question that should be asked more often in local government circles, in England as well as in Wales, is how much the Exchequer receives from the localities. If the Exchequer is indeed English, has not an "English hand" been in the pockets of thousands of Welsh taxpayers in the various localities which are resisting amalgamation?

It is true that the local authorities of Wales as a whole, as compared with England as a whole, receive a high proportion of their revenue in the form of grants: the sparsely populated counties of the "green desert" of Mid-Wales in particular benefit greatly from the equalisation element in the general grant. Since the War, Wales has consistently had about twice the unemployment rate and a much lower activity rate than England, to say nothing of the emigration of so many of the talented young people who might have been able to put this right. The legacy of ill health from the inter-war depression is still putting a big strain on her health and welfare services and she has a far greater leeway to make up in economic development than most parts of England. In other words, Wales can contribute less to, but needs more from, the Central Exchequer than any region of England with the possible exception of the North-East. In spite of all this, such evidence as we have shows that even Wales pays her own way in the world, a factor of immense significance for local authorities all over the United Kingdom. Since 1948, a research unit at University College, Aberystwyth, established and led for many years by Professor Edward Nevin, has been producing "social accounts of the Welsh economy" as well as it can on the basis of published statistics and intelligent estimates. The revenue accounts published show that, between 1948 and 1956, Wales received back from the central government about £4½ million per annum less than she had paid in taxes,[38] while, between 1957 and 1962, the Welsh surplus, as it were, was still over £1 million per annum:[39] and it should be emphasised that the Welsh receipts include the cost of defence establishments in Wales and the appropriate share of the national debt. No doubt the government made a much bigger profit out of most of the English regions.* No doubt Wales contributes proportionately very little (if more than countries like Eire or Finland spend under such headings)[40] to the overall cost of defence and diplomacy. But there is an immense difference between living off your neighbours in terms of expenditure on education, housing, health, welfare, roads and all the basic necessities of domestic government, and being unable to contribute very much to the defence of Hong Kong or the construction of nuclear submarines or the provision of that prestigious new embassy in Madrid. In terms of domestic expenditure, it seems, judging by the Welsh figures – possibly the least favourable of all to the localities – that most localities in the United Kingdom could finance out of their own taxable resources, not only their own local government services, but also the central services in their own area.

The leading industry of Pembrokeshire, agriculture, is not rated at all, and Pembrokeshire, with her frost free belt, is one of those counties where agriculture does pay. In comparison with the number of tourists and caravans, Pembrokeshire's second industry, tourism, contributes little directly to the

---

* The Labour Government claimed that Scotland receives back *more* than she pays but the fact that their Scottish "budget" was published on the eve of a by-election strongly contested by the S.N.P., coupled with very guarded comments by the Chancellor and with Dr. Gavin McCrone's opinion that the Treasury seriously underestimated the Scottish yield of income tax and of corporation tax (Dr. McCrone being an *opponent* of the S.N.P.) does not inspire confidence in this claim. It is perhaps worth mentioning here that the Welsh economist Dr. Nevin is neither a nationalist nor a party politician though, in 1967, he resigned from the Welsh Economic Advisory Council because of its ineffectiveness.

rates but involves local authorities in much extra expenditure. Again, even the rateable value of the oil refineries on Milford Haven only partially reflects the fact that, in Milford Haven, Pembrokeshire has, in terms of tonnage, the second most important port in the United Kingdom. Neither does the constant Irish traffic through Fishguard contribute much to the rates. In a less sophisticated age, when there were few objects for taxation apart from defence and diplomacy, it may have been reasonable to allow the central government the lion's share of taxable resources. In the welfare state would it not be more equitable and more humane to give the local authority first claim on a far greater proportion of the resources of its own area, leaving the central government to equalise by taking less rather than by returning more — equalisation from below as opposed to equalisation from above? As the *Local Government Chronicle* puts it, "unless the present overdependence on central grants is reduced, reorganisation will be a hollow facade as, with mounting population and other pressures, central control will grow and not diminish . . . the Government should apply here the White Paper's dictum about reorganisation — that there is no right solution and that whichever chosen must sacrifice some things in the interests of others. The sacrifices of local authorities should be matched by those at the centre".[41]

The Royal Institute of Public Administration has been advocating a local income tax since 1956 at least. Yet the claim of local authorities for a greater proportion of the taxable wealth of their own areas has never been pressed. Much has been made of the complexity of taxing locally, and even regionally, commercial systems based on London and other centres and of the problem of taxing commuters who earn in one area and live in another. The administrative problems involved are far from insoluble, however, particularly in the age of the computer, while the problem of just distribution is certainly susceptible of compromise. These are everyday problems in many countries and in Switzerland, administratively the most fragmented country in Europe, they are overcome by simple formulae such as "75% to the authority where you live, 25% to the one where you work"[42] and "by the ordinary courts of the land acting in particular cases". [43] Is it not willpower which has been lacking in the United Kingdom, where the local authorities so often defer to the civil service view and the civil service actually put, not ends before means, but means before ends – the convenience of the tax collector before local democracy itself.

The Royal Commissions' treatment of finance, divorced as it was from a radical reappraisal of functions, is naturally rather tentative: Redcliffe-Maud nevertheless emphasises the need for additional local taxes and draws attention to the Royal Institute of Public Administration's advocacy of a local income tax and local taxes on vehicles and fuel.[44] The Institute's evidence underlined the fact that the rating system is no reflection of the true wealth of an area: the South-East of England, including Greater London, accounts for 48.8% of the rateable value of property in England and Wales but only 35.5% of the motor fuel consumed and 39% of the car licences issued. All regions of England apart from the North-West would benefit relatively to London from taxes on cars licensed and on motor fuel consumed, while Wales, with only 4.1% of the rateable value of England and Wales in April, 1967, and 5.5% of the population, had 5.4% of the cars licensed in the quarter ended 30th September, 1966 and 6.00% of the fuel delivered in 1966.[45] The Institute considers that the transfer to local government of taxes generated by motor vehicles would not only be cheap to administer, but would reduce exchequer grants from 47% to 14% of the income of local authorities.[46] In a Research Study for the Scottish Royal Commission, Page and Canaway also conclude that, in large regional units which reduce daily inter-regional travel to the minimum, a local income tax at differing rates could be grafted on to the national system without undue complication: an income tax of 9d. in the £ would sustain the 1964/5 contribution from the private sector to local revenue in Scotland as a whole: for corporations it would be simpler to retain rating of property.[47]

Neither the Scottish nor the English Commission wished to

discuss the merits and demerits of specific taxation proposals. The Englishmen emphasise that all taxes have their disadvantages and that, in seeking the balance of advantage, the need of local authorities for an adequate local tax locally fixed, for which the representative authority is accountable to the electors, must be given great weight. The financial position of English Local Authorities, they state, has long compared unfavourably with that of local authorities abroad: in Sweden, for example, the local authorities are relatively rich because of the highly productive local income tax, and not surprisingly enjoy a large measure of freedom.[48] The Commission therefore conclude that "the central government ought . . . to recognise that a reasonable measure of financial independence is an essential in local democracy."[49] The Scots, who claim to be "advocating a complete transformation in relations between central and local government"[50] are much more positive: "the opportunity must be seized of reorienting the whole financial system in local government." The aim should be "to shift on to local government a substantial part of the burden now falling on the central Government." [51] Central control must be limited to what is necessary from time to time for the regulation of the economy as a whole. With this qualification, the level of spending by a local authority and, subject to recognition of certain minimum standards and broad national objectives, the allocation of spending between services, should be for the local authority to decide. [52]

V

The section on finance was not the English Royal Commission's only contribution to the discussion of matters other than size and area; the Commission also considered the management of local government and here again there is scope for radical reform by a reduction in the number and size of committees, by delegating the execution of policy to officers, by strengthening central management and curtailing departmentalism, and ultimately by the payment of members and the election of a few full-time ministers to take the place of committee chairmen. Many councillors fear that these processes are fundamentally anti-democratic; actually it is by seeing that such time as "amateur" members are able to devote to local government is taken up by a mass of administrative detail that chief officers are able to assume the main responsibility for policy making. Is it vital to democracy that a committee of thirty to forty members should have to vote, after inspecting several samples, on the particular brand of sock and Wellington boot to be issued to Leading Firemen? (In spite of the requirement, other things being equal, to accept the lowest tender, in spite of the guidance of the Chief Fire Officer, it is not unknown for such topics to be debated with some heat). Is it, on the other hand, consistent with democracy for a City Treasurer to advise his authority on the general aspects of a major political issue like self-government for Wales and give evidence on their behalf before the Crowther Commission — this happened in Cardiff recently and under the present system might have been difficult to avoid. In large authorities, one doubts whether anyone other than a paid minister — who might well be elected directly by the people instead of by the council — will ever gain the time and the expertise to be able both to overshadow an able chief officer and act thoroughly responsibly. Large departmental committees have their uses as sounding boards and educational bodies (for both officers and members). To give them executive responsibility for detail, however, leads to inconsistency and delay and provides a protective smokescreen for the officers. If all councillors had all the time in the world, it would be worth retaining them, but, unlike a full Council, they do not purport to represent either the politics or the localities of their area. It is in the fields of broad policy making, especially annual and supplementary estimates, priorities and key appointments, that the democratic process should be making itself felt and it is precisely here that the members so often lack leadership (unless it is the central leadership of a political party, which may at times only be the central ministry in another form.) The members lack leadership because they lack time and expertise and that kind of non-departmentalised information upon which decisions as to priorities ought to be based.

VI

There can be little doubt that radical reform along the lines advocated by Maud on Management would produce more effective, more enterprising and, in the field of policy, more democratically responsive authorities. Such authorities would, with a greater proportion of their area's taxable wealth at their disposal, and freedom from the *ultra vires* rule, be well equipped to take on a greater range of functions both in their own right and as the local agents of the central government. There is, however, no hint that either Royal Commission considered how the "efficient size" of an authority might vary with its managerial structure, its financial strength and its range of functions. At least as much can be done to strengthen a weak unit bu giving it more money, more work to do and better management as by giving it a greater area. Most county towns house the local offices of several government departments and nationalised industries, to say nothing of other local bodies like water boards and health executives. Could not some of the economies of scale be achieved by functional rather than by territorial amalgamation? Consider, for example, the position of Pembrokeshire (population 102,000). The Pembrokeshire Water Board has qualified accountants on its staff and often has to employ local solicitors. Across the road, the Pembrokeshire County Council, who administer the same area, have formidable legal and accountancy departments, to say nothing of an ICT 1903 computer. As things are, the two bodies are not infrequently in conflict over policy, accounts and questions of liability. Were they to be amalgamated, the same administrative structure would suffice for each body. There would be better co-ordination, a saving to the ratepayer and indeed a strengthening of local control. The same could be said if the County Council were to administer the Pembrokeshire Health Executive Council (which is responsible for the general practitioner service) and the hospitals of the county. Instead of letting it administer an estate of smallholdings alone, why not make the County Council responsible (as agent, if not in its own right) for agricultural advice and for the forests of the county? One service which should certainly be linked with the County Council's welfare service is public assistance: at present the lack of a uniform policy (no fault of the local administrators) is a constant source of confusion and inconsistency. For that matter, why not make the County Council the local agents for health and social security generally and for employment and productivity? There are local units of these services serving the same or a smaller area than the administrative county, while it seems probable that the major hospital in the county will soon be designated a district general hospital. Even the many defence establishments in Pembrokeshire might well be serviced by the County Council's administrative staff, to say nothing of the County Architect and the County Surveyor. If, as the Royal Commission implies, local authorities with fewer than 250,000 people cannot provide enough work for a really expert department of architects, why not give the County Architect of a small county sufficient central government work to make up for this? Even in the context of decentralisation, there is much to be said for the view of the Government of Northern Ireland in their *Further Proposals* for re-shaping local government that "the notion of a clear dividing line between local authority functions and the functions of central government (needs) to be challenged. The more considered approach undoubtedly is to regard public responsibility as one continuum stretching from Parliament through various authorities across to local government and sufficiently flexible to adapt itself to changing circumstances."[53] With extra functions, many of which could be taken on merely as agent, and with the financial resources allotted to those functions, every local government unit could provide itself with a more formidable administrative structure without acquiring a yard of extra territory, and both taxpayer and ratepayer might obtain some relief in the process.

If all this sounds to the reader like the wild dream of a local empire-builder, let him turn to a later chapter and reflect on the range of functions of Swiss cantons half the size of Pembrokeshire.

It is only within the conventions of the rating system and the doctrine of *ultra vires* that many of the smaller counties and towns of the United Kingdom should really be regarded as poor and weak. The unthinking acceptance of these conventions has been disastrous for local morale and it was refreshingly unusual to find one county council threatened with amalgamation for its own good telling the English Royal Commission, "Herefordshire is rich almost beyond compare."[54] By world standards, counties like Herefordshire are rich, rich enough to provide almost everything they need apart from sophisticated defence weapons, upon the deployment of which they can, in any case, have little influence.

Formally precluded from discussing functions other than existing functions for local government, not specifically charged with considering finance, neither Royal Commission discerned the extent to which the defects of small authorities are magnified by their lack of autonomy and authority to tax or the degree to which their shortcomings can be attributed to the central government itself. Their search for the right solution was inhibited by the traditional attitudes of the public service both local and central. Their recommendations might be acceptable in a static political context with all the emphasis upon the centre. They will not do if participation and decentralisation are to become serious issues.

Notes to Chapter 3

1. William A. Robson, *Local Government in Crisis,* 2nd revised ed., London, 1968, pp.13-16.
2. Report in *Local Government Chronicle,* 22nd February, 1969.
3. Leading article, 9th February, 1970.
4. Leading article, 10th July, 1970 (cf. The Ministry of Health and Social Security's refusal to increase supplementary benefit to meet increased council rents.)
5. Self-Government in Industry (1917), extracted in Henry Pelling (ed.), *The Challenge of Socialism,* London, 1954, p.225.
6. One of the most dedicated and influential educationalists in Wales, the Life Peer, Lord Heycock, is in fact an engine-driver by trade.

7.   Sidney and Beatrice Webb, *English Local Government, IV, Statutory Authorities for Special Purposes* (London 1922), 1963 ed., p.485.

8.   RCLGE, Minutes, I para.66.

9.   Emyr Humphreys reported in *Broadcasting in Wales in the Seventies,* report of an open conference at University College, Bangor, 7th February, 1970, p.5.

10.   Cmnd.4276, para.60.

11.   CCA, Second Green Paper on the Future Structure of the NHS, 23rd March 1970 Debate in the House of Commons, p.7.

12.   Ministry of Housing and Local Government Circular 44/68, para.6.

13.   Welsh Office Health Department Circular 26/70 (probably a replica of a London circular).

14.   Walter Bagehot, *The English Constitution,* with an Introduction by R. H. S. Crossman, London and Glasgow, 1963, p.59.

15.   *Ibid.* (Introduction), p.56.

16.   J. A. G. Griffith, *Central Departments and Local Authorities,* London, 1966, p.529.

17.   *British Government Observed,* London, 1963, p.14.

18.   *Ibid.,* p.34.

19.   *Decision in Government,* London, 1970, p.81.

20.   *Ibid.,* p.149.

21.   D. G. Watts, Milford Haven and Its Oil Industry 1958-69, *Geography,* Vol. lx, p.64.

22.   Malcolm MacEwen, The Third London Airport Problem, *New Statesman,* 6th March, 1970.

23.   *Western Mail* report, 21st July, 1970.

24.   *Future of Government,* CPC No.392, London, 1968, p.5.

25.   *Ibid.,* p.6.

26.   *Ibid.*

27.   *British Government Observed,* p.41.

28.   Future of the Welsh Office, *Planet,* August/Sept., 1970, p.86.

29.   RCLGS para.1052.

30.   Cyngor Cymru, Strategaeth Defnyddio Tir, Adroddiad Llywio, Caerdydd 1970 para.134. (Also in English)

31.   Sir Goronwy Daniel, *The Government in Wales,* Transactions of the Honourable Society of Cymmrodorion, Session 1969, Part I, p.126.

32.   Leading article, 7th February, 1970.

33.   J. P. Mackintosh, *The Devolution of Power,* London, 1968, p.99.

34.   "Gomer", Another National Park? 134 *Justice of the Peace and Local Government Review* (JPL), p.112. (cf. Gilbert Ellice, Not-so-National Parks, *New Statesman,* 1st August, 1969 for the more conventional view.)

35.   *Western Mail* report.

36.   *The Devolution of Power,* p.30.

37.   RCLGS, Short Version of the Report, (Cmnd.4150-1), H.M.S.O. 1969, p.1.

38.   Edward Nevin and others, *The Social Accounts of the Welsh Economy, 1948 to 1956,* Cardiff 1957, Table XVII.

39.   Edward Nevin, A. R. Roe and J. I. Round, *The Structure of the Welsh Economy,* Cardiff 1966, Appendix I, Table E (p.26). The Gross National Product of Wales in 1964 is put at £1,310 million in Table A.

40.   In 1964-65, the U.K. spent 7.9% of her Gross National Product on arms, Denmark 2.7% of hers and Finland 1.6% of hers. See "Wales" in Owen Dudley Edwards and others, *Celtic Nationalism,* London, 1968, p.286.

41.   Leading article, 7th February, 1970.

42.   George A. Codding, *Governing the Commune of Veyrier: Politics in Swiss Local Government,* Colorado 1967, p.78/9.

43.   Christopher Hughes, *The Federal Constitution of Switzerland,* Oxford, 1954, p.59.

44. RCLGE I, para.534 et seq.
45. S. H. H. Hildersley and R. Nottage, *Sources of Local Revenue*, London, 1968, p.40.
46. *Ibid.*, pp.39-41.
47. C. S. Page and E. E. Canaway, Local Taxation, RCLGS Research Studies I, Edinburgh, 1969, paras. 10 and 11 and Appendix 9.
48. RCLGE I, para.529.
49. *Ibid.*, para.532.
50. RCLGS para.1025.
51. *Ibid.*, para.1038 (a).
52. *Ibid.*, paras.1044-46.
53. Government of Northern Ireland, The Re-Shaping of Local Government, Further Proposals following discussions and consultations (Cmd.530), Belfast 1969, para.19.
54. RCLGE, Evidence of County Councils, p.97.

4. Conceding Democracy

"If people cannot have official democracy, they will have unofficial democracy, in any of its possible forms, from the armed revolt or riot, through the 'unofficial' strike or restriction of labour, to the quietest but most alarming form — a general sullenness and withdrawal of interest."
RAYMOND WILLIAMS

I

Whatever one may think of the Redcliffe-Maud belief in the relationship of large size ("within the range of 250,000 to not much more than a million") with good performance, there is no denying the persuasiveness of some of the geographical arguments for larger units which Redcliffe-Maud accepted and which Wheatley and Senior considered to be crucial — particularly if there is to be decentralisation of services now within the province of the central government. It is certainly more rational to plan a road and transport network in terms of a region than of a local community. In many regions too the ugliness and pollution which result from growth can only be controlled by land-use and investment planning over wider and wider areas. Land use and transportation are, moreover, critical factors in planning education, the health services and the hundred and one other services which government provides. Because of the importance of preventing the population explosion from overwhelming the amenities of Southern and Central England, because of the appalling housing situation in Glasgow and in other large cities — in part at least the result of central mismanagement, because of the need for economy as the demand for more and better services escalates, the

75

Commissions were, from the beginning, inclined to pay little attention to democracy as opposed to efficiency, to the convenience of representatives as opposed to the convenience of specialists. In a sense, they were seeking to meet an emergency by the traditional method of concentrating authority rather than seeking a just solution for all time.[1] Yet the basic question is not, whether there should be regional units and plans of some kind or other: the basic question is, what kind of regional units, monolithic, federal or co-operative, comprehensive or special purpose, autonomous or agent, and of what smaller units they should be made up.

Both Royal Commissions had to concede that few if any of the authorities recommended by them were "sufficiently close to the ground to give expression to the voice of individual neighbourhoods".[2] Both also had to recognise that the evidence of their own researchers showed, in the words of the Scots, that "almost everyone interviewed was able to think of his or her 'home' area only in very local terms indeed".[3] "This is one field," says Senior too, "in which a research study sponsored by ourselves has produced clear and decisive results."[4] The findings of the English Commission's community attitude survey showed indeed that, for the great majority of people living in big towns, the community with which the people can identify is very much smaller than that of the local authority area in question.[5] According to the survey, only in towns with populations of less than 60,000 does even a considerable minority feel a sense of belonging to the local government unit, whether borough or urban district. In the country too, the unit of community feeling is not the county or the rural district but the civil parish or an even smaller unit than that: only 2% of the people thought of the rural district as their home area whereas 85% thought of it as the parish or something smaller.[6] This appears to tally with what sociologists have been finding generally: according to Dr. R. E. Pahl, "most recent evidence suggests that it is the small group of eight to twelve houses which forms the focus of positive relationships of either friendliness or hostility,"[7] which suggests that even parishes and wards are too large.

Not that it is any easier to define community than to define individual or nation. To Ronald Frankenberg, "size is not the only key. Community implies having something in common,"[8] which is not always true of an urban housing estate but may, presumably, be true of a rural county. Frankenberg goes on to say that "those who live in a community have overriding economic interests which are the same or complementary" but perhaps he comes nearest to hitting the nail on the head later in the same passage when he says that those who live in a community "are never indifferent to each other" and that participation in community activities is more a matter of mutual obligation than of voluntary recreation.[9]

The direct economic interdependence of the peasant community is disappearing even in the country today. "What we have instead," according to Pahl, "is a degree of local social control and a community consciousness or local ideology so that people behave as if there was an autonomy which does not exist."[10] However, local planning problems, the local distribution of facilities, local variations on social status, can still provide objective bases for what Pahl prefers to call a "locality social system" rather than a community.[11]

In any case, "mobility is limited by class, career and life cycle characteristics," according to Pahl, and "will never destroy the importance of locality."[12] Neither, one might add, will it automatically destroy the distinction between town and country, even amongst the mobile.

It is easy for a suburban-bred administrator to underestimate the amount of local savour and sense of continuity which persists in many districts and which could be harnessed to local government. To assume, for example, that because a man commutes, he belongs to a larger unit, is something of an apathetic fallacy: in most Welsh county towns, a man commutes precisely because his ties with his original community are so strong. As a citizen, the commuter may still belong to his dormitory as surely as the seasonal commuter belongs to — and is acknowledged to belong to — the place where he leaves his wife and child. Mobility is indeed enabling more and more "rootless" people to choose their community — to put down

roots — and a parish citizen or countryman by choice tends
to be even more formidable than a parish citizen or countryman by birth. The case for larger units which encompass
work and leisure does not destroy the case for recognising
their constituent cells as autonomous units. To recognize
such cells and to develop them as communities in their own
right may be the only way of reducing congestion to a tolerable level in the towns. To fail to recognise them is to sanction, instead of tempering, the natural unrelenting imperialism
of the town.

There is little dispute that some kind of council at the level
of the parish or ward is necessary to make the local community
articulate. Such councils are an essential part of the Redcliffe-
Maud system for "the bigger the main authorities, the more an
effective system of democracy will require local representative
institutions capable both of rallying and giving expression to
local opinion and of doing a number of things for themselves."[13] These "local councils" would "not . . . provide
main services, but . . . promote and watch over the particular
interests of communities."[14] There would, however, be no
limit on their powers to levy a rate and undertake functions.
In the towns, as opposed to the country, where "Parish
Councils represent communities as Rural District Councils do
not",[15] local councils would be based on existing authorities,
i.e. upon the Boroughs and Urban Districts — some of them as
big as Bristol. This means that some local councils might take
on functions of substance and, in the view of the English
Commission's critics, seek to rival the new unitary authorities.
The "community councils" advocated by the Scottish Commission are more modestly conceived, dependent on grants
and donations, devoid of power to levy a rate, and "not . . .
part of the structure of local government."[16] It would be up
to a community to decide whether they wanted one or not —
to express their views, to improve the amenities of their area
and possibly to act as agents for the authorities proper. For
his part Senior, too, sees the need for "an organ of representative government at grass roots level": he calls it a "common
council," seeing in this term "the proper English equivalent of

its Continental counterpart, the commune"[17] – a significant comparison, as we shall see. Senior considers that his 148 second tier authorities would be small enough to enable the bigger towns to identify themselves with the local authority proper. There would thus be no need for the common council to help to administer statutory services and it would be "a quite different kind of animal from the service running local authority": localities with that "real feeling of community" which can support a common council do not exist everywhere, so common councils cannot have duties which have to be provided everywhere. Apart from voicing community feeling, their tasks would be in the field of recreation and amenity and in this field they would have a general power to act and to precept on the rates. They would also have a right to be consulted on planning matters and to nominate the majority of governors of schools in their area. The English Commission's discussion of local councils has an air of uneasy conscience about it: one must nevertheless agree with Senior that the concept of the local council is one of the most valuable to emerge from their discussions and that local councils could "do more to revitalise local democracy than anything else they could propose." As Senior puts it, "many thousands of able professional and business people who consider the administrative work of district or county councils a time-wasting chore are nevertheless willing to devote a great deal of attention to the parish pump."[18] And many thousands of able non-professional and non-business people too.

In advocating grass-roots councils, primarily as sounding-boards for opinion, the Royal Commissions were playing their own variation on a theme which is becoming increasingly popular, the theme of participation. Shortly before the Royal Commissions reported, the Government had received the report of the Skeffington Committee on Public Participation in Planning. This Committee had been established – rather belatedly in view of the fact that the first comprehensive Town and Country Planning Act became Law in 1947 – "to consider and report on the best methods, including publicity, of securing the participation of the public at the formative

stage in the making of development plans for their area".[19]
Participation, according to the Skeffington Committee, is
"the act of sharing in the formulation of policies and proposals".[20] In the introduction to their report, they express
the hope that, although their recommendations are set in the
field of planning, some of them will be of assistance in other
fields: planning is indeed the best point of entry to most of
those other fields. The principle of public participation "can
improve the quality of decisions by public authorities and
give personal satisfaction to those affected by their decisions".[21] It is particularly important at a time of brisk technological change in a densely populated island which somehow
has to accommodate a further fifteen million inhabitants
within the next three decades.

The main methods of participation advocated by the
Committee were, the supply of information to the public
throughout the process of formulating plans, the promotion
of community forums in which local organisations could
discuss issues of importance to a locality, and which might also
help with disseminating information and with opinion surveys,
and the appointment of community development officers to
"secure the involvement" of non-joiners. The job of the
community development officer would be "to work with
people, to stimulate discussion, to inform people in their
neighbourhood and to give people's views to the authority".[22]
Participation along these lines would be a costly process both
in material and in man-hours. Planning Departments in
particular would need sufficient staff to:

1. Arrange and attend public meetings;
2. Give talks and lectures to associations;
3. Meet individuals wishing to make representations;
4. Receive and evaluate letters;
5. Correspond with those making representations;
6. Staff exhibitions.[23]

In addition planning authorities would have to give grants to
community forums and pay community development officers.
Moreover, the whole process of planning would become more

complicated and the consideration of proposals by the authority and by the public would have to be very well synchronised if the delay traditionally associated with planning were not to become worse still, with owners and others kept in a state of uncertainty as to whether their property would or would not ultimately be affected and greater danger of "planning blight".

Even the mild form of participation advocated by the Skeffington Committee would result in more pressure than ever upon the elected member. To the Committee, "he is the man at the heart of the activity".[24] He will have to keep himself well informed on planning even if not on the planning committee itself; he will have to take part in participation projects, explain proposals and send forward comments from his own ward; and all this time he will have to think of his authority's area as a whole and not just of his own ward; he will also be involved in a good deal of extra evening work and so will the officers, especially the senior officers who bear the main burden of public meetings. At the same time — though Skeffington does not make this point — the growth of specialisms and sub-specialisms, each with its own technical jargon, and the general neglect of education in citizenship makes it more and more difficult for public and planners to communicate with one another. Communication is difficult enough amongst people on the same level educationally. How many transportation experts appreciate the viewpoint of the architect? How many town and country planners are versed in the niceties of political science? How many political scientists appreciate the basic issues of classical political philosophy? How many philosophers read poetry? Exasperation on the platform, despair in the body of the hall (or vice versa), is all too likely to prevail in a public meeting about planning: at the very least you must have on the platform elected representatives and chief officers of real authority and maturity to guide a meeting even at the level of a parish.

In spite of all this, neither the Skeffington Committee nor the Royal Commissions (who wanted consultation with community councils) appear to have appreciated that participation has implications for major authorities as well as for wards and parishes. If consultation is to be taken seriously, the deciding authority as well as the authority consulted has to have a manageable area. Even in a compact county like Pembrokeshire, holding meetings in all the localities involved in the reorganisation of schools, and on the variety of issues which flare up from time to time, involves the Chairman of the Education Committee and the Director of Education in many a long, arduous evening after a long day. Between 10th January, 1966 and 3rd March, 1966, for example, seventeen meetings with parents were held in connection with the introduction of comprehensive education at Haverfordwest, Milford Haven and Pembroke: 1,338 parents attended these meetings, while the attendance ranged from eight at the far-flung village of Angle to 265 at one of the two meetings in the county town.[25] Had four times the area of Pembrokeshire to be covered, as in the proposed county of Dyfed, such tasks would be impossible without wholesale delegation. Delegation is rarely acceptable to those consulted: they always wish to see the people who count and not some subordinate, however smooth. Delegation in the field of participation often leads to more misunderstanding and resentment than would have been caused by no consultation at all: there is a fatal lack of finality about meetings with subordinates.

Like Skeffington, the Royal Commissions also failed to appreciate that "participation" is very much more vital than a public relations exercise and that planning is much more than a matter of design. It is not only for the sake of responsive government and improving local recreational facilities and amenities that grass-roots units of government are necessary. The local community is still capable of giving as well as receiving. In many fields today the professionals are having to recognise that they need local help and that decentralisation is the only answer to the shortage of manpower and money and space at the centre — centralisation and decentralisation are often complementary processes. There is, for example, a new emphasis on community care in the social services — a recognition that individuals and families at risk usually belong

to a local community, that the community itself can contribute
both to their problems and to their re-habilitation: it may even
be the community, or at least its environment, which requires
treatment.[26] Social workers are thus becoming more and more
involved with community work, with participation and even
with pressure groups like Shelter; they are also becoming more
ready to recognise their dependence on the community to
help their clients, and more ready too to enlist volunteers.
The Meals on Wheels service has long depended on volunteers.
We are now arriving at the point where Home Helps will have
to be volunteers – or people of professional status earning as
much as General Practitioners. The need for them is not being
met at the moment and just before the General Election, the
Government were discussing the development of Good Neighbour Schemes and Voluntary Community Groups with the
local authority associations.

In the field of mental health, of prison after-care and of
care for the elderly and the handicapped, the emphasis is
decidedly on care in the community. Dozens of patients
have been discharged from some mental hospitals and now
reside in small hostels which look like any other house. A
county council's children's home may be just another council
house for a largish family.

Again, in the field of education, most of the demand for
play groups and nursery schools is having to be met by the
local community. Schools proper too are being opened in
various ways to the public, with the joint use of halls and
sports facilities and the provision of facilities by parent-
teacher associations: the Professor of Education at York has
even said that parents should be allowed to help in the classroom. At the same time, as the Schools Council's project on
social education shows, more children are being trained to
observe and identify with and even participate in the social
work of, their own locality – and also in improving the
physical environment, work which has its adult counterpart in
the civic societies, of which nearly 500 have been established
since 1957.[27] Even in the museum field, the tendency is to
move out into the community. Even in the fire service, there

is a recognition that the limitation of loss depends mainly, not on the extension of cover, but on fire prevention measures, publicity and education,[28] all of which need local backing to be effective: the same could be said of other services concerned with safety.

More social workers are being attached to local schools, health centres and social services centres. Even in the general hospital field, it is being suggested that "many people now in hospital would be at least as well off in their own homes or even at work".[29] A high proportion of the cases dealt with by hospital consultants and other staff in outpatient and casualty departments never enter hospital and it would be much more logical to bring more hospital services out into the local health centres, which could be given instant access to distant computer terminals in order to keep and retrieve their records.

One result of instituting a unified health service and a unified social service might be to speed up the progress of care in the community but it cannot be speeded up if the sense of community continues to decline. There can be no doubt that it is better for many old, disabled and sick people to live amongst their friends instead of being in some strange institution, however humane. This will be much more difficult if there is no basic feeling of community left in the localities: there is, for example, little point in setting up an "ordinary" hostel for the mentally handicapped in an entirely self-centred community which ostracises them — local volunteers have a role to play as opinion leaders as well as providers of help.[30] With the increasing mobility of the population, the family is becoming less and less capable of giving succour to its members. We shall have to rely more and more on territorial as opposed to family or religious sense of community. And as Sir Goronwy Daniel put it recently in discussing the problems of replacing the twenty-two local authorities of East Glamorgan by one unitary authority, "many voluntary workers are most interested in making their services available close to their own home and within their local community. Not only their interests but practical considerations of the time they can make available and the cost of extensive travelling incline them in this direction . . . they are normally anxious to get on as directly and simply as possible with the job they are interested in and are not as a rule over-fond of form filling and report writing . . . community councils . . . having no professional staff of their own . . . will not be able to provide a local link between the voluntary and professional worker . . . it is important to the general health of society that people with . . . a contribution to make should be given ready opportunities for making it and it would be a great tragedy if the need for this were to be neglected as the result of bureaucratic considerations".[31] If people with a contribution to make are becoming fewer and if the bond of neighbourhood is losing its force, should we not be considering how to halt and reverse this process? Taking genuine decision-making political institutions further away from the localities will not help us to preserve local self-respect or to focus local feeling and co-ordinate local effort. Responsibility without power can be just as debilitating as power without responsibility.

Another factor which should make us reluctant to move the town hall or the county office further away from most communities is the constant and growing need of the citizen for information and interpretation and know-how. The administrative problems which can arise and which require some expertise in knowing to whom to turn for help, let alone in actually helping, are innumerable in every locality today. It is not in spite of centralisation that there is an emphasis on local consultation today: it is because there is so much more. When governments did little more than wage war with the help of a professional army and keep order with the help of a voluntary magistracy, it did not matter so much that the ordinary citizen had little part to play in public affairs. Now that the Government is omnipotent and ubiquitous, its finger in every pie, a citizen who has no personal contact with the authorities can become utterly bewildered or blissfully irresponsible. Even in a sparsely populated rural area of a few square miles — an area as uncomplicated in its economy as it is possible to imagine in the United Kingdom today — a certain county official can vouch for having been personally

approached within the space of five years for official advice —
advice normally only available in a county town at least fifteen
miles away — on substantial problems in the following fields:

> Registration of Common Land;
> Enclosure of Common Land;
> Ownership of Waste Land;
> Housing a family at risk;
> University entrance;
> Training facilities in Social Service;
> Petition for improved hospital facilities;
> Stopping of unemployment benefit (welfare aspect);
> Staffing ratio at village school;
> Repair of bridge;
> Improvement of dangerous bends;
> Necessity for certain road signs;
> Qualification for registration as elector;
> Return of election expenses;
> Planning permission;
> Repositioning of Telephone Kiosk;
> Delay in provision of street lighting;
> Unauthorised dumping;
> Extension of water supply;
> Unsatisfactory working conditions;
> Compulsory removal to hospital;
> Grants for apprentices;
> Preservation of building of special interest;
> Status of footpath;
> Trust deed of village hall, and grant for its improve-
> ment;
> Securing forms in the Welsh language;
> Complaint of unbalanced parent against school;
> Positioning of public convenience on manorial waste;
> Grant for local eisteddfod.

To say that such problems can be dealt with over the
telephone or by correspondence is completely unrealistic even
in the case of eloquent conversationalists and inveterate letter
writers. Invariably, the further away the headquarters, the

more difficult it is to obtain satisfaction – and the less likely it is that the organisation in question is in close touch with the many other organisations likely to be involved in any administrative issue.

This brings us to another point which Skeffington only hints at – that participation is not a matter for planning departments alone or for any department in isolation but rather for the local government service as a whole: "what is thrown open for public debate must be a comprehensive policy for the whole environment, in its functional as well as its visual aspects, and not just a policy for the use of land."[32] If the participants are to be capable of conceiving of their community as a whole, they must represent small territorial units rather than sectional pressure groups organised over wide areas. If they are to stand any chance of giving as good as they get in the discussion, they must have some professional assistance in preparing for it. And if they themselves are to be able to feel the pulse even of their own small community, the people they represent must be able to turn to their office for help with all those odds and ends of government which affect their daily lives.

II

"Until August 1914," says A. J. P. Taylor, "a sensible law-abiding Englishman could pass through life and hardly notice the existence of the state, beyond the post office and the policeman."[33] Today there are as many civil servants in Wales as there were in the whole United Kingdom a century ago[34] – 40,000 – and hundreds of regulations to go with them: from para.1b of the Schedule to the Food Standards (Tomato Ketchup), Order, 1949, which states (*inter alia*) that "tomato ketchup, catsup, sauce or relish shall be so strained, with or without heating, as to exclude seeds or other coarse or hard substances," to para.4 of Schedule 7 of the Finance Act 1967, which prudently enacts that if the clerk to licensing justices should fail to render a return of certain matters to H. M.

Customs and Excise, he shall be liable to a maximum fine of
£5. In this "age of interference", people will often feel
annoyed, frustrated or bewildered without easy access to a
government office simply because they do not understand
what is going on. In some cases — decisions about the siting
of motorways, airports, oil refineries or reservoirs, for example,
and, equally, decisions not to allow development in the
interests of beauty and recreation — the extent of public
dissatisfaction will sometimes force a government to choose
between ineffectiveness and repression. The number of
decisions of this kind is multiplying rapidly and it is no use
allowing people to participate in some process of consultation
unless they feel that they do have power to influence the
ultimate decision. "Unless the local people have power to
achieve or boycott something," says Pahl in his attempt to
define "community", "the community-in-the-mind is simply a
common delusion, shielding local people from the real
world."[35] Consulting people before the authority has come
to any firm conclusion and before attitudes have hardened on
each side is important but does not go nearly far enough. In a
masterly essay on Public Involvement in Planning, Senior has
criticised the Skeffington Committee for advocating participation at the stage when the planning authority has already
decided (admittedly without commitment) which solution it
prefers, rather than at the preceding stage of "identification of
choices available," with the authority explaining "what each
alternative implies in terms of the subordination of one
possible objective to another" and the public making the
value judgements which only the ordinary citizen has a right
to make. Senior accepts too that such judgements should be
the province, not of community forums of sectional organisations or of community development officers working amongst
the non-joiners, but of elected local councils concerned with
the well-being of the community as a whole and prepared "to
make necessary changes which no sectional interest wants, and
to withstand pressures which no sectional interest opposes."[36]
What Senior does not suggest is that the value judgements of
a community council should be in any way binding upon the

planning authority, even initially and subject to further
negotiation and appeal, or even in relation to the design plan
alone. Yet if participation is to be more than a public relations
exercise, the people of a locality need to feel that there is a
real chance of their case being accepted as well as being heard.
And where their voting strength could never count for much
on a national or continental scale, they need the kind of
security whcih a formal written constitution might give them,
a recognition that some degree of sovereignty over its own
area remains with the local community.

The concentration of power in the United Kingdom today
might well lead most of us to give up all hope of influencing
events. As Professor Keeton puts it, "a single chamber has
unlimited competence . . . the government, who are leaders of
the dominant party in the House of Commons, may over a
period of approximately five years make legislative changes of
unlimited extent."[37] Much of the authority of the government
itself has to be delegated to the civil service, a civil service
which can be given only limited suprevision and which is liable
to become increasingly resentful of "political" interference as
its decision-making becomes more systematic — though a
question in parliament or a personal contact may bring something he has delegated to the notice of the Minister, even he
has to work as a member of a team both within and outside
his department: with the best will in the world, he cannot
afford continually to upset his servants in the department or
his colleagues in the Cabinet. As for delegated legislation, after
the summer recess of 1968, the statutory instruments committee of the House of Commons found more than 500
Orders awaiting their examination.[38] And though in some
cases ministerial decisions are subject to judicial review, the
number of decided cases which may be relevant in a search
for the law on a particular point is formidable indeed: as long
ago as 1916, there were 6,836 volumes of British law reports.
The capacity of judges to defend the citizen may be severely
restricted in the near future by dependence on a central
computer, and those who programme it, for knowledge of
the law.[39]

The success of the movement against making Stansted London's third airport is sometimes quoted as an example of the way in which a determined local community can still defeat the civil service. Was not Stansted's success due, however, to the fact that some influential local residents had friends at court? The Government's initial decision to designate Stansted is more significant: this reversed conclusions reached at a public local enquiry which lasted over 39 days and which involved the Essex County Council in heavy expenditure, both at the inquiry itself and in an attempt to gain acceptance for the inquiry's conclusions. Eventually the Roskill Committee was set up to report on alternative sites for the airport but, by October 1968, a further statutory instrument (No.1623 of 1968) had been made to enable the British Airports Authority to carry out major developments at their airports without first having to receive planning permission.[40] The privileged position of public bodies such as the nationalised industries in the field of planning control has also been highlighted by the case of the Abingdon gasometer. In this case the regional Gas Board, having decided to build a gasometer in a grossly unsuitable place, were able to obtain a very large sum of money from Abingdon Borough Council in consideration of their putting it elsewhere! Only after prolonged negotiations with the Government department concerned were the Council able to have the sum reduced to one that they could just afford. Cynicism about the good faith of nationalised industries and departments of state is widespread: few objectors attend an enquiry with any real hope of success.

In theory, of course, the present political system is self-righting, but consider the experience of the Liberal Party in the General Election of 1964. It put up 365 candidates; it was given the status of a major party on television and in the press; it polled respectably in every constituency. Yet it actually won only nine seats: 11.2% of the votes gained only 1.4% of the seats. In England, properly excluding Cornwall as well as Wales and Scotland, the position was even more ludicrous: 2,714,068 votes and only two members.[41] In most constituencies, a vote for the Liberals was quite literally wasted, and this is an indictment, not of the Liberal Party but of the British Constitution, which, without proportional representation, only allows our complex society to choose the lesser of two over-simplified evils.

If the British Constitution is unfair to a historic third party like the Liberals, it is positively oppressive towards any fourth, fifth or sixth parties which wish to present a case. At a time when the main debate takes place on television, Plaid Cymru, fighting every seat in Wales, and the Scottish National Party, fighting most of those in Scotland, have to be content with 4 minutes 40 seconds each to put their case and scarcely a mention on the main news bulletins and discussion pro-grammes, which concentrate on the two rival presidents. Yet if the candidates for any one constituency were to appear on the same platform, no democrat would dare suggest that two of them should speak for fifty minutes, one for thirty and one only for five. In a large, impersonal, over-centralised field like broadcasting, injustice can easily pass for convenience or realism but there is a direct connection between this kind of injustice and the fact that some nationalists think it naive of Gwynfor Evans and Plaid Cymru to believe that self-government can be attained by constitutional methods alone — must we accept Camus' provisional verdict on rebels: "if they retreat, they must accept death; if they advance, they must accept murder."

The increasing power of television and of the few daily newspapers which are now economically viable does mean that the right of freedom of speech is far less valuable for minorities than it was a century ago.[42] "The massive popular press," according to Richard Hoggart, "must restrict itself to the appeals and attitudes which are most popular."[43] The growing proportion of people employed by the state and other large organisations also means that it is becoming less and less "popular" to stick one's neck out: whatever formal rights one may have, the best way to advance is to keep well in with everyone of any consequence. Shortly before the last General Election, even *The Times* and *The Guardian* did not see fit to print a letter from leaders of the religious denominations of Wales drawing attention to the injustice to Plaid Cymru in the matter of election broadcasts[44] (See Appendix 1). "Where all are pals," says Herbert Butterfield, "there's no need for censorship."[45] And by this he means, not so much a deliberate conspiracy as an unconscious condition of society.

To appreciate fully the crucial importance of grass-roots participation and community feeling, one has to consider issues far wider than local government reform. Both Royal Commissions appear to have regarded community and local councils as a kind of optional extra not vital to the survival of the local government system. Had they given more weight to the increasing amount of governmental interference in ordinary life, to the increasing impact of governmental decisions upon local communities as a whole, and, above all, to the increasing alienation of masses of people from any sense of identification with government, might they not have concluded that the problem of the local community was, in fact, the major problem which lay before them? The evidence before them showed conclusively that most local government units are already too big to command the loyalty of their citizens. If some of them are small from the point of view of economy, larger units may well be impossibly big from the point of view of democracy. Both Royal Commissions assumed that all the average citizen requires is efficiency but neither asked what sort of citizen society is producing.

In spite of the fact that so many people feel helpless in the face of the authorities, we are certainly not living in a planner's paradise in which a well informed and rational government always has its own way. For all its power, the Government is often at the mercy of comparatively small groups who are sufficiently determined to break the law or to damn the consequences to others, or who are sufficiently young to be able to question the very legitimacy of authority. People who are reasonably well fed, clad and housed are more than willing to go on strike out of a sense of relative, rather than crying, injustice — schoolmasters and doctors as much as steel workers and dockers. As for the really powerful lobbies like T.U.C., the B.M.A. (making the most of their discreet collective power of life and death), the nationalised industries and the international corporations, they often appear to give the orders rather than to take them.

Crime has never been better organised; neither have those means of escape from humanity, the drug industry, the drink industry and pornography — five years ago, according to Charing Cross Hospital casualty department, a drug addict was a rarity: now they treat ten to fifteen a day and the number is increasing, most of the patients being young people destined to suffer agonisingly and to die within a few years at the longest.[46] Intelligent and idealistic students, from the most disinterested if the least experienced section of the community, appear to reject our very conception of society.[47] Perhaps we should welcome a good deal of the unrest which is being expressed, however rudely and violently; from the point of view of preserving community, angry interaction is better than no interaction at all and the most ominous feature of our society is not occasional anarchy so much as general apathy. An excess of television not only sanctifies the trivial but separates performer and spectator to such an extent that the whole of life becomes a mere spectacle.

Those who are content to base local government reform on the thesis that "very few people indeed worry about who provides services so long as they are properly provided"[48] (which begs the whole question anyway) might consider a murder committed in a "staid, middle-class, tree-lined" street in a quickly growing part of New York at about 3.20 a.m. on the night of 13th March, 1964.[49] The murderer stalked his prey, a young woman, Catherine Genovese, for over half an hour. He stabbed her to death at the third attempt, having twice been interrupted by the switching on of lights and the sound of voices which followed her screams for help. Fifteen minutes later, one man telephoned the police: only when detectives made enquiries did it transpire that no less than 38 respectable people had watched the whole incident. Practically everyone gave the same excuse for not calling the police after the first attack, let alone taking action themselves: "I did not wish to get involved." If this is an extreme case, this is only because, according to the Metropolitan Editor of the *New York Times,* "38 did that night what each alone might have done any night without the city having known or cared."

Writing these lines in the idyllic Pembrokeshire countryside in May, with little personal experience of violent disorder or of hard times, it is hard not to feel that the dangers to society are too remote to affect my generation or my children's, that the very process of retailing news highlights the trouble in the world. But the prevailing wind blows from across the Atlantic and there is no room for complacency. After the shooting dead by National Guardsmen of four students on the campus of Kent University, Ohio, an American professor wrote to *The Guardian:* "Students and faculty, having tried other means to improve American life, now feel they must resort to self-destruction to prove the intensity of their frustrations . . . if English universities are to double in size by 1980, as has been announced, and if the quality of life regarding immorality, impersonality, financial care, and rising unemployment are to continue in England, then Englishmen may expect similar conditions on their own campuses in the 1970's."[50] Again, Sir Alec Clegg, Chief Education Officer of the West Riding, warned us in a recent lecture that "from January this year, police in Washington have patrolled junior and senior high schools. Lest anyone say that it could not happen here let him bear in mind that crimes of violence among older adolescents have increased by just under 1,000% in the last 18 years".

Then there are the reports of New York construction workers systematically beating up students in Wall Street, while the police looked on, and forming flying columns to plunge into other areas of the city "to punish anyone remotely in favour of America abandoning the war in Vietnam and Cambodia".[51] People of substance are concerned about police brutality and lawlessness, not only in America, but in Wales and in Australia, while secret police activity, the keeping of dossiers and electronic surveillance have aroused William O. Douglas, a Justice of the United States Supreme Court itself, to throw his weight behind the "forces of dissent" in their protest against prejudices and attitudes "that prepare us to think alike and be submissive objects for the regime of the computer".[52] Hardly had Justice Douglas' book been published when President Nixon asked his Department of Health, Education and Welfare to study proposals that all six-year-old children in the United States be given psychological tests to determine their potential for criminal behaviour, followed in appropriate cases by "massive psychological and psychiatric treatment." It does not diminish one's misgivings to know that the authority who made the proposal had seen Pavlovian methods effectively used in the Soviet Union.[53]

Marx's view that the very process of industrialisation and division of labour would create a proletariat alienated from society is more true than the lack of militancy of that proletariat might lead one to imagine. Though social barriers have become less rigid, the sheer geographical distance between classes is being extended: most of the goals set up by television and the press are such that few people can aspire to them except by chance (the chance industry is another which is thriving). Education too is becoming more divisive as equal opportunity mops up those pockets of intellect which used to leaven the life of the steel works, the construction site and the road gang: when a working farmer or a redundant quarryman wins the Chair at the National Eisteddfod of Wales, it is now regarded as something of a miracle but to Simone Weil there was something "woefully wrong with the health of a social system when a peasant tills the soil with the idea in his mind that, if he is a peasant, it is because he was not intelligent enough at school to become a schoolteacher." Universal literacy is little help: "a very large number of people have been held down at an appallingly low level in their reading."[54] says Hoggart, who fears that mass-publications are keeping working people in "a new and stronger form of subjection," in chains "both easier to wear and harder to strike away than those of economic subordination,"[55] and that we may eventually move towards "a new caste system, one at least as firm as the old".[56] Hoggart has said that, since he wrote *The Uses of Literacy* thirteen years ago, "the tendencies towards processing human beings and making us more and more a centralised, meritocratic, machine-tooled society"[57] are going on as fast as he thought, if not faster — though he also acknowledges that he underestimated the capacity of some people to fight back. In *The Uses of Literacy,* he maintained, from experience, that the English working class was alienated from government and mistrustful of even the benevolent forms of authority: even the younger people, less actively hostile and less deferential, had contracted out of any belief in the importance of the bosses' world, while, in the division between "us" and "them", "them" included "those civil servants or local authority employees whom the working classes meet — teachers, the school attendance man, the corporation, the local bench."[58] Raymond Williams came to much the same conclusion independently of Hoggart and in spite of a rather different type of working class background, rural and Welsh, in which it was nothing unusual for the sons of poor families to go on to the university and become teachers and preachers: "the fact is that working-class people cannot feel that this *is* their community in anything like the sense in which it is felt above them ... What 'they' decide is still the practical experience of life and work,"[59] while "few men can give the best of themselves as servants; it is the reduction of man to a function".[60] Williams himself sees the remedy, not in exhortation, but in "conceding the practice of democracy".[61] Small units induce democracy. This may or may not make them less efficient from day to day. From decade to decade, however, it probably makes them more stable and in the long run efficiency itself depends on stability: "only freedom can make security secure."

The ordinary citizen today is in an extraordinary position. On the one hand he has neither a formal written constitution or a faith in democratic institutions to protect him; on the other the decisions imposed upon him are seldom the result of bureaucratic consensus, let alone systematic management. As more and more people are willing to have recourse to industrial action, to publicity stunts and to breaking the law, the hope of achieving consensus, of obtaining government by discussion and consent and of making certain constitutional rights sacrosanct becomes more and more remote.

Both Royal Commissions accepted that the basic units they advocated were too big to cater for civic identity and for democracy. They ignored signs that lack of faith in democracy is already threatening the ordinary processes of government, and that the remoteness of the welfare state is destroying that very sense of community which gave it birth. They made mountains of the inefficiency of local authorities which, compared to the leviathan of central government, are mere moles. They did not even consider the inefficiency of the political structure as a whole. On being challenged to produce evidence of local government inefficiency, the civil service tend to say that they were considering, not so much present capacity as capacity to meet future demands. But it is no use trying to project how many cars there will be in 1999 unless you consider also what sort of people will be driving them. What does the future hold and, more important, what do we want it to hold? If it holds increasing centralisation in store, may this not also involve a backlash of violence or disorder until the local community has once again to police itself or remain unpoliced? If it holds rapid economic growth in store, does this not also involve increasing pollution and ugliness and uniformity for many areas, and artificial sterilisation for some — congestion here and atrophy there — unless the local community condemned has the power and the self-respect to call a halt? For decades now, central government has had immense power to shape our society. It has done badly and has lost its hold on people's hearts. It is time that local government, with the active participation of local people, was given the opportunity of doing better.

In itself no amount of democratic local government can protect a country from the diminishing of man but there can be no doubt that local democracy tends to work against that diminishment, while centralisation facilitates it. To spend a great deal of energy (and according to Cheshire County Council's consultants, £200 million)[62] on creating a uniform pattern of large local authorities at a time like this may well be fiddling when Rome is about to burn. Should we not be bringing people into government, not taking them out? The absentee landlord, the class which cuts itself off from its roots, eventually has to account, not to elected representatives but to the mob. And if every generation in turn thinks that mankind is going to the dogs, there is a strong body of opinion, as we shall see in the next chapter, amongst those who look at present trends from a less transitory point of view than most of us which is gravely concerned about centralisation. This body is more worried about over-large units than about setting the lower limit to the ideal unit. "What does the citizen want" is too superficial a question; the basic question must be, what he is.

Notes to Chapter 4

1.   Cf. Bernard Crick, *In Defence of Politics,* Pelican 1964, p.28, where "the problem of how to maintain a state through time (which is a problem of spreading power)" is held to be more normal than that of "how to preserve it in crisis (which is a problem of concentrating power)."
2.   RCLGS, para.717.
3.   *Ibid.,* para.591.
4.   Senior, para.442.
5.   RCLGE, III, Appendix 7, para.98.
6.   RCLGE, I, paras.233-35.
7.   *Patterns of Urban Life,* London 1970, pp.119-20.
8.   *Communities in Britain, Social Life in Town and Country,* London 1966, p.238.
9.   *Ibid.,* p.239.
10.   *Patterns of Urban Life,* p.107.
11.   *Ibid.,* pp.107-113.
12.   Is the Mobile Society a Myth? *New Society,* XI, pp.46-48.
13.   RCLGE, I, para.371.
14.   *Ibid.,* para.12. See also paras.379-392.
15.   *Ibid.,* para.375.
16.   RCLGS, para.865. See also paras.845-871.
17.   Senior, para.426 *et seq.*
18.   *Ibid.,* para.449.
19.   *People and Planning,* H.M.S.O. 1969, para.1.
20.   *Ibid.,* para.5(a).
21.   *Ibid.,* para.2.
22.   *Ibid.,* para.253, VI.
23.   The list is from *ibid.,* para.217.
24.   *Ibid.,* para.43 *et seq.*
25.   Pembrokeshire County Council, *A Unitary Authority for Pembrokeshire,* Haverfordwest 1970, p.11 and Table III.
26.   Anthony Forder and Sheila Kay, Recent Developments in Social Work: a Survey Article, *Social and Economic Administration,* Vol.3, No.2 (April 1969) p.89 *et seq.*
27.   Dilys M. Hill, *Participating in Local Affairs,* London 1970, p.202. And see Anne Corbett, Community School, *New Society,* Vol.13, No.335 (27 February 1969).

28. Departmental Committee on the Fire Service, Report (Holroyd Report, Cmnd.4371) H.M.S.O., 1970, paras.3, 5 and 14.

29. George Teeling-Smith, The Role of Hospitals in Community Care, *Social and Economic Administration*, Vol.3, No.3 (July 1969) p.193.

30. Lady Serota, Family Health and the Social Services in the Seventies (The Fourth Eileen Younghusband Lecture), London 1970, p.13.

31. Participation in Community Life, Opening Address to the Seventh British Conference on Social Welfare, Swansea, 11 April 1970.

32. Derek Senior, Public Involvement in Planning, in Robson and Crick (ed.), *The Future of the Social Services*, London 1970, p.101.

33. *English History 1914-1945*, (1965) Pelican 1970, p.25.

34. Sir Goronwy Daniel, The Government in Wales. *Transactions of the Honourable Society of Cymmrodorion*, Session 1969, Part I, p.101.

35. *Patterns of Urban Life*, p.102.

36. *The Future of the Social Services*, p.102.

37. G. W. Keeton, United or Disunited Kingdom? *Current Legal Problems 1969*, London, 1969, p.41.

38. *Ibid.*, p.35 (quoting *Tht Times*).

39. Julius Stone, *Law and the Social Sciences*, Minneapolis, 1966, pp.68-69.

40. Keeton, pp.34-35.

41. For an expansion of this theme see my article. Democracy in 1966, *Welsh Dominion*, No.1, Summer 1967, p.2 *et seq.*

42. Cf. James D. Halloran, Philip Elliott and Graham Murdock, *Demonstrations and Communications: a Case Study*, London 1970, p.300 *et seq.*, which shows how practically all the media focused on one limited aspect of a certain demonstration (some violence) thus giving a wholly negative impression of those participating in it — and this, not through bias as such but through the preoccupation of the media with incidents as opposed to background.

43. *The Uses of Literacy*, Pelican ed. 1968. p.192. Mass culture also makes it "harder for people without an intellectual bent to become wide in their own way."

44. Editorial, *Barn*, No.93, July 1970.

45. *History and Human Relations*, London, 1951, pp.197-98.

46. Anne Robinson, *The Sunday Times*, 3 May 1970.

47. See Richard Hoggart, The End of the Protestant Ethic, *The Listener*, 9 April, 1970.

48. J. A. G. Griffith, Maud and Senior, in Andrews (ed.), *Welsh Studies in Public Law*, Cardiff 1970, p.116.

49. This paragraph derives from A. M. Rosenthal, Thirty Eight Witnesses, *New Society*, Vol.4, No.102 (10 September 1964) pp.11-15.

50. George S. Rousseau, *The Guardian*, 13 May 1970. See also a letter from a "faculty wife" at Kent, *The Sunday Times*, 24 May 1970.

51. Cal McCrystal, *The Sunday Times*, 17 May 1970.

52. The American Way of Protest, an extract from Justice Douglas' newly published book, *Points of Rebellion*, in *The Times*, Saturday Review, 16 May 1970. On the police in Australia, see Graham Parker, The Police and the Public, 134 *Justice of the Peace and Local Government Review*, pp.292-3; in Wales "Gomer", *Ibid.*, p.432.

53. 134 *Justice of the Peace and Local Government Review*, p.339.

54. *The Uses of Literacy*, p.192. Mass entertainment offers "nothing which can really grip the brain or heart."

55. *Ibid.*, p.201.

56. *Ibid.*, p.281.

57. *The Listener*, 9 April 1970.

58. *The Uses of Literacy*, p.53 *et seq.*, and pp.79-80.

59. *Culture and Society 1780-1950*, Pelican ed., 1961, pp.316-17.

60.   *Culture and Society 1780-1950*, p.317.
61.   *Ibid.*, p.304.
62.   *Local Government Chronicle*, 16 May 1970. The work was carried out independently by the Local Government Operational Research Unit and P. A. Management Consultants Ltd.

5. Efficiency, Humanity and Freedom

"... people know less of their neighbours than ever before in history. The pursuit of efficiency, ... is directed towards reducing the dependence of people on each other, and increasing their dependence on the machine ... by a gradual displacement of human effort from every aspect of living, technology will eventually enable us to slip swiftly through our allotted years with scarce enough of physical friction to be certain we are still alive."
EDWARD J. MISHAN

I

WE have seen that the efficiency of large local units was exaggerated by the Royal Commissions, that it may be possible to overcome the disadvantages of existing small units by giving them more functions and finance instead of more territory and that, even from the point of view of the Royal Commissions themselves, a tier of councils based on the smallest communities of all is necessary to the smooth running of the system. It is time to consider the problem from the opposite direction. To many thinkers, local democracy and local identity are positive virtues to the maintenance of which it might be worth sacrificing some efficiency, whether in the form of higher taxes, delay, friction, or even lower standards. Other thinkers question the whole concept of efficiency if, by efficiency, we mean continually trying to increase the gross national product. Perhaps the most serious weakness of all of the Royal Commissions was that they never considered to what extent their solution involved throwing out the babies of liberty and identity with the bath-water of inefficiency and sentimentality. Obliged by their terms of reference to examine local government outside its context in government generally, they chose also to ignore the wider social context. The short-term economic problems of the United Kingdom loom large in their reports: one looks in vain for any recognition of those long-term social trends which worry and which have long been worrying political philosophers, planners, poets and theologians.

Liberty is an unfashionable word today. To assert that the price of liberty is eternal vigilance is to invite many readers to assume that one knows nothing of management techniques: even the permissive society hesitates to permit local authorities to challenge the national minimum standards of civic respectability. Liberty is freedom to be different and freedom to be wrong. If man is a social animal, it is freedom for a community to be different and for a community to be wrong, not because there is any virtue in being wrong but because human judgement is so fallible, so fickle, so relative, that it is dangerous to impose the same human judgement everywhere. Professor J. A. G. Griffith himself concedes in his great work, *Central Departments and Local Authorities,* that "many, in some fields most, of the important national advances — both in policy and technique — have originated in the minds of the officers and members of local authorities, receiving a wider dissemination through the departments."[1] Anglesey was free to go comprehensive twenty-five years ago and Leicestershire has been free under successive governments to experiment with a two-tier secondary system. Might not the imposition of the comprehensive system generally have prevented some other Anglesey from demonstrating, for the benefit of all, that the weaknesses of the selective system can be countered in other ways or even that the present system is, in the less socially rigid type of society which is evolving, the lesser of two evils? In some areas, the premature imposition of the comprehensive system has merely substituted one type of discrimination for another: discrimination between Grammar School children and Secondary Modern children has given way to discrimination between the children of one district, who attend a superb new purpose-built school, and the children of another — predominantly working class perhaps —

who have to make do with old secondary modern buildings. There are enthusiasts for comprehensive education who think it bad for their own cause to make the change before the right buildings exist in the right place. There are those who, preferring the comprehensive system themselves, consider that you cannot legislate for equality and that a trend which began with directing local education authorities could end up with the oppression of religious minorities. There are those who believe that society depends on the early cultivation of outstanding talent: "the only children whose talents, according to the Donnison Report, entitle them to separate treatment are potential ballet-dancers," says Professor Beloff, "Frivolity and cynicism could go no further."[2] Whether he is right or not is, for the purpose of the present argument, beside the point: what is important is that there *are* two points of view and that even the Department of Education and Science of the United Kingdom of Great Britain and Northern Ireland is not infallible. At present the Department is able to distil the fruit of decades of local experiment, local perspectives, local traditions of excellence: an excess of central planning and of local sycophancy — on the part of the National Union of Teachers as well as on the part of the Department itself — could soon dry up the sources of new life.

Politicians often testify that one of the strongest forces with which they have to contend is the demand that there should be equality between the various parts of the United Kingdom, that nobody should suffer because of his place of birth. Have they not mistaken a telling debating point for a political principle? People do not live their lives according to the principle of equality alone. In the last resort, not a few prefer being unemployed in Blaenau Ffestiniog to earning good money in Wolverhampton, or consider that the intangible benefits of living in Pembrokeshire are worth the loss of a few hundred pounds a year in salary, and the addition of a few score miles from major centres of shopping, medicine and high life. Naturally, such people strive for the best of both worlds and demand the amenities of Cardiff in addition to those of St. David's — ironically, it is the apostles of uniformity

in Cardiff, and, *a fortiori,* London, who usually deny them
these. But there comes a point when a man must choose and,
to our great good fortune, men do not, as yet, choose alike.
That freedom to choose should be reflected in the decisions
of local communities and local governments. Indeed, if his
community has less freedom, the individual himself has less
opportunity to put his own freedom into practice, less capacity
to maintain the differences which he appreciates, less self-
respect. Only to his immediate community is the average man
capable of contributing a first-hand opinion; in a sense it is
from his immediate community that he derives his humanity.
All too often now, when the lives of the inhabitants of a
certain locality are made miserable by some nuisance by way
of smell or noise, all they can do about it is to write angry
letters to a remote administrative centre and, when that
administrative centre ignores their complaints, shrug their
shoulders and carry on with bad grace. Were the decision to
permit or to tolerate the nuisance to be in their own hands,
they might well find that the matter was far from simple.
They might well find neighbours championing the perpetrators
of the nuisance and learn to respect them. They might even
be forced to the same conclusion as the remote authority
themselves. But it is always preferable to have the opportunity
of interpreting the force of circumstances for oneself, rather
than have to take the word of some superior for it.

Over large areas of the world today, men identify themselves
with very large units, units of many millions of people, while
the mass media certainly play up this process. A man's
relationship with a large state is nevertheless more sentimental
than real. Nazi Germany is only the most extreme of many
examples of how horrifyingly and dangerously unreal a large
unit can be, and if the cult of loyalty to the unitary state could
become so monstrous in the country of Haydn and Beethoven
and Brahms, could this not happen anywhere in the course of
time? Even in the United Kingdom, according to Raymond
Williams, England's position as an imperial power has tended
to limit the sense of community to national lines.[3] Most men
only have experience of dealing with small groups. How can

they adapt themselves to the scale of the modern industrial state, a state which is itself having to adapt continually to changes in technology? "The weakness of parliamentary democracy," says G. D. H. Cole, "has been that it has presented the ordinary man with problems much too remote for him to solve rationally. As he must solve them somehow, he solves them irrationally . . . Democracy in the state was a great aspiration but in practice it was largely a sham." The democratic movements of the last century tended to distrust local authorities as strongholds of conservatism. They tried to create a direct but essentially artificial personal relationship between the individual and a monolithic state. Not only the civil service but the corresponding voluntary associations, including the trade unions and the political parties, were organised from the top down. And how, in many countries, even the grass roots of society have to be cultivated by organisers from the centre. Local dialects are preserved today by national societies centred on capital cities. Mobs descend upon the localities by central direction, often on a national scale. As a practising citizen, the individual is lost without that small political community which central propaganda does so much to belittle. More and more he has to express himself through central professional and sectional groups which cannot express the whole man and which, today, pose a much greater threat to human understanding than territorial parochialism: a parish is at least a microcosm of humanity as a whole, with the great advantage that the various fractions within it do meet face to face. At this level, direct observation does have some chance to prevail against the cultivated image. Where the party political label counts for little one sometimes sees a man magnanimously voting for what he did not previously support because of the good case put up by a person he knows and respects. Where party does matter you may see the same man voting against what he does support purely because it has been put forward by a centrally organised party other than his own. "If the citizens of a state are to judge and to distribute offices according to merit, then they must know each other's character," said Aristotle, who held that the right population for a state was "the largest number which suffices for the purpose of life *and can be taken in at a single view*." (my italics)[4] Even at the national level, according to a social analyst who considers that "the problem is not to grow but to stop growing," modern techniques have only extended "the population limit of healthy and manageable societies from hundreds of thousands to perhaps eight or ten million."[5] Television has certainly not put us back in the position of the Greek city state. On the contrary, modern image-making and simplifying techniques are far more likely to distort the truth than the most vicious old-fashioned whispering campaigns.

The great advocate of the small unit as a training ground for democracy is, of course, Alexis de Tocqueville, a philosopher to whom tremendous lip service is paid in university courses. When one considers that he is not so much as mentioned in the report of either Royal Commission, one wonders whether there is any point at all in teaching political philosophy. Tocqueville's belief in local autonomy as an antidote to the featureless equality and despotic tendencies of modern democracies goes deeper than this, however. It is not so much demagogery and the political police that he fears so much as a type of oppression "different from anything that has ever been in the world before" for "that same equality which makes despotism easy, tempers it".[6] The incipient despotism of a democracy would be "more widespread and milder: it would degrade men rather than torment them".[6] The leaders would not be "tyrants, but rather schoolmasters",[7] and though this is rather unfair on schoolmasters, one cannot help thinking in this context of Mr. Stewart advocating a quick military solution in Biafra and protecting Anguilla from international gambling or of Mr. Short seeking to impose immediate transfer to the comprehensive system on every local education authority. In America itself, Tocqueville's worst fears appear to have been uncannily accurate: "most organisation men," says William H. Whyte himself, "see themselves as objects more acted upon than acting — and their future, therefore, determined as much by the system as by themselves."[8]

Every arts or social science undergraduate should know the sixth chapter of Part 4 of Volume II of Tocqueville's *Democracy in America* (America being principally a hook upon which to hand a treatise on democracy in general) but it seems that few think about it after being appointed to Royal Commissions. What Tocqueville foresaw was a mass of men "alike and equal, constantly circling about in pursuit of the petty and banal pleasures with which they glut their souls."[9] To each, mankind would consist only of his own family and friends. As for the rest of his fellow citizens, "he touches them but feels nothing". A benevolent state regulates everything: "it gladly works for their happiness but wants to be the sole agent and judge of it". This state "does not break man's will but softens, bends and guides it . . . never drives men to despair but continually thwarts them and leads them to give up using their free will". Little by little the exercise of free choice becomes so restricted as to be pointless. Consoling themselves with the idea that they are sovereign, the people actually become incapable of making a choice. The occasional opportunity of electing the central power is insufficient to develop their political sense: having given up managing affairs which they can comprehend, they are unlikely to make a good job even of that. Disillusioned, they will either "create free institutions or fall back at the feet of a single master". Since they have already been slowly falling back "below the level of humanity," it is the latter solution which is the more likely. "It is not easy to fight benevolence".

Democracy in America was published in 1835. A century and three-quarters later most of Tocqueville's predictions have an all too familiar ring. Is it not our own experience that "as conditions become more equal among people, individuals seem of less and society of greater importance;"[10] that this "naturally gives men in times of democracy a very high opinion of the prerogative of society and a very humble one of the rights of the individual . . . the interest of the former is everything and that of the latter nothing"; that "most . . . think that the government is behaving badly but . . . all think that the government ought constantly to act and interfere in

everything;" that "not only are (men) by nature lacking in
any taste for public business but they also often lack the time
for it;" that a man's "needs and even more his longings
continually put him in mind of (the State) and he ends by
regarding it as the sole and necessary support of his individual
weakness" and that "every central government worships
uniformity; uniformity saves it the trouble of enquiring into
infinite details, which would be necessary if the rules were
made to suit men instead of subjecting all men indiscriminately
to the same rule"? Raymond Aron recently stated that, of the
three great sociological thinkers of the last century — Comte,
Marx and Tocqueville — it is Tocqueville whose vision "most
closely resembles Western European societies today."[11]

Tocqueville's belief in intermediate levels of power as an
antidote to uniformity, centralisation and a more powerful
state, is all the more persuasive in that he himself thought it
"both necessary and desirable that the central power of a
democratic power should be both active and strong".[12] His
argument is that governments should try a little more to make
men great rather than to do great things with men, that
flabby and feeble people cannot make an energetic nation
and that both anarchy and despotism spring from general
apathy. That is why he pleaded for liberty in the face both of
those who believed it to be dangerous and of those who
believed it to be impossible. Because, with the levelling of
social conditions, it was becoming so much easier to establish
absolutism he was indeed "disposed to worship liberty."[13] "In
the dawning centuries of democracy," he says, "individual
independence and local liberties will always be the products
of art. Centralised government will be the natural thing."[14]

Tocqueville does not, in the second volume of *Democracy
in America,* go into detail about the type of intermediate
authority which is necessary. One of the things which lay at
the back of his mind was, however, the New England township
(with, generally, two to three thousand inhabitants) which he
described in the first volume and which drew from him the
much quoted remarks, "the strength of free peoples resides
in the local community. Local institutions are to liberty what

primary schools are to science; they put it within the people's reach; they teach people to appreciate its peaceful enjoyment and accustom them to make use of it. Without local institutions a nation may give itself a free government but it has not got the spirit of liberty".[15] There were as many as nineteen "main officials" in these New England townships and each inhabitant was bound on pain of a fine to accept office. Most of those who did so received some remuneration, so that poorer citizens could devote time to public office without loss and the maximum possible number of people had some concern with municipal affairs.[16] In origin, each township had been almost "a little independent nation".[17] Instead of receiving powers from the state, it was the township which had surrendered powers to the state and that only when there was "some interest shared with others" — "I do not think one could find a single inhabitant of New England," says Tocqueville, "who would recognise the right of the government of the state to control matters of purely municipal interest".[18] Each township had, it is true, certain obligations to the state but even here the government merely laid down principles and, in putting them into practice, the township resumed all its independent rights: "taxes are . . . voted by the legislature but they are assessed and collected by the township; the establishment of the school is obligatory, but the township builds it, pays for it and controls it."[18]

Within its own sphere the New England township had the power and the independence to "excite men's interest," independence in itself supplying "a real importance not warranted by size or population".[19] Indeed the New Englander is attached to his township "not so much because he was born there as because he sees the township as a free, strong corporation of which he is part and which is worth the trouble of trying to direct". The county, an administrative unit with no real political existence, could not rival the township; even the state was only of secondary importance, while few men could aspire to participating in the federal government. A man's taste for power and self-advancement and esteem was thus concentrated on the township and was far less trouble-

some since it had to be exercised so close to home: "In
America it is not virtue that is great, but temptation that is
small . . . It is not disinterestedness that is great, it is interest
that is taken for granted". Because all the voters had to take
the main decisions, and administrative power was so well
distributed amongst elected officials subject only to judicial
control, government really did "emanate from the people".
Out of a sort of parental pride in the distinct identity of his
township, the citizen saw that, for all its defects, it got along
somehow. In this process, he "gets to know those formalities
without which freedom can advance only through revolutions,
and becoming imbued with their spirit, develops a taste for
order, understands the harmony of powers, and in the end
accumulates clear, practical ideas about the nature of his duties
and the extent of his rights." Greater centralisation might
lead to more immediate efficiency but, in the long run, the
nation's power would be diminished, its citizens incapable of
being deeply stirred: "In America, the force behind the state
is much less well regulated, less enlightened, and less wise,
but it is a hundred times more powerful than in Europe".[20] In
other words, the political advantages of decentralisation and
a general civic pride and lack of apathy, outweigh any administrative and economic disadvantages. Tocqueville rebukes a
writer who compares American budgets unfavourably with
the methodical municipal budgets of France – all drawn up
on what we would call the same prescribed form – in these
words: "I wonder if the same cause may not be responsible
for the prosperity of the American township and for the
apparent disorder of its finances, and conversely, for the
wretchedness of the French commune and for its immaculate
budget".[21] The very lack of central supervision means that
"municipal bodies and county administrations are like so
many hidden reefs retarding or dividing the flood of the popular will."[22] They guard against that tyranny of the majority
which, if unrestricted, ends up either by reducing all men to
the level of fawning courtiers or by driving minorities to
desperation and anarchy.[23] Even the majority should not be
granted that "power to do everything" which one would

refuse to a single man.[24]

On the face of it, Tocqueville's New England township of 1835 may seem to have little relevance to the problems of local government at the end of the Twentieth Century — though, as it happens, the Swiss commune retains to this day an uncanny resemblance to the old New England township.[25] Yet the dangers which de Tocqueville sensed are infinitely greater today than they could have been in the Nineteenth Century and many of the best minds of our own time are followers of his, conscious or unconscious. In Sweden, and Sweden is the avant-garde of Europe, a thinker and statesman of the experience of Gunnar Myrdal is adamant that "we should not make peace with bureaucracy."[26] Looking "beyond the welfare state", but in a far more immediately practical way than the Marxist who prophesies its withering away, Myrdal sees that autonomy is securely realist in its very self-interest. He accepts that the task of the state is to lay down fundamental economic and social policies but regards interference with the day-to-day running of a locality as an indication that there has been *insufficient* fundamental planning.[27] In our urge to improve society, we would be short-sighted to place "an almost exclusive trust in continual extension of state regulations": indeed, much of the state regulation practised today is a legacy from the time of the first drastic efforts to bring order to a completely uncoordinated industrial society, or from a still earlier era, more autocratic and stratified and less educated and open-ended.[28] Myrdal nevertheless warns us that "bureaucracy has its own will to survive" and that "to give up autocratic patterns, to give up administrative controls and to dismiss personnel employed in managing them and generally to withdraw willingly from intervening when it is no longer necessary, are steps which do not correspond to the inner urgings of a functioning bureacracy".[29]

Myrdal insists that to leave more and more actual government to public and private organs beneath the state level is a real goal and he implies that, in the Scandinavian countries, there are already auguries that the next phase in the develop-

ment of the welfare state will bring "an actual decrease of
state intervention — and with this, a strengthening of
provincial and municipal self-government, a balanced growth
of interest organisations and, in both these fields, intensified
citizen participation."[30] In the United Kingdom, however,
we seem to be in a vicious circle, for that lack of education
in civic affairs which results from lack of participation means
that reformers see direct state intervention as the quickest
route to their goal. Christopher Price, the Education Correspondent of the *New Statesman,* for example, considers
that one of "the many lessons" which Sweden has to offer
educational reformers in England is that government should
be able to pass detailed laws about the shape of the curriculum
and the pattern of schools. But the total population of
Sweden is only seven million and is not the fundamental
reason for their success the fact that, as Price himself puts it,
"the Swedes are lucky in being the sort of cohesive community
in which you can carry out rational reform"?[31] In terms of
the United Kingdom, the success of Sweden is an argument
for decentralisation, not against it, as is the way in which
mental welfare is organised nationally in Denmark, with her
population of 4½ million.

In the United States too, somewhat ironically, the pro-
gressives tend to favour further centralisation: even in
Tocqueville's day, the townships became less democratic as
one travelled southwards[32] and it was after his day that
immigration made its biggest impact and that the problem of
integrating the Negro (about which Tocqueville himself was
so pessimistic) became acute. Myrdal, who has considerable
experience of America, is well aware of this but feels that "it
is rational to take risks and even to make temporary sacrifices
in the endeavour to spread out ever wider and deeper the
roots of democracy in the national community."[33] Without
this there is a risk of reaction against the welfare state itself,
against planning, against all humane causes — who has not
heard people who work hard, for less money than others
receive gratis from the Social Security offices, urging that nobody should be allowed to eat who is not prepared to work?

More insidiously dangerous still, according to Myrdal, without participation − and education for participation − the people become less and less propaganda safe and more and more susceptible to manipulation by an oligarchy of big corporations, and by a communications industry whose services only the wealthy and the influential can engage. Unfortunately, the people themselves are mainly organised as producers demanding higher wages, rather than as consumers wanting to keep prices down or as communities which cut across callings. Only education in democracy, particularly practical education by participation, can strengthen their awareness of the common interest in stabilising the price level.[34] Only with participation from below can we hope to convert a multiplicity of hurried and often ineffective acts of state intervention into overall co-ordination and planning proper.

Are not these views of Myrdal's a contemporary social democratic version of Tocqueville's classical liberal championship of the small unit as a defence against tyranny? Be that as it may, it is striking how many distinguished thinkers echo Tocqueville today, whether they are to the right of centre like T. S. Eliot and F. R. Leavis, or to the left like Myrdal and Hoggart and Raymond Williams − or neither of the left or the right, like Simone Weil, of whom it has been said, "if she had any predilection, it was towards anarchism and syndicalism."[35] Some of these thinkers are more concerned with conserving the social environment than with liberty as such. Tocqueville's desire to "ennoble equality" has, however, much in common with the Leavisite idea of civilisation through literature which, paradoxically, is much more necessary to modern industrialised society than it was to the organic community which Leavis himself has tended to idealise.[36] It is symptomatic of that very specialisation and sub-specialisation which is fragmenting society and its territorial communities that the great English literary tradition itself, with its sensitive human values, its preference for weighing men rather than counting them,[37] its concern with "the man whom we behold with our own eyes" and with "men as they are men within themselves" is hardly reflected in current thinking about local government in England.

II

The "conservative" approach to the appreciation of the small unit has much in common with Tocqueville's fear of tyranny through degradation but is concerned more with the sanctity of separate identity than with liberty as such. Fundamentally this approach too begins with the individuality, the uniqueness, of every human being: humans are social beings: to destroy or neglect the particular community to which they belong is to impair their very individuality: to deprive the individual of his own distinct community is to diminish him as an individual: so is to deprive him of the stimulation of making contact with other distinct communities. It is perhaps the poet and the theologian who put this point over most convincingly but, essentially, conserving the social environment is a cause as popular as it is aristocratic. In the welfare state, travel is one of the greatest popular pleasures but there may soon be little point in it except for a change of climate. Even the tourist industry is beginning to dread a Europe in which more and more people see the same advertisements, dress in the same fashion, eat the same meals, drink the same drinks, put up the same kind of houses and offices, speak the same common language – or at least use the same vocabulary whichever language is being used – from Lapland to Asturias: the first move of every cosmopolitan who opens a souvenir shop in Wales is to call it Welsh Crafts and bespatter it with red dragons and Welsh hats. Paradoxically, it is the ultra-large, nationalistic nations like Russia and America which, under similar pressures to become more powerful, tend to become uniform and alike. "We may race up and down the entire North American continent," says Leopold Kohr, "and see nothing but Main Street all over again, filled with the same kind of people, following the same kind of business, reading the same kind of funnies and columnists, sharing the same movie stars, the same thoughts, the same laws, the same morals, the same convictions . . . if in several European vast-area states such as Italy, France or

Germany, so many exciting though rapidly dwindling differences are still experienced on relatively short journeys, it is because the medieval small-state diversity has left so lasting an imprint that no unifying process has as yet been able to wipe it out".[38] It is the number and the ingenuity of the variations which can turn a theme into a work of art: how much interest would there be in cathedrals and churches if they had all had to be built within Department of Education cost limits, in consultation with the departmental architects? In nature, in science, in art, it is infinite variety which makes life worth living and lends charm even to classification.

Individuals, however mobile, nevertheless need roots. MacDiarmid has a poem in which he enthuses over the fantastic variety of plant life within a small patch of ground on some bare Highland hill and then suddenly remembers the Scots who consider Scotland herself to be too small to contain their talents and ambitions, too small to govern herself with distinction:

"Scotland small? Our multiform, our infinite Scotland small?"

MacDiarmid — formally a Communist — can see the creative possibilities of the *small* nation and the importance and uniqueness of every community even within a united, proletarian world. On the Right, Yeats, in *A Prayer for my Daughter*, stresses an individual's need for the particular protection of and loyalty to one place:

"O may she live like some green laurel
Rooted in one dear perpetual place."

And Simone Weil, free of political attitudes but having seen at close quarters more aspects of society than most intellectuals, attributes the end of natural equality to *déracinement*, the loss of roots, the loss of sustenance from the past, for the future can only take and cannot give and the state has "morally killed everything, territorially speaking, smaller than itself."[39] In a rootless society, rootless in time as well as in space, nobody knows where he is or who he is. Everyone's rightful place is the next place up. Work becomes no more than a means of obtaining a wage (the psychological need is to earn it). Rights take precedence over duties. With a remote state the sole purveyor of welfare, we live in "perpetual mendacity," while centralisation transmits dullness to every corner. The only choice before the uprooted is lethargy or a paranoic aggressiveness towards those who have kept their roots (this is very close to Tocqueville). Pre-war France chose the former, pre-war Germany the latter — one can only wonder what the outcome will be in the United States and, a few decades hence, in the European Community.

According to T. S. Eliot, Simone Weil's *L'Enracinement* "belongs to that category of prolegomena to politics which politicians seldom read and which most of them would be unlikely to understand or know how to apply."[40] For them, perhaps it is more to the point that the great sociologist Karl Mannheim's diagnosis has much in common with Simone Weil's: he too believed in the cultivation of "primary groups" to give individuals a feeling of belonging, to modify the emphasis on monetary reward and to reassert the role of reason in democracy.[41]

The Welsh philosopher J. R. Jones, originally a Marxist, eventually came to the conclusion that the main threat to humanity is no longer the economic oppression of capitalism but the spiritual oppression of mechanisation and standardisation.[42] As more and more of the things we use are produced in identical units, he argues, the danger is that human beings too will be treated as units rather than unique beings. Neither can the uniqueness of individuals be considered apart from the uniqueness of the nations and communities within which they have developed and apart from which (in spirit) they tend to lack integrity and significance. Not entirely satisfied by Simone Weil's treatment of the question of why man needs roots, J. R. Jones nevertheless maintains that man is never rooted unconditionally in any earthly territory.[43] His "essential homelessness" on the earth is at once the reason why he needs an anchor in a particular community and place and vocation and the source of that moral power which enables him to resist the monolithic state in its efforts to deprive him of his manhood and condemn him to meaninglessness: the nation or community in which he seeks roots is not an end in itself: it is his link with eternity.

III

The intuition of poets and philosophers often precedes the postulates of political scientists and the practice of men of action: administrators and professional politicians are usually the last to jump on to the bandwagon. There is some evidence that the call for decentralisation which led to the institution of the Crowther Commission was not merely a reaction to central indifference but the first political stirrings of a positive approach to the region and, by implication, to the local community. During the thirties Lewis Mumford was beginning to develop and popularise the work of pioneers of this movement like Patrick Geddes: it seems possible that, had the impact of his most immediately political work, *The Culture of Cities* (1938) not been muted by the Second World War, Mumford's brand of regionalism would have gained much more momentum. In Mumford's view, our environment is being dehumanised as a result of the mechanised outlook of the Nineteenth Century and of the "psychological complexes that have been deliberately built up around the idea of national sovereignty and centralised government."[44] Human communities should be based on the region, "not found as a finished product in nature, not solely the creation of human will and fantasy,"[45] and though isolation is, in the modern world, a delusion, it is frontiers which must be cheapened, not local loyalties. No longer must the capital city of a large state be allowed to "monopolise advantage or substitute its activities for those of the whole".[46] Every cell is important and inter-regional co-operation must take the place of directives sent down from above: instead of concentrating in one Capital, the *élite* should travel from region to region.[47] In delineating the region, the aim must be, not to make men more powerful, but to make them more human, to emphasise, not the mechanistic, but the organic, to unify, not by suppression, but by inclusion.[48] An organism has an environment not only in space but, "through the biological phenomena of inheritance and memory",[49] in time. Even the "outer environment" itself becomes, through long association, part of the "inner environment" too: "one must not confuse the region, which is a highly complex human fact, with arbitrary areas carved out to serve some single interest such as government or economic exploitation. The country within fifty miles of a metropolitan centre is not a region just because it is a convenience for a metropolitan advertising agency or newspaper or planning board to call it so".[50] Regionalism is thus a political and a cultural movement as well as an exercise in administration and economics: in Denmark, it meant "the recapture of the native heritage of the ballads and the folk literature, the founding of folk high schools in the countryside and the growth of the co-operative movement in agriculture. In Czechoslovakia, it meant the founding of an independent political state."[51] Where the region has no inner environment, or where the inner environment has been obliterated by a centralised state, the region must be "politically and culturally re-willed"[52] and though, in many cases, any sort of boundary defining the limits of obligation and interest is better than no boundary at all,[53] one must be careful not to over-simplify the administrative pattern for the sake of convenience, "sacrificing accuracy and comprehensiveness to the practical needs of the moment". Even geography is an insufficient base in itself for though "primitive regional differences may diminish with intercultural contact ... emergent differences become more profound unless the region itself is disabled by the metropolitan effort to wipe out every other mode of life except that which reflects its own image".[54] In conceiving a region therefore, one should strive towards a balance of communities of different interests, as well as a geographical base small enough to keep those interests in focus as the subject of collective concern: "the sort of regional planning that seeks some simple arbitrary pattern more closely fitted to the convenience of the political or industrial administrator is regional in name only".[55] Neither will the region, except on an island or in the high mountains, have definite physical boundaries: its limits will be shadowy at the margin and there will be considerable inter-relationship.[56]

Mumford is well aware of the political difficulties of regionalism within a large state: "the fact is that real communities and real regions do not fit into the frontiers of the ideological pattern of the national state. The state is usually too big to define a single region ... and it is too small to include a whole society like that of Western Europe or the North American continent, which must ultimately become the sphere of a larger system of co-operative administration".[57] He traces the beginnings of regionalism to the founding of the Félibrige — a society for the restoration of the language and cultural life of Provence — by Mistral and six other young men on Sunday, the 21st of May, 1854, and he might well have quoted from their first manifesto to convey the sort of spirit that is lacking in mere "decentralisation by central direction":[58]

"Le Félibrige est établi pour conserver toujours à la Provence sa langue, sa couleur, sa liberté d'allures, son amour national et son beau rang d'intelligence ... Le Félibrige est gai, musical, fraternel, plein de simplicité et de franchise; son vin est la beauté, son pain est la bonté, son chemin la verité ..."[59]

Mumford's list of other peoples similarly striving to keep their identity and extend their autonomy suggests that regionalism has made little progress during the last hundred years: "the Bretons and Provençals in France, the Czechs and Slovaks in the old Austro-Hungarian Empire, the Irish, Welsh and Scotch (*sic*) in Great Britain, the Basques and Catalans in Spain, the Flemings and Walloons in Belgium."[60] It could nevertheless be argued that the nationalism of the Scandinavian countries, which, with Belgium and Holland, Mumford considers "have contributed far more to the development of modern life than colossi like England and Germany"[61] is essentially regionalist in Mumford's sense. There is perhaps more hope today than when Mumford was writing

that Auguste Comte's prediction of a Europe of 160 regional
entities may come about.[62] For if regionalism or, as it might
be more accurately described in Europe, the humane nationalism of small nations, is incompatible with the large national
state, it is compatible with larger continental systems like the
European Economic Community which, in their ideal conception, depend on breaking down the authority of the
national state. Before 1914, both regionalism and internation-
alism were working with the grain, and now again a "New
European" like Anthony Sampson can write, "for so many
modern purposes the nation (i.e. the large state) is either too
big or too small . . . why cannot the regions go direct to the
real masters of technology in America, Geneva or Brussels?"[63]
So successful have the centralisers been in their attempt to
identify the regional and the local with the narrow, the backward and the unbrotherly that such thoughts shock many
good "internationalists." Yet it was the revolutionary com-
munards of 1870 who cried "Paris for the Parisians" and laid
down in their manifesto, "The autonomy of the commune
will have for its limits only the equal autonomy of all other
communes adhering to the contract."[64] Proudhon himself was
such an extreme federalist as to oppose the unification of
Italy:[65] "In a little state, there is nothing for the bourgeoisie
to profit from . . .". And to Leopold Kohr, the only way to
solve the problem of international government is to break up
"the great powers, those monsters of nationalism" and
replace them by small states for "only small states are wise,
modest and, above all, weak enough to accept an authority
higher than their own."

As a planner, Mumford accepts the autonomy of the region
and the community. Just as, in the building of a house, the
architect has to rely upon the autonomous skill of the builder
and the builder upon the craftsman and the labourer, a plan
is not "a substitute for intelligent choice, decision or invention
on the part of those who must execute it in detail. It rather
assumes the existence of these qualities and organises the
milieu in which they can most effectively work."[66] Like
Tocqueville, Mumford fears that civilised man will not

survive unless there is a "general reduction of the area of arbitrary compulsion and restoration of the processes of persuasion and rational argument. Political life instead of being the monopoly of remote specialists must become as constant a process in daily living as the housewife's visit to the grocer or the butcher, and more frequent than the man's visit to the barber."[67] And for the regionalist's process of survey, evaluation and planning to succeed, it must begin at school so as to increase the possibility for rational judgement: this is vital to Mumford's whole conception. "All rational politics must begin with the concrete facts of regional life, not as they appear to the specialist, but as they appear first of all to those who live within the region".[68] This is the remedy both for the politics of slogan and for the extreme specialisation of the highly sophisticated. We have to make the landscape as a whole mean as much to the citizen as his garden to the householder: "these people will know in detail where they live and how they live. They will be united by a common feeling for their landscape, their literature and language, their local ways and, out of their own self-respect, they will have a sympathetic understanding with other regions and different local peculiarities".[69] And though a region with a radius of forty to a hundred miles may be a reasonable catchment area for the minority who attend a university, a central reference library, or a completely equipped hospital, limitations on size, density and area, are absolutely necessary to effective social intercourse and, therefore, rational democratic planning: the answer is to open the whole region for settlement, with a cluster of towns forming a "regional city", focused upon a mother city which provides facilities for which the towns are too small:[70] it is the same vision as that of Ebenezer Howard, who was far more than the founder of Letchworth and Welwyn. The fathers of regional planning saw the region in terms very much more subjective and tentative than those advocates of the "city-region solution" who would merely substitute commuter-flow units for existing administrative units, and who harp on the obsolescence of ancient boundaries. Neither can one deduce from their enthusiasm for regional planning any wish to impose plans rather than agree them. To them, developing a feeling of loving care for one's own region was the crucial factor — all the more crucial today because of the urgent need to conserve the physical environment against pollution, to conserve natural resources in the face of a world population explosion and a diminishing food supply and to conserve the social environment in the face of substitute living, the impersonal and the trivial. Mumford foresaw the need for conservation in the thirties. Conscious that the moving frontier of America had already reached its limit in 1893, he could write in *The Condition of Man,* "Utopia can no longer be an unknown land on the other side of the globe: it is rather the region one knows and loves best reapportioned, reshaped and recultivated for permanent human occupation".[71]

IV

The question of pollution has at last reached the headlines and the danger now is, not that pollution will remain the concern of a few ecologists and idealists, but that it will become the object of that universal, conventional type of concern which is the particular responsibility of nobody. Preserving the balance of nature requires a complete change of heart amongst races hitherto bent on exploiting and dominating nature rather than living in harmony with it, and that more as a result of Christian theology than of any fall from grace. The dangers appear to be very great. Between 1942 and 1967, according to Professor Barry Commoner, the annual United States consumption of chemical fertiliser increased from less than half a million tons to six million tons, and though chemical fertilisers increase crop yields, unlike manure they fail to maintain the organic nitrogen content of the soil.[72] Even when combined with straw, an appreciable part of the fertiliser ends up in the air and in the water or in the crops themselves and, therefore, in animals and in man. And animals and humans, especially infants, are susceptible to certain harmful effects from the conversion of nitrate to nitrite by bacteria. Thus the strain on the nitrogen soil balance is transmitted to human health: "it is entirely possible," according to Professor Commoner, "that infants' diets now sometimes exceed the recommended nitrate limits". The effect on the nitrogen balance in water is even better known. Not only is the natural self-purifying system of water affected but also the treatment of sewerage by man, which is based on the natural system. Thus Lake Erie, for thousands of years a beautifully clear inland sea, is becoming "a rank muddy sink", fouled by algae fertilised by the nitrate washed from the soil. Again, the stress upon the nitrogen cycle of the air, much of it caused by nitrogen oxide from the chimneys of power stations and from car exhausts, produces smog and further deposits on land and water. And this is only one of the problems of pollution. The effect of industrial combustion on the carbon cycle could produce toxic levels of carbon monoxide in cities or increase the carbon dioxide level in the atmosphere sufficiently to influence the earth's temperature or to deprive us of oxygen. If a new power station is not built immediately in New York, by 1974 the city will not have enough power to run itself. If it is built, its fumes may, in spite of the latest extraction techniques, be responsible for "countless cases of lung disease and even death."[73] Such dilemmas are likely to multiply all over the world. In the United Kingdom, which only has one acre per person as opposed to twelve in the United States,[74] industrial waste, much of it toxic, is expected to treble in amount by the end of the century, and it must be accommodated somewhere. As for unspoilt countryside, the very type of person who deplores the existence of frontiers between nations is now advocating the erection of frontiers around the National Parks. With technology continuing to develop so rapidly, all this calls for tremendous restraint on the part of mankind as a whole, for a general slowing up of "progress," for population control, for a curb on mobility and for an effort to break down the barriers between various professions and interests, and between basic and applied sciences, so that the environment can be considered as a whole: special knowledge of one part is an unreliable guide to the behaviour of the whole. Without this revolution in thinking, "we run the risk of destroying this planet as a suitable place for human habitation".[75] Without an informed body of citizens committed to understanding and protecting their own local environment, shall we ever achieve such a revolution?

Changing from a growth-oriented economy to a conservative system has its relevance for any local government reform based on "efficiency", particularly when the final appeal of the English Royal Commission stressed the need to economise in the face of the balance of payments crisis then current and the fact that "Britain is now more vulnerable than ever before both to economic forces and to military aggression,"[76] and when the "greatest challenge to urban local government"[77] which they could foresee was the increase in the number of cars within the next ten to fifteen years, from one car to five persons, to one car for every three. That the change will come, that the small unit will become increasingly relevant to the type of problem to be faced, is suggested by the fact that economists are now joining the poets and the ecologists in challenging the very concept of growth itself.

Dr. E. J. Mishan in particular has challenged the protagonists of growth on their own terms by stressing our failure to put a cost on external diseconomies, i.e. the damage inflicted on third parties or on the community as a whole by any particular process of production — as we have seen in considering pollution, this problem is becoming greater and greater. In spite of the increased use of cost-benefit analysis, the increase in noise and dirt rarely has a figure put on it, or certainly not a figure that anyone would have to pay. Yet if we could work out a system of legal recognition of amenity rights and of compensation for their loss, many of the worst effects of growth would be priced out and a far greater choice of environment could be presented to people.[78] According to Mishan, "it is just not possible for the economist to establish a positive relationship between growth and social welfare."[79] His argument is based on the fact that, in the words of Anthony Crosland, then Secretary of State for Local Government and Regional Planning, "although in this country we have had one of the slowest rates of economic growth in the world, even the growth we have had has been achieved at an appalling cost in terms of environment,"[80] that, by 1983, the United Kingdom will have to accommodate five million more people and 50% more cars, and that, in assessing growth, and the gross national product, economists tot up the value of the goods produced without making any allowance for bad side-effects such as "development blight, the erosion of the countryside, the accumulation of oil and sewerage on our coasts, contamination of lakes and rivers, air pollution, traffic congestion and shrieking aircraft." The public cannot be said to have deliberately chosen to put up with these spillover effects in return for the corresponding benefit: one cannot stop aircraft noise by choosing not to travel by air oneself. Freely negotiated settlements are sometimes possible between highly organised groups but if the damaged group consists of hundreds of families dispersed over a wide area, like the victims of aircraft noise, negotiations are not practicable, In any case, at present, the law is, in general, permissive of spillovers, while the need for faster economic growth is uncritically accepted by the establishment, aided and abetted by the technocrat and the advertiser, not only as the cure for all social ills, but as "inevitable," as "economic necessity," as "progress."[81]

Under the present system, most of those whose welfare is adversely affected by spillover effects are not compensated, while the more familiar spillovers — aircraft and traffic noise and pollution — fall most heavily on the lower income groups: "the distribution of welfare is ... more regressive than the distribution of income".[82] In theory, the Government could regulate the position in such a way as to arrive at the ideal amount of, say, traffic flow, by way of a congestion tax or, indirectly, by cost-benefit analysis. The cost of calculating a tax would be great, however, while in practice cost-benefit analysis seldom, if ever, takes account of equity: few of those at whose cost in noise and ugliness a flyover is built can be compensated, and none of those who directly benefit from it have to pay to travel along it.[83] At present, the law says that if a house is destroyed by the local authority, the proprietor must be compensated. If, however, a motorway passes fifty yards from a house, making it virtually uninhabitable, there is no compensation and the house becomes impossible to sell. The Greater London Council — and, for that matter, the Pembrokeshire County Council — wish to extend the payment of compensation if only the law could be amended, but even if the Government eventually bring in a bill along the lines of the Planning Blight and Worsenment Bill which recently failed to get a Second Reading in the Commons, not all those who live in the huge areas depressed by motorways will be compensated, while the depressed classes who come to live in them later will not come into the reckoning at all. More than this, the worst effect of all of the London motorways, according to Douglas Jay, is the loss of housing space: 60,000 people will be displaced, so that 60,000 slum dwellers will lose the chance of being re-housed and another five to ten years will be added to waiting lists.[84] There can be no compensation for persons who cannot be identified as affected, while many spillover effects in fact elude measurement: in a cost-benefit analysis, most of the benefits can be quantified in great detail, while many of the costs have to be content with a sentence or two by way of surmise. When the Ministry of Transport decided to build a six-lane highway through Soltram Park, Plymouth, an "inalienable" National Trust property, no figure could be attached to the loss, not only to the present but to posterity, of rare natural beauty, while plenty of figures could be produced to establish the "economic necessity" of the scheme.[85]

In principle, one could, of course, try to calculate the minimum sum each family in the country, both now and in future generations, would be willing to accept to reconcile it to the destruction of an area of natural beauty, or to the advent of a new spillover such as the supersonic boom. What Mishan proposes is, however, a more objective scheme which is entirely in accord with the principles of a market economy and of a society which believes that men should be free to pursue their own interests provided that, in doing so, they inflict no harm on others. If the law were to be changed so as to give men basic rights to such amenities as quiet, privacy, clean air and unpolluted water and, therefore, to compensation for any interference with these rights — with the cost of negotiating an agreement falling on the transgressor — the market mechanism itself would tend to cut out spillovers unless they really were essential. "Under such a dispensation", says Mishan, "the costs of operating the Concorde over Britain would have to include compensation for inflicting on us the plague of sonic booms. As an economic proposition it would be a dead duck".[86]

Mishan has to concede that an alteration of the law to make it *prima facie* prohibitive, rather than permissive, of spillovers may not be enough — firstly, because there may be insufficient information about the long term consequences of various types of polution; secondly, because it is future generations who may suffer most, as in radio-activity.[87] There are other difficulties. In practice the amount of compensation owing to any one individual might be too small to be a deterrent unless those affected acted collectively. And then there is the question of whether amenity rights should themselves be susceptible to compulsory purchase. This in itself suggests that many, if not all, the amenity rights to be protected in law should be vested, not in individuals, but in the lowest tier of local government. There is, however, a more important reason why the negotiation of amenity compensation should be related to the local community rather than to the individual. In a poor area, the interests of that community as a whole might lie with the developer, a developer difficult enough to attract without his having to compensate individual objectors: one recalls that the Merioneth branch of the Council for the Protection of Rural Wales itself decided not to object to the Trawsfynydd Nuclear Power Station because of the amount of unemployment in the county: if the principle of amenity compensation had been recognised, a few wealthy individuals might have been able to make the project uneconomic. The law should, however, provide that a local authority, instead of waiving its amenity rights, may be compensated by amenity bodies or by the Government for insisting on them and foregoing development. The vesting of water rights in the local communes of the Grisons has resulted in some communes receiving compensation for the exploitation of those rights and of others being compensated for refusing to have them exploited.

This is not the place to discuss the legal implications of Mishan's proposals and the possible variations upon them but the extension of amenity rights seems likely, in some form or other, in the near future, not only because of the growing concern about general pollution but also because more and more individuals are having their lives spoilt by corporations who cannot, as the law stands, be expected to compensate them. To create a positively good environment on the basis of such rights, however, we must have local enthusiasm at the level of the village or the street. To obtain informed, organised, responsible insistence on respect for community rights, we must indeed have a local authority with residual sovereignty over its own locality, answerable to the people as a whole. The possibilities of local sovereignty have recently been demonstrated by Kanton Zürich's ban on night flights from the busy international airport at Kloten, the enactment of which will, however, be the subject of litigation before it is clear whether it was within the competence of a canton.

In a sense, pollution, of all problems, is the one which requires a world solution. Unless the regions and localities of the world are legally and politically strong, however, the great powers will always be tempted to accept second-best solutions, acceptable to the "vast majority" but intolerable for certain small groups and individuals, and to push the worst pollution on to some less influential community. For the sake of vigilance as well as for the sake of equity, central co-ordination must be allied to local rights. If it can be argued that only a superpower will be able to deal with some of the immense international corporations which are developing, it can also be argued that, unless one can retain the spirit of local independence, and ensure that the superpowers are built up on the basis of hundreds of autonomous localities, those superpowers will tend to work in collusion with the super-corporations and will lack any real conception of what the destruction of a locality can mean, let alone any spirit to fight a locality's battles.

If Mishan is primarily concerned with the quality of the environment, his arguments tie in with J. K. Galbraith's celebrated exposure of conventional economic wisdom in *The Affluent Society* and in *The New Industrial State*. To Galbraith, the problem, in the United States at least, is not the ability to produce but the willingness to allocate product-ion to the right social goals. "Production for the sake of the goods produced is no longer very urgent ... we sustain a sense of urgency only because of attitudes which trace to the world, not of today, but into which economics was born".[88] Production is indeed important in so far as it affects economic security: "when men are unemployed society does not miss the goods they do not produce ... but the men who are without work do miss the income they no longer earn."[88] It follows that, "if the things produced are not of great urgency ... the process by which they are produced ceases to be an over-riding consideration."[89] Thus, in dealing with the problem of a declining locality, the efficient solution of en-couraging the people to leave for better placed regions need not have precedence over the humane solution of allowing them to keep "the ties of family, friends, pastor and priest, country-side and mere inertia."[89] "Are we desperately dependent on the diligence of the worker who applies maroon and pink enamel to the functionless bulge of a modern motor-car?"[90] asks Galbraith. "If the goods have ceased to be urgent can we sternly command men to leave their homes and produce them with maximum efficiency?"[91] Need we indeed deprive them, in the name of efficiency, of the satisfaction of electing their own local councils; need we deprive those councils of the power and the financial resources to make decisions of consequence?

Galbraith, like Mishan, is scathing about the acceptance of the growth of the gross national product as an over-riding goal for it is only "because the goals of the industrial system are so narrow that they lend themselves to precise statistical assessment".[92] Not only does large industry manipulate rather than reflect what the consumer chooses — it is bound to do this.[93] The heavy capital requirements, sophisticated technology and elaborate organisation of modern industry cannot be put at risk in a competitive market. Planning must replace the market and, in the United States as well as in the Soviet Union, the large scale organisation, though it requires a large measure of autonomy, is dependent on the state to stabilize wages and prices, and provide the trained and educated manpower upon which industry is now as dependent as it once was on capital. The close identification of the industrial system with the state, the growing recognition that it is only marginally subject to the market and to consumer sovereignty, provides an opportunity to substitute more sensible goals for the goal of mere growth. The increasing intellectual demands of the system, its dependence on more and more highly-educated personnel, provides some hope that the opportunity will be taken.[94] Better educated people may not be prepared to subordinate all belief to the needs of the industrial system. On the contrary, they should be able to see that it is only part of life, a subordinate part. Galbraith's fear of "the benign servitude of the household retainer who is taught to love her mistress and see her interests as her own"[95] is pure Tocqueville, as indeed is Galbraith's sense of the "oneness" which underlies the apparently opposite political systems of the U.S.S.R., and the United States. Where Tocqueville had no confidence in the spirit of liberty which seemed to animate his contemporaries, however, Galbraith is much more confident that the industrial system itself is bringing into existence, to serve its intellectual and scientific needs, "the community that hopefully will reject its monopoly of social purpose".[96] Is Galbraith putting too much weight on the virtues of secular vocational education? Tocqueville considered that political freedom worked in America because it went hand in hand with the moral discipline of religion. If the goals of the new intellectual community are to be more humane than those of a robot industrial system, their education must at the very least include politics, and not political theory alone (this is where the French Revolution went wrong according to Tocqueville) but practical training in dealing with real issues and real people in a locality small enough to be comprehended as a whole. If, as is often maintained, one of the problems of a highly developed industrial system is the problem of leisure, we can look forward, not only to an educated society, but to an educated society with the leisure to devote to public life. Whether that society chooses to devote its leisure to public life is another matter: it depends to a great extent on having local and regional units which can evoke, not merely respect, but dedication and pride.

Galbraith himself implies that his work is relevant to England as well as to the United States. To those who say that his ideas are excellent for the United States, which is very rich, but inapplicable to the United Kingdom, with its balance of payments problem, he states that the essence of the problem everywhere is, not ability to produce, but willingness to allocate.[97] That this is indeed so seems probable from Mishan's attack on governmental preoccupation with the balance of payments and on the "atmosphere of vague but persistent economic foreboding"[98] in England (which is reflected in the Redcliffe-Maud Report). According to Mishan, the excess of imports current in 1967 — between £250 and £400 million — represented no more than one to one and a half per cent of the total national income, well below the average real increase per annum.[99] To him, all this necessitates is coaxing foreigners into buying a little extra or reducing the import of inessentials such as French cheese, Italian shoes or Belgian chocolate, or investing less abroad: none of these courses need cause particular hardship at home or provoke considerable reprisal abroad[100] (at the moment of writing the government claims to have solved the problem in any case). There can, however, be no presumption that faster economic growth improves the balance of payments:

the reverse might in fact be true — the optimum volume of
trade is practically impossible to determine.[101] It appears
then that the balance of payments problem is no more a
matter of life and death than the import of Brie and
Camembert. The crux of the problem is "the psychological
one of being unable to break free from long-established
habits of thought".[102] In reality, the United Kingdom is "a
wealthy and resourceful country" which has many alternatives
to the policy of increasing growth and exports for their own
sake. Its citizens have already been deprived of much of the
"aesthetic and instinctual gratification" which sweetened life
two centuries or so ago but it is still open to them to keep
what they hold.

If economists like Mishan and Galbraith are right, the price
of "inefficiency" is no longer dirt and disease and poverty but
a little delay, a little less luxury or a little more effort, all for
the sake of making more contact with other human beings
instead of with things — a process which can only be bene-
ficial to the minority who still are really poor or neglected
and who, in recent years, appear to have been getting
poorer.[103] And even if large local government units were
more efficient, we should still have to ask for whom they were
more efficient, in the long run as well as in the immediate
plans of those who advocate them. Aneurin Bevan once said
that he would rather have his life saved in a remote, cold,
central hospital than die amid gushing sympathy in an old-
fashioned local one. Within the limits of surgical medicine,
that was a wise remark. The basic question in local government
reform generally is, however, the contribution which local
government can make to maintaining the humanity of man,
so that a man's life will always be considered worth saving
and will always take precedence over machines and systems:
a society which always puts efficiency first may eventually
find it inefficient to keep some of us alive at all. If the
economic problems stressed by the Royal Commissions are less
serious than they assumed, the problems which they overlooked and the evils which they accepted as inevitable are
much more serious. These cannot be overcome without

enormous self-discipline on the part of individuals and nations, without political education in small communities and without strong campaigning to bring such communities to life. The proposed reorganisation of local government will only maintain, by rationalisation, the present, centralised system. The radical solution is to bring the existing units to life.

Notes to Chapter 5

1. *Central Departments and Local Authorities,* p.18.
2. Max Beloff, Minority View, *The Times,* 4 June 1970.
3. *Culture and Society,* p.313.
4. *Politics,* London (O.U.P.) 1942, VII, 3, p.1326b.
5. Leopold Kohr, *The Breakdown of Nations,* London 1957, p.108. Kohr attributes the universal cause of modern social difficulties to the overgrowth of societies: I have not taken as much advantage of his theories as I might in this work, preferring to work from the facts as I see them. The reader is nevertheless strongly advised to read Kohr, a writer as entertaining as he is important.
6. *Democracy in America: II,* Fontana ed. 1968, p.897.
7. *Ibid.,* p.898.
8. *The Organisation Man* (1956), Pelican 1963, pp.363-64.
9. *Democracy in America: II,* pp.898-899. The following passages are taken from these pages and from the rest of the chapter.
10. *Ibid.,* p.868. The following passages are taken from pp.868-874.
11. *Main Currents of Sociological Thought I* (1965), Pelican 1968, p.192.
12. *Democracy in America: II,* p.904.
13. *Ibid.,* p.903.
14. *Ibid.,* p.874.
15. *Ibid., I,* p.74.
16. *Ibid.,* p.78.
17. *Ibid.,* p.79.
18. *Ibid.,* pp.79-80.
19. *Ibid.,* p.81. The following passages are taken from pp.81-84.
20. *Ibid.,* p.112.
21. *Ibid.,* p.113, Note.
22. *Ibid.,* p.324.
23. *Ibid.,* pp.318-322.
24. *Ibid.,* p.310.
25. Ioan Bowen Rees, Local Government in Switzerland, *Public Administration,* Winter 1969, pp.446-47.
26. *Beyond the Welfare State: Economic Planning in the Welfare States and its International Implications,* London 1960, p.70.
27. *Ibid,,* p.67.
28. *Ibid.,* pp.70-71.
29. *Ibid.,* p.71.
30. *Ibid.,* p.68. See also the last para. of p.74.
31. Sweden's New Comprehensives, *New Statesman,* 24 April 1970.
32. *Democracy in America: I,* pp.97-98.
33. *Beyond the Welfare State,* pp.72-73.
34. *Ibid.,* pp.78-86.
35. E. W. F. Tomlin, *Simone Weil,* Cambridge 1954, p.13.

36. Daniel Jenkins, *The Educated Society,* London 1966, p.28. For the organic community see Leavis and Thompson, *Culture and Environment, The Training of Critical Awareness,* London 1933.

37. Hoggart, in his television interview, The End of the Protestant Ethic, touches on this and quotes Coleridge's refusal to discuss the dispossession of the Scottish Highlands in economic terms: "Men, I think, have to be weighed, not counted." The other quotes are from Wordsworth's Prelude (1805).

38. *The Breakdown of Nations,* pp.136-37.

39. Simone Weil, *The Need for Roots, Prelude to a Declaration of Duties towards Mankind,* (Trans. A. F. Willis), London 1952, p.117.

40. *Ibid.,* Preface p.xi.

41. Jean Floud, Karl Mannheim (1893-1947) in *The Founding Fathers of Social Science* (ed. Raison) London, 1969, esp. p.211.

42. Gwerthoedd Cenedl, a Harlech Television interview with Gwyn Erfyl, published in full in the Welsh language newspaper *Y Cymro,* 15 and 22 July 1970, shortly after J. R. Jones' death. Apart from work in the academic journals, J. R. Jones' writings were all in Welsh. When he died, he had been Professor of Philosophy at University College, Swansea for eighteen years but it was only about four years ago that he emerged from his study and began to exert an extraordinary influence over the youngest generation of Welsh nationalists.

43. Yr Angen am Wreiddiau, in the collection, *Ac Onide,* Llandybie 1970, pp.154-165.

44. *The Culture of Cities,* London 1938, p.358.

45. *Ibid.,* p.367.

46. *Ibid.,* p.358.

47. *Ibid.,* p.368.

48. *Ibid.,* pp.310-11.

49. *Ibid.,* p.301.

50. *Ibid.,* p.367.

51. *Ibid.,* p.305.

52. *Ibid.,* p.369.

53. *Ibid.,* p.309.

54. *Ibid.,* pp.313-14.

55. *Ibid.,* p.314.

56. *Ibid.,* p.315 and pp.367-68.

57. *Ibid.,* pp.351-52.

58. It is T. S. Eliot who says that decentralisation by central direction is a contradiction (*Notes Towards a Definition of Culture*).

59. Emile Ripert, *Le Félibrige,* 3rd ed., Paris 1948, p.70 (cf. J. E. Jones' constant emphasis on much the same qualities as the binding force of Plaid Cymru from its earliest days, in *Tros Gymru,* Swansea 1970, e.g. pp.46 and 271).

60. *The Culture of Cities,* p.350.

61. *Ibid.,* pp.355-58.

62. *Ibid.,* p.351.

63. *The New Europeans,* London 1968, pp.430-31.

64. George Woodcock, *Pierre-Joseph Proudhon, A Biography,* London 1956, p.276-77.

65. *Ibid.,* pp.246-49. To Proudhon, the principle of confederation began at the local level; above this level, "the confederal organisation becomes progressively less an organ of administration than of co-ordination among local units," all affairs being settled by "mutual agreement, contract and arbitration."

66. *The Culture of Cities,* p.380.

67. *The Culture of Cities*, p.382.
68. *Ibid.*, p.383.
69. *Ibid.*, p.386.
70. *Ibid.*, pp.486-493 but see Pahl, *Patterns*, pp.114-119, for doubts as to the validity of Mumford's subjective opinion that 5,000 is the upper population limit for a "neighbourhood" and of his assumption that physical proximity reduces social difference. See also Robert E. Dickinson, *The City Region in Western Europe*, London 1967, pp.295-98 for Mumford's relevance to the practice of regional planning today.
71. *The Condition of Man*, London 1944, p.403.
72. Sabotaging Nature, *Resurgence*, Vol.2 No.10 (Nov./Dec.1969) pp. 11-17. Most of the facts in the ensuing paragraph are taken from this well-documented article.
73. Joyce Egginton, 'Ultimate Madness' Strikes New York, *The Observer*, 16 August 1970.
74. Lord Kennet (then Parliamentary Secretary to the Ministry of Housing and Local Government) quoted by the Local Government Correspondent of *The Daily Telegraph*, 20 December 1969.
75. Commoner, p.17.
76. RCLGE I, para.33. See also paras.37-41.
77. *Ibid.*, para.40.
78. E. J. Mishan, *The Costs of Economic Growth* (1967), Pelican 1969, Chapters 4 to 9. See also Mishan's less academic *Growth: The Price We Pay*, London 1969.
79. *Ibid.*, p.151.
80. Quoted in Mishan, The Spillover Enemy, The Coming Struggle for Amenity Rights, *Encounter*, XXXIII, No.6 (Dec, 1969), p.3. This is a brilliant summary of Mishan's position.
81. *Ibid.*, p.4.
82. *Ibid.*, p.3.
83. *Ibid.*, pp.6-7. On the dangers of cost-benefit analysis, see also Peter Self, Nonsense on Stilts: The Futility of Roskill, *New Society*, Vol.16 No.405 (2 July 1970).
84. The Cost of Urban Motorways, *Town and Country Planning*, Vol.38, p.99.
85. The Spillover Enemy, p.7.
86. *Ibid.*, p.8.
87. *Ibid.*, pp.8-9.
88. *The Affluent Society* (1958), Pelican 1962, p.165.
89. *Ibid.*, p.232.
90. *Ibid.*, p.235.
91. *Ibid.*, pp.233-34.
92. *The New Industrial State* (1967), Pelican 1969, pp.387-88.
93. See esp. *Ibid.*, Chapter 19, The Revised Sequence (i.e. instead of the Accepted Sequence of demand flowing from consumer to market to producer, which still holds good outside the main industrial system of large corporations. If the consumer is not in fact the real boss, the case for tolerating squalor – and autocracy – for the sake of industrial efficiency disappears).
94. See esp. *Ibid.*, Chapter 35, The Future of the Industrial System.
95. *Ibid.*, p.399.
96. *Ibid.*, p.400.
97. *The Affluent Society*, Preface to the Pelican edition, p.10.
98. *The Costs of Economic Growth*, p.42.
99. *Ibid.*, p.42, note.
100. *Ibid.*, pp.47-52.
101. *Ibid.*, pp.45-46.
102. *Ibid.*, p.61.

103. See discussion of views of Professor Peter Townsend (Professor of Sociology at Essex and Chairman of the Child Poverty Action Group) in *The Sunday Times*, 22 March 1970. Townsend is quoted as saying that the actual number living in poverty had increased during the life of the Labour Government and that certain groups of the poor had got relatively poorer.

6. Government by Commune: Local Government Abroad

"Es gibt keine Freiheit ohne Risiko" (There is no freedom without risk)
MAX FRISCH

I

IF local government was the preserve of a small, sociable but hierarchical profession like the Bar and an essential bastion of the Establishment, it is probable that "British local government" would enjoy much the same kind of reputation as "British justice" – possibly with more justification. The fact that there is no myth about "our wonderful system of local government" was not enough, however, to save the Royal Commission from geographical as well as functional insularity. In spite of the fact that Dr. A. H. Marshall had provided the Maud Committee on Management with an admirable volume on Local Government Administration Abroad (Volume 4 of their Report), neither Royal Commission appeared to think that it had much to learn from other countries, more successful than the United Kingdom in promoting economic growth, in enhancing the quality of life or in both. The Scottish Commission did visit Norway, Denmark, Sweden, the Faroe Islands and Holland, but, having "gained a great deal from all these visits",[1] only saw fit to make one reference to local government abroad in their whole report: they state that they were not diverted from their view that the education service should not be divided by the example of a divided system in Scandinavia, "however well the system works", because a divided system in the United Kingdom would result in greater

137

central control:[2] they do not say why. That the example of Scandinavia was highly inconvenient to the preconceived notions of the Commission is suggested by the Note of Reservation on the Island Problem in which Miss Betty Harvie Anderson and Mr. Russell Johnston accept the Zetland County Council view that the dynamism of the Faroes is related to the "considerably greater degree of self-decision which they enjoy, as compared with our island groups".[3]

Any consideration of local government abroad suggests that, if there is indeed "something . . . seriously wrong"[4] with local government in the United Kingdom, little of the blame can be attributed to the size of authorities. By Western European standards, and even by United States standards, they are already large. And though there is undoubtedly a trend in most, if not all, of these countries towards the amalgamation of small authorities, this is more relevant to the parish than to the county, or even the county district, in the United Kingdom. "Here", says Professor Gowan, "we are thinking of population ranges of between 250,000 and 1,000,000 for our unitary authorities. In most other countries, even in the developed world, most of the population lives in "municipalities" or "communes" with a population of less than 2,000".[5]

In Sweden, even when the second series of amalgamations since the Second World War has been completed, there will be, for a population of 7½ million, three 'county boroughs', twenty-five counties, 93 rural communes and 188 towns[6] — and it is the smaller authorities which have "most of the duties of government"[7] and which are regarded as "*the* local authority". Dr. Marshall has nothing but praise for Swedish local authorities, and says that they have more independence than any others known to him. He does himself anticipate a further grouping of small units but the desirable minimum population at present is only 8,000, a figure selected with reference to primary education.[8] Eight thousand is also the minimum now being sought after in Finland.[9] In Norway, with a population of 3¾ million, there are *following* a re-organisation which took effect on 1st January, 1968, 454 communes (as opposed to 732 in 1960) with an average population well under 10,000: the number of counties remains at twenty. Here too it is the commune which is the primary authority and an American author comments that the Norwegian commune engages "in a wider sphere of activity than is the case in less socialistic countries".[10] In Denmark, with effect from the Spring of 1970, the minimum population for a commune has been set at 5,000: in the opinion of Professor Gasser, reorganisation even to this extent would have been rejected by the Danish people had it been subject to popular referendum but was pushed through Parliament by the political parties, all of which hoped that larger communes would be able to provide *paid* offices for their local stalwarts.[11] Iceland, with a population of only 199,000, is divided into 16 provinces, 14 towns and 313 communes. Eire (population 2.8 million) has twenty-seven county councils and four county boroughs, together with second-tier urban authorities, about three to a county: education is, however, a national service, as is police.

The eight Länder of Western Germany (population 59 million) have between them 24,444 communes (*Gemeinden*), 20,000 of which have fewer than 2,000 inhabitants. They all have a general competence though, outside the larger towns (some 140), there is a two-tier system with 425 counties (*Kreise*, with an average population of 75,000) taking over functions which the communes cannot undertake themselves.[12] In addition, there are numerous joint authorities for particular purposes. There is much talk of reform (with a minimum population for a commune of, say, 5,000 and also regional planning authorities) but reform of the financial structure to reduce the dependence of local authorities on grants has taken precedence over the alteration of areas.[13] Dr. Marshall regards the number of small authorities as a handicap but nevertheless considers the West German local government system to be "a smooth running, efficient machine",[14] with the local government service – hardly distinguishable from the federal and state services – a strong binding influence.

In the Netherlands (population 12 million), there have

been as yet no proposals for the overall reform of local government and there is a tradition of local resistance to central authority. The eleven provinces are divided into 939 municipalities, nearly 850 of which have fewer than 20,000 inhabitants and some of which are very small. The municipalities form a single tier within the provinces and have general competence and a high standing. To Dr. Marshall, Dutch local government gave "an impression of stability and efficiency". In Belgium (population 9½ million), the association of communes itself advocates the grouping of the 2,586 communes into 165 federations for "planning and equipment": the minimum population would be 10,000.

In 1967, the number of communes in France was no less than 37,954, only 2,433 of which had more than 2,000 inhabitants: there were 95 *Départments* and 322 *Arrondissements*.[15] In spite of their comparative lack of autonomy, the recent proposal of the Ministry of the Interior to group all communes into 3,500 *Communautés de Programme* with populations of between 2,000 and 8,000 — virtually joint boards to undertake tasks for which the communes are too weak — was received with great misgiving, particularly as a commune not prepared to join in would not receive grant aid, while joint action for particular purposes is already common. The Deputy Mayor of Perpignan, Paul Alduy, described the proposed new structure as "la création d'une super fiscalité anonyme et sans aucune responsibilité politique"[16] — this in a centralised country, faced with units within the population range 2,000-8,000! It has been truly said that "decentralization cannot be based on skeletal communes, without people, without problems, without means."[17] But it is quite one thing to support the amalgamation of French communes into units within the population range 2,000-8,000, quite another to support the amalgamation of local authorities in England.

And then there is Yugoslavia, a federation of six republics — each with a right to secede and some with autonomous provinces within them — embracing between them two alphabets, three major religions, four languages and five nationalities, and within each republic and autonomous province, not merely autonomous communes and federations of communes but autonomous and democratic factories, schools and other institutions of all kinds, so that each commune has, not only a political council but a council of working communities, while the republics and provinces have five councils: political, economic, educational and cultural, social and health and so on. Authorisation planning has formally been abolished: actual plans multiply – each level of government exchanges information and has to work within the frame which the levels above are providing.[18] To what extent the whole system would break down without the unifying influence of the Communist Party, one does not know, but one hears that the police are less in evidence in Yugoslavia than in Wales. The experiment of cutting down the state proceeds and Yugoslavia is obviously a country to watch. It may be that the problem of the future for us all will be, not so much decentralisation as the tensions between territorial democracy and syndicalism. For the present, the example of Switzerland is 'fantastic enough for anyone accustomed to the United Kingdom.

II

It is dangerous to generalise about local government in the United States. Each of the fifty states has its own system but the typical citizen lives under a two-tier system supplemented by separate School Boards and other *ad hoc* bodies, particularly for fire protection, soil conservation and drainage.[19] In some rural areas, the county is the only authority; elsewhere rural counties are divided into towns or townships, mostly of declining importance. In the urban areas – and it is estimated that about three-quarters of the 260 million inhabitants of the United States in 1980 will be living in metropolitan areas[20] – the county tends to be less important, while the municipality (under various names) is the general-purpose unit. Including *ad hoc* boards (for 34,678 School

Districts and 18,323 Special Districts) there were no less than 91,185 local government units in the United States in 1962. [21] And though there has been a distinct trend in recent years to consolidate school districts, together with a small decrease in the number of townships, only in two cases in this century have counties been amalgamated. [22] During the past two decades, the number of municipalities and special districts has actually increased: the increase in the number of special districts is, of course, evidence of consolidation rather than fragmentation. One authority who considers that, in general, there are far too many units, considers the "incorporation" of some new municipalities within urbanised counties to be reasonable: "while it is difficult to obtain co-operation among local planning agencies for regional planning purposes, it is even more difficult to extract the same degree of co-operation from a number of landlords who reside in an unincorporated area". [23]

As in the United Kingdom, there seems to be a general feeling amongst academics and civil servants in the United States that local authorities should be larger — possibly with more reason, since American cities are quickly losing their more prosperous citizens and their taxes, while the rural areas proper are also failing to provide the leadership for which they were once so famous, and are neglecting to use their powers. The phrase, "too many local governments, not enough local government", [24] is often quoted and over two decades ago William Anderson put forward a scheme for the elimination of most *ad hoc* boards and for the reduction of the remaining units to 17,800: 200 "city-counties", 2,100 rural counties, 15,000 "incorporated places" and 500 miscellaneous units. [25]

In spite of such plans, what strikes one about the local government reform movement in the United States is its slow pace and its moderation, its willingness to recognise the other side of the question, and the way in which the problems seem related more to the nature of a unit's population than to its size as such. "The defects of our system", says Herbert Kaufman, ". . . are in many ways the source of its accomplish-

ments and proudest claims".[26] He admits that a multiplicity
of decision centres facilitates "deadlock, delay and obstruction", movement "by drift rather than by direction" and
"narrower perspectives" but points out that a single ruling
clique or a single hesitant official in a large unit can also
display the same weaknesses, with more danger to everyone.[27]
More than this, state and local governments, particularly in
the urban areas, "have been exceedingly inventive and
flexible with regard to organisation and procedure" and
"have risen dramatically to the challenges of the post-World
War II world, increasing their expenditure and their functions
at a far faster rate than the federal government has expanded
its non-war budget and activities".[28] Each locality and state
is free to push ahead in the areas it considers important. Every
group has an opportunity to defend its own interests. There
is broad access to officials and ample opportunity to extract
concessions. Dr. Marshall makes the point that in both Canada
and the United States the citizen is more actively associated
with the routine of government than in Europe: "citizen's
committees, local research associations, pressure groups, the
close contacts of councillor and elector, the intense interest
of press and radio, all testify to the involvement of the public
in the daily round."[29] And when Dr. Marshall concludes his
study with the words, "in an atmosphere so permeated with
enterprise and so rich in experiment, the visitor may be a
little confused; but he can hardly fail to be stimulated
. . . ,"[30] one is again reminded of Tocqueville's preference of
American confusion to French formality.

Geoffrey Smith, the assistant editor of the *Local Government Chronicle,* on a visit to Connecticut, appears to have
been astonished at the number of municipal enterprises at
Poughkeepsie (population about 50,000) and West Hartford
(75,000): the latter has, in addition to 22 schools, six swimming pools, two golf courses, ice skating rinks, picnic areas,
and baseball, tennis, football and soccer facilities: of Granby
(6,000), "the equivalent of a small English rural district —
with far more powers," he comments, "I thought it much too
small for the powers it has — but it is a delightful place and

has every appearance of being well governed".[31]

That there is a good deal more confusion in America now than in Tocqueville's time is apparent from an article by Mr. J. K. Boynton, the Clerk of Cheshire County Council, about a study visit to American local authorities. Each bottom-tier authority in California decides for itself what services to provide on its own and King County (population one million) proved to have 250 special tax districts, the State of California itself to have 3,500: the town of Evetyville, with about 2,500 inhabitants, even had its own police force and fire brigade. Yet the visitors were assured that reforms were politically impossible, while the computer appears to be making the system more tolerable: the very fragmentation of the system encourages the integration of data-processing, and the widespread use of terminals to answer inquiries and update the file information. Computers, according to Mr. Boynton, are "helping state and local government to achieve what ideally should be achieved by structural and political reform".[32] Or is it that, in the United Kingdom, we are using the sledgehammer of drastic structural reform to crack problems which could be overcome more humanely by co-operation, facilitated by the computer?

If there is little enthusiasm for local government reform in America, the federal idea too appears to have survived the onslaughts upon it in the thirties and the continuing extension of federal aid to the states — federal aid "with strings". Governor Rockefeller of New York follows Bryce in seeing the sovereignty of the states in terms, above all, of dynamism and initiative and creativity. According to him, the "major and most successful" measures of social reform of the New Deal itself had been anticipated by particular states: "the ferment of ideas and innovations worked itself up through the federal system — often from private initiative".[33] More recently, it was the State of New York which took the initiative in promoting the peaceful uses of atomic energy, the field of atomic energy having previously been, in effect, monopolised by the central government and kept in isolation for military purposes.[34]

Significantly, Governor Rockefeller regards federal grants as a means of averting the growth of central authority rather than of enforcing it (Wyoming draws almost one-third of its revenue from grants): similarly, he regards grants by the states to local authorities as a way of enabling them to continue to administer services close to the people.[35] The same kind of point has been made by the Secretary of the Netherlands Advisory Council for Municipal Finance, who says that grants, though they make up no less than 84% of municipal costs, help to *preserve* municipal autonomy in his country.[36] It is, after all, the attitude of mind of those who make the grants which is crucial, not the proportion they form of expenditure. And in the United States, it seems that states can take the initiative in promoting joint action on regional problems between the federal government and themselves without any loss of face. The American preference for joint action by authorities at different levels, or joint boards between authorities at the same level, rather than for central- isation and amalgamation, looks untidy but at least, in Governor Rockefeller's words, "the federal government . . . has not become an uncontrollable colossus".[37]

If the Presidential system, the current emphasis on defence questions and racial tension and the *de facto* centralisation of American culture have highlighted the twin dangers of anarchy and apathy in the United States, it seems fair to conclude that the democratic element in their local government system is one of the more hopeful features of American life. At the same time, it has to be conceded that, to an observer as independent as Professor Beloff, the states are "ineffective as instruments for dealing with some . . . major internal problems" − notably pollution − and the real problem of America today is to provide more effective, expert and co- herent government without sacrificing the substance of democracy.[38] But again, it is one thing to put the emphasis on greater effectiveness in a sprawling country which is already federal, quite another to emphasise effectiveness in a central- ised state like the United Kingdom.

III

If the local government unit is both smaller and stronger in Scandinavia than in the United Kingdom, it is smaller and stronger still in Switzerland, easily the most fragmented and, except sometimes for Sweden, the most prosperous nation in Europe. There is indeed no such thing as a *Swiss* local government system: each of the twenty-five cantons* is responsible for its own system. The cantons could tentatively be divided up into five or six groups with much in common but the difficulty of generalising means that little has been written on local government in Switzerland for the general student, let alone the general reader. To a Swiss, cantonal government is not local government: in popular parlance, the cantonal government is *the* government, the canton *the* state, Switzerland itself being known as the Federation. Yet by

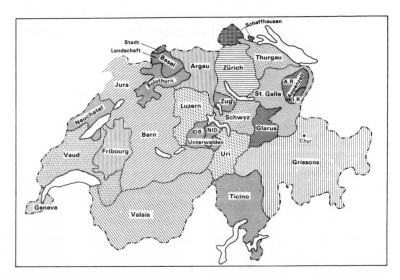

Map 4. The Cantons of Switzerland.

* Six of the twenty-five are "half-cantons": each of these is as autonomous a state as a full canton but in Federal matters has only half a vote, and thus only one seat, not two, in the second parliamentary chamber, the Council of States.

United Kingdom standards, few cantons have the population even of a large county (see Table I). Of the twenty-five cantons, only Zürich and Bern have a population approaching one million: each is nevertheless smaller than the administrative county of Cheshire. The third largest canton, Vaud, is smaller than Wiltshire, the remainder very much smaller again. Over half the cantons are as small as or smaller than the rural counties of Wales now threatened with amalgamation. In spite of the rapid growth of population, sixteen fell short of 200,000 in 1960, nine of 100,000: seven of the latter had fewer than 53,000 inhabitants. Appenzell Inner Rhodes, with 12,943, had some 5,000 fewer people than Radnorshire and was the only canton with fewer in 1960 than in 1950 (by 3.6%).[39]

The number of local authorities proper in Switzerland, and there is in effect only one tier, the commune, strains all belief. In Switzerland as a whole there were, in 1960, 3,095 political communes for a total population of 5,429,000, only 65 of these having a population greater than 10,000. Neither has the number of units been reduced much as the countryside loses population to the towns and the towns spill over into the country. Six communes disappeared between 1950 and 1960, six between 1941 and 1950, eleven between 1930 and 1941. During this period, though the number of inhabitants per square kilometre in Switzerland increased from 98 to 131, the number of communes with fewer than 200 inhabitants also increased from 570 to 629. In Graubünden (the Grisons) where the commune is particularly autonomous as well as particularly small, there are no less than 221 communes, only six fewer than in 1854: only 34 have over 1,000 inhabitants, the average population being 667. When the population of the canton was 127,000, about the size of Caernarvonshire, 70 communes had fewer than 150 inhabitants, 34 of them fewer than 100. The *Zwerggemeinde* is not peculiar to Graubünden and the average commune is even smaller in Fribourg. In fact, two-thirds of the communes in Switzerland have fewer than 1,000 inhabitants, almost a third fewer than 300. Neither is fragmentation confined to the

Table I. Swiss Cantons Ranked in Order of Population

Range	Canton (1960 population)		No. of Communes	Certain English or Welsh Administrative Counties for comparison (mid – 1966 population)	
I				Lancashire	2,366,020
				Cheshire	1,023,730
over	Zürich	952,304	171		
				Hampshire	905,060
750,000	Bern	889,523	492		
				Hertfordshire	872,100
II				Warwickshire	556,880
500,000-				Somerset	555,603
750,000				Northumberland	501,380
III				Wiltshire	471,350
250,000-	Vaud	429,512	388		
500,000	Aargau	366,940	233		
				Cornwall	351,420
	St. Gallen	339,489	91		
				Salop	321,720
	Genève	259,234	45		
	Luzern	253,446	107		
IV				Oxfordshire	239,260
100,000-	Basel-Stadt	225,588	3		
250,000	Solothurn	200,816	132		
	Ticino	195,566	253		
				Denbighshire	179,150
	Valais	177,783	169		
	Thurgau	166,420	201		
				Flintshire	160,560
	Fribourg	159,194	284		
				Lincolnshire (Kesteven)	149,580
	Basel-Landschaft	148,282	74		
	Neuchatel	147,633	62		
	Graubünden	147,458	221		
				Herefordshire	139,790
				Caernarvonshire	120,050
V				Pembrokeshire	97,060
				Isle of Wight	97,050
Under	Schwyz	78,048	30		
				Westmorland	67,410
100,000	Schaffhausen	65,981	35		
				Anglesey	55,950
	Zug	52,489	11		
	Appenzell A.Rh.	48,920	20		
				Montgomeryshire	43,700
	Glarus	40,148	29		
				Merioneth	37,750
	Uri	32,021	20		
				Rutland	27,950
	Obwalden	23,135	7		
	Nidwalden	22,188	11		
				Radnorshire	18,300
	Appenzell I.Rh.	12,943	6		

Sources: *Statistisches Jahrbuch der Schweiz, 1967. County Councils Association Year Book 1967-68.*

mountains: some communes around Zürich have amalgamated with the city but Greater Zürich is still composed of 40 communes, while the canton of Geneva, which is almost entirely built-up, has 45.

In spite of all this, the really striking feature of Swiss government is not so much the number of small administrative units as the power and the prestige which attach to each one of them. The example of the cantons suggests that, if the problems of English local government have anything at all to do with size, it is because the functions of the English county are too light, not because they are too onerous. The status and the power of a Swiss canton are incomparably greater than those of an English county. Insofar as its sovereignty has not been limited by the Federal Constitution, a canton is indeed a sovereign state and although the Swiss, with their high standards of decentralisation, now think it superficial to lay stress on the sovereignty of a canton,[40] it would be just as superficial for an outsider to ignore the savour of sovereignty which persists where formal power has passed to the centre. Even outside the important fields of government still left mainly to them, the cantons enjoy extensive residual and delegated powers at home and considerable – sometimes decisive[41] – political influence in federal affairs. Constitutional revision as such requires the support by referendum of a majority of the cantons as well as a majority of the people and the outlook of many national councillors is essentially cantonal.

During recent decades the Federal Government has, it is true, been steadily acquiring new powers – of the 62 constitutional amendments between 1874 and 1959, 43 extended its competence. Nationally organised interest groups now rival the cantons in their influence over policy.[42] The cantons nevertheless employ the language of sovereignty without much fear of ridicule. They have their own citizenship, professional qualifications, banks and churches. Subject to certain safeguards, the constitution still permits them to make treaties with foreign states on matters within their competence.[43] Under delegated powers, they have a greater share in the administration of local army units than an English police authority have in running their police force.[44] Prisoners are still "extradited" from one canton to another.[45] When, at the annual meeting of the Graubünden *Grosser Rat* or Parliament, the president reviews the course of the year, he may well refer to world crises almost as if his canton was still the power it was in European diplomacy during the Thirty Years War. Indeed, the whole atmosphere of the cantonal buildings at Chur, from the chandeliered room where the five ministers meet formally every Monday afternoon, to the state wine cellar below, suggests a ministry, even a palace, as opposed to the county hall of as august a county as Lancashire.

In many ways, a cantonal government is indeed a government as opposed to a local authority. Even after the amendments of 1947 had given the Federal Constitution a new emphasis on welfare,[46] the cantons had to be consulted on economic affairs and social security and, as a rule, to execute any legislation. In these fields responsibility is divided and a cantonal government has many of the functions of the United Kingdom Ministry of Agriculture, Board of Trade and Departments of Employment and Productivity and Health and Social Security. Again, if the criminal and civil codes are matters for the Federation, the administration of justice is largely under the canton, the Federal Tribunal being mainly appellate in character, the federal police concerned with aliens, espionage, treason, forensic science and the like. As for fields traditionally associated with local government in the United Kingdom — education, health, welfare, highways, planning — the cantonal department is very much a ministry, its relations with the federal authorities almost as remote in some fields as those of an English county council with the High Court. Even when a canton is executing federal legislation, it usually has a free hand within certain basic principles.

Nothing illustrates the contrast between Switzerland and the United Kingdom so well as education. To Professor Griffith, the Department of Education and Science is the clearest example in the United Kingdom of "a department with a positive, promotional attitude to local authorities".[47]

To Professor Hughes, on Switzerland, "the supremacy in this field belongs to the cantons":[48] in a recent work on educational administration in Switzerland, indeed, the short chapter on administration at the federal level begins, "there is no federal education authority in Switzerland."[49] With the exception of the Federal Technical University at Zürich, even the universities are cantonal institutions. The only duty imposed upon the cantons by the Federal Constitution is that of providing adequate primary education, free, compulsory, inoffensive to any creed and under civil control. The Federal Government has a duty to take measures against cantons which fail to fulfil their obligations and also to provide subsidies, but "organisation, control and supervision"[50] are to remain with the cantons. In 1882, the Federal Government tried to introduce inspection but their proposals were defeated in a referendum by 318,000 votes to 172,000, never again to be revived.[51] Neither has the federal subsidy ever been withheld in order to bring a cantonal government into line with Federal wishes. Only indirectly, through the necessity for national recognition of leaving examinations and through the examination of recruits by the military authorities (military service being compulsory for men) can the Federal Government bring some pressure to bear. Recently, the Federal Government joined the cantons in setting up a central information office for educational questions,[52] while the Ministry of the Interior began to co-ordinate the expansion of the universities. Essentially, however, central control of education, such as it is, is a matter of dealing judicially with individual complaints about cost and religious bias, not of preserving standards.

It follows from all this that the relationship between central and local taxation in Switzerland is vastly different from that prevailing in the United Kingdom. Originally, almost all that the cantons yielded to the Federation was customs duty, and ever since this ceased to suffice, the Federation has had to struggle hard to obtain a reasonable share of revenue. From 1914 to 1958, the Federation depended on what was essentially emergency legislation for its direct taxation, legislation often of doubtful validity at that.[53] In 1958, a constitutional amendment put the validity of the federal defence tax beyond doubt but merely allowed it to be prolonged until 1964, by which time it was hoped that Cantons and Federation would have agreed on a permanent solution. In 1963, however, all that could be agreed was a further extension of the existing regime up to 1974.[54] To some extent, therefore, the increasing functional competence of the Federal Government has been offset by its failure to obtain adequate finance for its new powers: the Federal share of direct taxation only comes to about 15% and there is no alternative to using the cantons as agents for the execution of federal policies.[55] Federal expenditure, even including subsidies, still falls well short of that of the cantons and is less than half that of the cantons and the communes together. (See Table II.) The cantons have managed somehow both to retain their hold on direct taxation and to obtain an increase in federal subsidies.

Table II. Public Expenditure

Switzerland in 1965 (Population—Dec. 1964 — 5.9 million)

	SF million
Communes	3,959
Cantons	6,945
Cantons and Communes	10,920
Federal Government	4,920
Federal Subsidies to Cantons	651

The United Kingdom in 1964-65 (Population—June 1965 — 54 million)

	£ million
Local Authorities	4,129
Central Government	7,713
Central Grants to Local Authorities	1,139

Sources: *S.J.B.S. 1967*, pp.403, 409, 429, 431; *Whitaker's Almanack, 1968*.

IV

If Switzerland as a whole is still very much a federation of twenty-five cantons, most of the cantons are, in a sense, federations of communes: it has even been suggested that the cantonal parliaments are, in effect, assemblies of communal officials[56] – elected officials such as mayors, it is true, but many of them paid. Switzerland has indeed been built from the bottom up. About such a fragmented country, it is, however, dangerous to generalise and in the French-speaking cantons, in particular, there is, by Swiss standards, a more authoritarian approach to the commune. In Vaud and Fribourg the communes in each *Bezirk* are supervised by a prefect appointed by the canton. The great canton of Bern also has prefects, a *Regierungstatthalter* in each *Bezirk* but here, as in some other cantons, the fact that the prefect is a cantonal official is offset by the fact that he is elected by the people of his *Bezirk*.[57] In most cantons the government has imposed a certain amount of uniformity on the communes by means of statutes comparable to the United Kingdom Local Government Act 1933. Eight cantons have no such statute however, and, in one of them, Graubünden, the people decisively rejected a local government bill in 1945, and again in 1966, by a smaller majority.[58] Significantly, the latter bill was more moderate than that of 1945 but the cantonal government is unlikely to put it up again for another twenty years and it is to one article of the Cantonal Constitution itself that one must turn for the only general law of local government.

According to article 40 of the Cantonal Constitution of Graubünden, each commune has sovereign authority within its own area and the right to govern itself. The commune may legislate as long as its laws are not repugnant to cantonal and federal law and there is a general power of taxation in accordance with equitable principles and, where they apply, cantonal rates of progression: the usual practice is to add a percentage to cantonal direct taxes. The commune must administer its affairs efficiently and appoint such officers as are necessary, but education and care for the poor are the only functions singled out for mention. The only other reference in the Constitution to communes comes in Article 41, on education. It states that, in spite of the canton's responsibility for promoting education, the provision of (roughly, in practical English terms) primary and secondary modern education is, in the first place, a matter for the commune.

The autonomy of the commune is particularly deeply rooted in Graubünden for it was only in 1854 that the canton itself became a unitary state, as opposed to a federation of forty-eight *Gerichtsgemeinden,* originally grouped into three loose alliances. When, in 1854, the cantonal government provided a precedent for communal constitutions, it was almost entirely ignored and the government received for ratification constitutions the number of articles in which varied from five to 148.[59] And when, in 1872, the cantonal parliament attempted to impose a minimum size for the status of commune, there was general uproar and the attempt came to nothing.[60] The Graubünden commune is an extreme case but there appears to be agreement among Swiss scholars that Swiss communes generally are self-governing rather than self-administering areas. There is argument about which of a commune's functions are delegated and which it exercises in its own right: it is not in dispute that each commune has a certain residue of power in its own right.[61] In any case, whatever the position in law, even in the delegated sphere, the canton exercises only an intermittent corrective, rather than a constant preventive, type of control.

Because the population of a commune can be anything from 50 to 500,000, the real status of a commune obviously varies greatly in practice. Basically, the Graubünden commune provides education, supports the poor (including, subject to certain inter-cantonal agreements, its own citizens outside the commune) maintains minor roads, provides water and sewers, controls streams and avalanches and regulates the communal pastures and forests.[62] It is also the legislative as well as the executive authority for building standards and for planning.

At one end of the scale, the city of Chur undertakes most of the functions of a well developed English county borough. At the other, a group of tiny communes may combine to provide even the primary school. Some communes run their own electricity undertakings, delimit nature reserves, promote cable railways and ski-lifts, provide sites for industry, run clinics or join together for "regional" planning. Some act as agents of the canton in the collection, if not the assessment, of taxes and in land registration. All provide the link between national servicemen and their units and execute federal and cantonal civil defence regulations.[63]

Historically, the strength of the small commune is due to the large amount of communal property, which not only provided revenue but ensured that able men took an interest in local government. Most of the alpine pastures in Grau-bünden are owned by a commune, as are 90% of the forests, almost all of which are being put to use — until a recent recession in the timber trade, these made an important contribution to communal funds. As recently as 1952, twenty-nine communes were able to cope without taxation though one must add that the then Secretary of the Kleiner Rat (the cantonal cabinet) described these as "mostly selfish and unenterprising".[64] In small communes, communal labour is still an important factor and may be compulsory. All water rights are vested in the commune and many mountain com-munes have become prosperous by granting concessions to hydro-electric power undertakings from whom they receive, for the use of their water, first a lump sum and then royalties and free electricity, often distributed by the com-mune and charged for. The deferential way in which reservoirs are sited and communes compensated is itself a perfect example of the respect paid to "insignificant" local-ities by the highest authorities of the Swiss Federation and by its richest cities. In addition to all this, the communes have at their disposal almost the whole range of taxes open to a state: twelve are listed in the recent finance statute of a commune of 2,200 inhabitants[65] — they range from income tax, property tax and purchase tax to estate duty and a tax on dogs.

The amount of control exercised by the cantonal government of Graubünden over the communes is very limited. The
necessity for ratification of communal constitutions and
statutes by the *Kleiner Rat* means only that these documents
are scrutinised for repugnancy: it does not mean political or
administrative control. Neither does the canton have much
opportunity to interfere under specific statutes of its own:
exceptions are the approval required for sewage disposal, for
compulsory purchase, for the plans of grant-aided school
buildings and for the broad lines of the school curriculum.
As might be expected, it is in the sphere of finance that the
cantonal government has most opportunity to influence a
commune, though here again, communes which neither qualify
for an equalisation grant (as opposed to a subsidy available
generally) nor run into financial difficulty, remain immune
from inspection or central audit: the cantonal government
complain with reason that this means they are often called in
too late.[66] In 1966, sixty-one communes, about a quarter,
were subject to cantonal inspection,[67] but here again control
is respectful to the point of being welcome. The Ministry of
the Interior's inspectorate consists of a chief and three
assistants and they are easily accessible for informal advice.

Article 40 of the Cantonal Constitution does provide the
Kleiner Rat with one ultimate sanction: a commune whose
administration is contrary to law may be placed under a
custodian. In 1966, three communes were in this position,
one having been so for ten successive years.[68] Another of
these communes was recently discovered to have raised no
taxes and held no election for ten years: the President had
managed to carry on alone on a bank overdraft! When one
considers the size and limited resources of most communes in
Graubünden, the surprising factor by United Kingdom
standards is that so few fall by the wayside. If there are weaknesses in the Swiss system, if the size of the unit is anywhere
reduced to absurdity, it is in Graubünden that this is most
likely to become apparent. Even in that sparsely populated
canton, however, the force of communal pride is enough to

carry most communes through their difficulties.

In spite of the fact that, in a country as small as Switzerland, the general consensus of official and professional opinion has a good chance of reaching the remotest corners, it must not be thought that the autonomy of the small Swiss unit is purely formal and that the official federal or cantonal view can be superimposed upon it by a corps of like-minded officials. Yet another astonishing feature of Swiss government is, not merely the small size of its units, not merely the degree of decentralisation, but the combination of these factors with a degree of direct democracy and lay participation which puts officials at a distinct disadvantage. More than a bare majority of Swiss live in communes with under 10,000 inhabitants and, in these, in German-speaking areas especially, what an Englishman might describe as a parish meeting is still the supreme authority. In 1967, only 3% of the communes of German-speaking Switzerland had abandoned their assembly, as opposed to 25% in the Latin cantons.[69] In Vaud, a commune with a population over 800 has to be content with a council of between 45 and 100 members, while in every canton the assembly has been given up in the largest towns. Communes as large as Olten (21,700) nevertheless still have an assembly and it should be emphasised that elsewhere most of the powers of an assembly devolve, not upon the council, but on the electorate as a whole and are exercised by referendum and initiative.

The referendum and the initiative are features of cantonal and federal as well as of communal government in Switzerland. If the legislative power is firmly in the hands of the people, however, the executive authorities elected by them seldom become bogged down in committees in the way so characteristic of English local authorities. Yet it is the lay element which predominates, even in the executive. Most communes and all the cantons are led by a strong collegiate executive directly elected by the people and usually paid, but nevertheless representative of each of the main political parties in the area. Each of the half-dozen or so members of the collegiate executive is responsible for a particular department of his

authority's work, but all major decisions are the collective
decisions of the executive as a whole. The presidency rotates
from year to year. In the cantons and the large towns, most of
the ministers make a career of government and, though they
are essentially politicians rather than civil servants, their own
officials play a manifestly subordinate role: in the small
communes, there are, of course, very few, if any, officials at
all. If, in the United Kingdom today, participation is seen as
officials consulting the people, in Switzerland it means, and
has always meant, not only the ultimate decisions being taken
by the people at every level of government, but also active,
effective, lay participation in administration proper.

V

Enough should have been said about Switzerland by now
to horrify, not only the English civil service, but also the
local government establishment itself. According to everything that we have been taught in the United Kingdom, the
principal features of local government in Switzerland are a
recipe for disaster. Think of Sir Herbert Andrew, the
Permanent Secretary of the Department of Education and
Science, speculating before the Royal Commission that "there
is nothing to chose between 3 million and 50 million as a
unit of educational administration"[70] — and then of the
half-canton of Appenzell Outer Rhodes which is, with a
population of barely 49,000, not only an unsupervised unit
of educational administration but a unit of educational
legislation! And this is not all: Appenzell Outer Rhodes has
not, in fact, gone to the trouble of legislating for education:
each of its twenty communes is virtually self-governing in
this field. "Each of the communes takes such advantage of
its freedom", says a Swiss teacher, "that the canton presents
us with a truly colourful list of examples of what can be done,
of what should be done, and of what should not be done in
the field of educational administration".[71] Yet the teacher in
question does not on balance consider the lack of an education

statute to be a weakness: communal pride and professional pride ensure that the communes compete with one another in making the most of their freedom from administrative restraint.

The Swiss experience tends to shatter any confidence one may have had in the importance of creating bigger units, of controlling them strictly from a centre and of seeing that real power is in the hands of officials you can trust rather than of a "bunch of ignorant laymen" (let alone the public at large). The Swiss are nevertheless well versed in the type of problem which created a demand for larger units in the United Kingdom. The phenomenal population explosion in the Mittelland — an increase of 63% between 1950 and 1960 in the communes around Zürich and of 82.8% in those about Lausanne[72] — has led to a demand for regional planning in many fields and for more planning at the national level too. To the Swiss, however, this does not mean that the small units which command the basic loyalty of her citizens should lose all power. They prefer to change the functions of a unit than to change its boundary. They favour co-operation as opposed to amalgamation: co-operation in the disposal of refuse, say, amongst suburban communes; co-operation between the cantons of St. Gallen and Graubünden, for example, to found a polytechnic at Buchs. The independent state of Liechtenstein is also a partner in the latter scheme, while the Federal Government itself co-operates closely with the Scandinavian countries and with the Netherlands in running Swissair. The tram system of Basel even runs over two national boundaries, into France and into Germany. Nowhere in Graubünden is the idea of amalgamation opposed as strongly as at Mathon (population 73). This attitude is not felt to be in the least inconsistent with providing the school jointly with two other communes or belonging to an association of sixteen communes for the joint negotiation of concessions for water rights and the joint distribution of the proceeds:[73] although it is difficult to say where Mathon begins and the next village ends, the people of Mathon do not want to lose the opportunity for direct access to the cantonal government. Where there are many boundaries, boundaries themselves are apt to be lower than in countries with comparatively few units, all of which aspire to a certain status in the world.

Significantly, co-operation developed more rapidly within the less authoritarian German-speaking cantons than in the Suisse Romande: by 1969 there were nevertheless as many as 91 joint associations in Vaud alone, involving 233 of its 388 communes[74] — the objects of such associations vary from land-use planning to water supply, from secondary education to refuse disposal.

One of the tenets of English thought on government seems to be that every local authority of the same class should possess the same powers and more or less the same population. In the opinion of the County Councils Association, the way in which the number of people per acre varies so much within England creates "a terrible problem in re-organising local government", so that "you have to allow some parts of the country to have comparatively small units, as low possibly as 40,000 in population, simply from the geography point of view".[75] This is no problem at all in Switzerland: to some extent it is the commune itself which determines which services are appropriate to it alone, which services require co-operation with other communes and which should be left to the canton. It is not always with the same set of neighbours that a commune co-operates in every field and the complicated pattern of Swiss local government would create nightmares for any ministry at Bern which had to keep abreast with the activities of every commune. The variations in terminology from canton to canton create problems even for experienced Swiss students of government, while the variety of ways in which education is organised makes it fortunate indeed that there is no ministry of education at Bern to be confused. But Switzerland has no Ministry of Education and no Ministry of Local Government. The only civil servants concerned are those of the canton. Their offices are within about forty miles of every commune at the very most (usually much closer) and they appear to be more ready to trust the leaders of a commune than to watch and inspect and exhort them continually.

If there is, in many fields, little pressure towards uniformity from above, what about pressure from below? Swiss society is becoming increasingly mobile but the variations in educational administration from canton to canton are often reflected in the curriculum. Curricula variation between the Länder of West Germany has, according to Kloss, resulted in a great deal of criticism from parents and strenuous measures to iron out the difficulties. The very much greater variations within the very much smaller country of Switzerland are, on the other hand, accepted with some equanimity by parents.[76] People do not expect uniformity there, while the schools themselves allow new pupils plenty of time in which to adapt themselves to a new system. Even in the world of planning, the communes of some Swiss cantons, including the greater part of Zürich,[77] are at the moment perfectly free in law to do nothing to control development. If the Federal Government recently obtained a constitutional amendment giving it power to lay down guide-lines in the field of land-use planning, this is more because the Swiss aspire to higher standards than because they are falling behind other countries: according to Ian Nairn, at any rate, "nowhere in Europe, apart from the German part of Switzerland and the Flemish part of Belgium, is the landscape really in tune with the life that is lived there". It is intriguing to reflect that about 80% of Switzerland speaks German, that the Romansch parts are, if anything, more tasteful still in their building, and that it is the French-speaking parts which place most emphasis on the control of commune by canton. How elementary the recommendations of the Skeffington Committee seem compared with the current practice in Switzerland! It was with the public that the Swiss began, with the Parish Meeting, as it were, passing its own planning statute and approving its own development plan. Swiss planning reports can indeed "be read with a certain complacency by those sheltered by U.K. planning legislation"[78] but who can be complacent about the results?

Sometimes, in Switzerland, one feels as if one had entered

a different dimension, rather than a different country. No variation is too small to be overlooked. As a result of a federal referendum in 1938, even the Romansch language, spoken by barely 40,000 people in a handful of valleys in Graubünden, was recognised as one of the four "national languages" of Switzerland, along with German, French and Italian. Unlike the other three languages, Romansch is not an "official language" in the sense that the federal (as opposed to the appropriate cantonal and communal) authorities are obliged to take the initiative in using it on all occasions — for example, in warning passengers on the Federal Railways not to lean out of the carriage window. It is, nevertheless, paid very much more attention than is paid to Welsh (a stronger and more viable language in every way) in the United Kingdom: there is nothing exceptional in the fact that the notices in the main pavilion of the Swiss National Exhibition at Lausanne in 1964 were in Romansch as well as the other three languages. To fully appreciate the Swiss respect for variety and capacity for consideration, however, one has to examine the position of Romansch in its home canton. There one finds, not only that it is spoken, but that it is written, in five or six distinct dialects and that, though it is possible to make do with two versions of official cantonal pronouncements in Romansch, there have to be four versions of every Romansch primary school text-book. Those concerned readily admit that this creates difficulty, but the difficulty is overcome. And in a tourist resort like Pontresina where, owing to an influx of German and Italian speakers, only 20% of the population now speak Romansch, Romansch is still, by a decision of the village assembly, the medium of instruction of the primary school:[79] such is the respect of the Swiss for the historical language of a particular locality.

Perhaps it is the tiny village of Bivio at the foot of the Julierpass which best symbolises the utter fragmentation (and the corresponding unity) of that most fragmented canton of Graubünden: on the face of it, it is a singular Italian-speaking enclave north of the Alpine watershed and a Protestant, or at least ecumenical, enclave in a Roman Catholic district: the commune officially recognises both faiths. The language pattern of Bivio is, however, far more complicated than one might at first suppose.[80] The most recent families to settle (attracted by its winter sports potential) speak German. The Italian-speaking families represent two distinct waves of emigration and may speak a Lombard dialect or the dialect of the Val Bregalgia. Before the Reformation, However, this was a Romansch-speaking village and a handful of the original families still speak a Romansch dialect peculiar to Bivio, while others speak the more general Romansch dialect of the Oberhalstein: all this amongst a population of about 200, almost overwhelmed in the winter sports season by some 800 visitors – and with only two volumes in the Bivianer Romansch to help to keep that dialect alive, both by Rudolf Lanz, schoolmaster, poet, horsehandler, businessman and president of the commune and the *Kreis* at the turn of the century. With such communal awareness, no wonder that detailed economic statistics are kept on a communal basis in Switzerland, and that the president of a commune of a few hundred people can tell you without hesitation what proportion of his citizens is employed in each of the main sectors of employment, how this compares with the cantonal proportion, what changes have occurred over the past decade, and what his executive is trying to do about it. No wonder that, even in Geneva, where the power of the commune is comparatively limited, and the canton appoints the teachers and administers the instructional side of education, the commune spent (in 1965) no less than SF8600 (i.e. about £860) on its annual School Prize Day, "one of the more important functions of the year in the commune".[81] No community in Switzerland is insignificant. This means that a small commune can – and sometimes does – hold up a motorway. And also that a small commune can – and sometimes does – save itself from economic stagnation by its own efforts. And why not? The result is neither poverty nor chaos.

Sometimes, the variations from canton to canton or from commune to commune in Switzerland do reach the very root of government and human rights. In the Canton of

Solothurn, for example, private schools are forbidden,[82] while, in Graubünden, in one commune alone – the commune of Chur – have women the right to vote at the communal level. The variations which would be regarded least favourably of all in the United Kingdom are probably those which hit the pocket – in particular, variation in rates of taxation. In 1965, the percentage of SF10,000 of earned income paid in income tax by a Swiss husband without children varied from 6.5% in Fribourg to 1.9% in Riehen, a commune of Basel, taking into account communes with over 10,000 inhabitants alone. In £ sterling, the range of variation is as much as from £52 to £120, on an income of £1,500, and from £400 to £900 on an income of £5,000. All this is anathema to most economists, but the most heavily taxed cantonal capital, Chur, is booming: its population increased from 18,424 in 1945 to 28,385 in 1965 and is still increasing, while, as we shall see, the people of Basel-Landschaft recently rejected a proposal that they should join the most lightly taxed canton of all, Basel-Stadt.

The fact has to be faced that the dire consequences which English civil servants presume will ensue from lack of central control and lack of uniformity just do not come about in Switzerland.

Notes to Chapter 6

1.   RCLGS paras.24 and 25.
2.   *Ibid.,* para.351.
3.   *Ibid.,* p.287, para.10.
4.   *Ibid.,* para.1.
5.   Ivor Gowan, review of Humes and Martin, *The Structure of Local Government, A Comparative Survey of 81 Countries,* The Hague 1969, *Local Government Chronicle,* 2 May 1970.
6.   A. H. Marshall, *Local Government Administration Abroad* (Management of Local Government, Vol.4), H.M.S.O. 1967, Sweden, para.15.
7.   *Ibid.,* para.14.
8.   *Ibid.,* para.11. The second series of amalgamations is itself a voluntary process and, according to *Local Government Abroad,* Nov. 1969, there are still 850 communes in being.
9.   Unless there is an indication to the contrary, it can be assumed that the figures in the following section have been taken from the *IULA Newsletter* Nov. 1967.
10.   James A. Storing, *Norwegian Democracy,* London 1963, p.173.
11.   Letter to the author dated 25 August 1969.
12.   Marshall, *ibid.,* The German Federal Republic, paras.15 and 16.

13. *Ibid.*, para.179.
14. *Ibid.*, para.193.
15. André Voisin in *L'Elu Local* (Paris), Septembre 1967, p.11.
16. *Ibid.*, p.14.
17. *IULA Newsletter*, Nov. 1967.
18. Roger Dehem, *Planification Économique et Fédéralisme*, Geneva, 1968 p.121.
19. George S. Blair, *American Local Government*, New York 1964, p.44 et seq.
20. *Ibid.*, p.591.
21. *Ibid.*, Table I, pp.46-47.
22. *Ibid.*, p.594.
23. *Ibid.*, p.595.
24. *Ibid.*, p.52. The phrase was coined by the Presidential Commission on Intergovernmental Relations (1955).
25. *Ibid.*, pp.57-58.
26. *Politics and Policies in State and Local Governments*, Englewood Cliffs, 1963, p.115.
27. *Ibid.*, pp.113/4.
28. *Ibid.*, p.114.
29. Marshall, *ibid.*, The United States and Canada, para.196.
30. *Ibid.*, para.198.
31. Citizen Participation in Connecticut, *Local Government Chronicle*, 15 November 1969.
32. Local Government Information Systems in North America, *ibid.*, 31 January 1970.
33. Nelson A. Rockefeller, *The Future of Federalism*, Cambridge (Mass.) 1962, p.16.
34. *Ibid.*, pp.39-41.
35. *Ibid.*, pp.43-45.
36. Quoted in R. H. A. Chisholm, *Local Government Finance*, Papers Presented at I.U.L.A. Conference, Brighton, 1968, p.5.
37. *The Future of Federalism* pp.45-46.
38. Max Beloff, *The American Federal Government*, 2nd edition, Oxford 1969, pp.162-3.
39. It may be assumed unless the contrary is apparent that all statistics relating to Switzerland are taken from the 1967 Edition of the *Statistisches Jahrbuch der Schweiz* and that population figures relate to the census of 1960.
40. e.g. F. R. Allemann, *25 mal die Schweiz, Panorama einer Konföderation*, rev. ed., Munich 1968, pp.9-10.
41. K. J. Allen in *Regional Policy in EFTA*, p.133.
42. Anton Bellwald, *Raumpolitische Gesichtspunkte der industriellen Standortswahl in der Schweiz*, Zürich 1963, p.62.
43. Hughes, *Federal Constitution*, p.12. (See Chapter 2.)
44. *Ibid.*, p.19.
45. *Ibid.*, p.77.
46. *Ibid.*, p.33.
47. *Central Departments*, p.522.
48. *Federal Constitution*, pp.28-29.
49. Heinz Kloss, *Schulverwaltung*, p.81. (See Chapter 3.)
50. Bundesverfassung der Schweizerischen Eidgenossenschaft, Art.27. bis.
51. Hughes, pp.28-29.
52. Kloss, p.83.
53. Hughes, pp.48-50; G. A. Codding, *The Federal Government of Switzerland*, Boston 1961, pp.147-150.
54. Roger Dehem, p.102.
55. Dehem (p.113) puts it the other way round — that cantonal agency has

concealed the degree of centralisation!

56. Adolf Gasser quoted in Kloss, p.56.

57. A. Gasser in M. Bridel (Ed.), *Die direkte Gemeindedemokratie in der Schweiz* (DGD), Zürich 1952, pp.57-58.

58. For text of bills and case on their behalf see Abschied des Grossen Rates des Kanton Graubünden zur Volksabstimmung vom 22.4.1945 and do. vom 24.4.1966.

59. F. Pieth, Bundnergeschichte, Chur 1945, pp.470-71.

60. *Ibid.*, pp.469-70.

61. Z. Giacometti, Schweizerisches Bundesstaatsrecht, Zürich 1949, p.68, Note; H. P. Matter, Die Legitimation der Gemeinde zur staatsrechtlichen Beschwerde, Bern, 1965, p.15.

62. cf. G. A. Töndury, Studie zur Volkswirtschaft Graubündens, Samedan 1946, pp.189-196.

63. Bundesgestz über den Zivilschutz vom 23.3.1962.

64. J. Desax, Untersuchung über die Volksversammlungen im Kanton Graubünden, in DGD, p.118.

65. Steuergesetz für die Gemeinde Samedan vom 16.7.1965, Art.I.

66. Abschied des Grossen Rates, 1945, p.2.

67. Bericht des Kleinen Rates des Kantons Graubünden, 1966, p.14.

68. *Ibid.*, p.15.

69. A. Gasser, L'Autonomie Communale en Suisse, I, *L'Élu Local,* Septembre, 1967, p.38.

70. RCLGE, Minutes, V para.535.

71. Hans Knecht, Aspekte des ausserrhodischen Schulwesens, Der Kanton ohne Schulgesetz, *Schweizerische Lehrerzeitung* 1961, quoted in Kloss, p.33.

72. Bellwald, p.39.

73. B. Mani, Die Gemeindekorporation Hinterrhein, *Terra Grischuna, Zeitschrift für bündnerische Kultur, Wirtschaft und Verkehr* (TG) 1963, pp.47-50.

74. *Le Tribune de Genève* du 25 mars 1969.

75. RCLGE, Minutes, XIII, para.1413.

76. Kloss, pp.21-22. An intercantonal agreement is nevertheless pending.

77. Kanton Zürich, Baugesetz für Ortschaften mit städtischen Verhaltnissen vom 23 April 1893 (as amended to July 1967), Art.68.

78. T. H. Elkins, review of Barbier and others, La région Haut-Léman Chablais, *Town and Country Planning,* July/August 1970, pp.358-359.

79. G. Deplazes, Die Schule und das Rätoromanische, TG, 27, (1968) p.315.

80. E. Simonett and R. Arquint, Bivio, Vergangenheit und Gegenwart, TG, 27, p.270 et seq.

81. Codding, Veyrier, p.75.

82. Kloss, p.130.

7. Discussion and Consent: Reorganisation in Switzerland

"*Der Kleinstaat ist vorhanden, damit ein Fleck auf der Welt sei, wo die grösstmögliche Quote der Staatsangehörigen Bürger im vollen Sinne sind ... der Kleinstaat hat überhaupt nichts als die wirkliche tatsachliche Freiheit, wodurch er die gewaltigen Vorteile des Grossstaates, selbst dessen Macht, ideal vollig aufwiegt; jede Ausartung in die Despotie entzieht ihm seinen Boden ...*"[1]

JACOB BURCKHARDT, 1868

"*... der Kleinstaat bietet − ich scheue mich vor dem Wort: Freiheit − einen grösstmöglichen Spielraum für persönliches Denken, weil der Kleinstaat, ohnmächtig wie er ist, kein Götze werden kann, dem der Einzelne sich zu opfern hat.*"[2]

MAX FRISCH, 1966

I

PROFESSOR Christopher Hughes, the leading English authority on Swiss Government, is quite prepared to demolish Swiss myths where necessary. He nevertheless states in his *Federal Constitution of Switzerland*, "I rate Swiss Government, particularly Local Government, very highly." For all her arcadian features, Switzerland has to live in the limelight of contemporary Western Europe and is manifestly an advanced country in standard of living, in humanity and in design: in 1963, she was ahead even of Sweden in gross national product per head. A reliance on the tourist industry means that she must ensure high standards of sanitation and planning in the remotest corners. The Zermatt typhoid epidemic, at the height of the winter sports season of 1963, was a tremendous blow to Swiss hygienic prestige. It occurred through the contamination of the water supply for a few hours by the action of one infected man near the source of supply, but by the end of the

167

two to three weeks' incubation period, most of those affected had been scattered all over Europe. How many people by comparison know of the epidemic at Aberdeen in 1964, which gave rise to 396 cases as compared with the 329 at Zermatt?

Again, Switzerland's lack of natural resources and of any outlet to the sea makes her particularly dependent on technical advance and therefore upon a high standard of education.[3] She has to deal with congestion in her cities and with depopulation in her mountains but she copes at least as well as her large, centralised neighbours. Indeed, it is more fashionable to criticise Switzerland for super-efficiency than for any lack of it and some Swiss tend to suffer from an "artist in Philistia" complex. Switzerland leads Europe in the number of computers per head of population. In spite of having an incomparable railway system, she spends a greater proportion of her gross national product on roads than any other European country apart from Finland. In Professor Donnison's study[4] of the government of housing, she comes at, or near, the head of the European league table by every standard adopted (not that there is no housing problem in some cantons). Architects who visited Switzerland after World War II encountered "a standard of architecture which technically was comparable only to that of Sweden, Finland or the United States."[5] If one sometimes hears people criticising congestion on Swiss roads one can be certain that they have not visited certain parts of the United Kingdom; if some Swiss technocrats voice fears that the educational system cannot sustain further growth, one should remember that, if the Swiss sometimes appear self-satisfied, they are rarely complacent. The whole success of Switzerland during the past two centuries has depended upon that readiness *selbst das Neue ergreifen* — that readiness to undertake new development yourself instead of waiting upon events — which is so characteristic of Swiss commerce.[6]

The structure of Swiss government itself is not without its critics today. Even the great champion of local autonomy in Europe, Adolf Gasser, accepts that, if in most countries the problem is to protect the localities from anonymous, authoritarian, central power, the problem of Switzerland is still the reverse: to induce the localities to consider their problems in terms of much larger areas.[7]

In 1967, the Federal Government set up a Commission headed by Professor Wahlen to consider the general revision of the Federal Constitution, including the distribution of power between the Federal and the Cantonal Governments. It is hoped that the Commission will, amongst other things, suggest an answer to the vexed question of providing the central authorities with adequate permanent sources of taxation, and some method of regulating the economy as a whole. There is growing pressure from technocrats for a more comprehensive national road network, for nationally imposed sanctions against river pollution, for national standards in the preservation of beauty, the development of school curricula and the tapping of the pool of ability. If there is too much centralisation in most states today, the problems of Switzerland appear to be at the other extreme and it is certainly conceivable that the report will advocate a further shift of power from the cantons to the centre. At the same time, it is most unlikely that the Commission will advocate any amalgamation of cantons or that the Swiss people as a whole will accept drastic changes of the kind necessary to put them in the position of a country like Sweden, let alone the United Kingdom.[8] In the re-shaping of government to meet modern conditions, in Switzerland, as in no other country, the local is at least as formidable as the central in the prestige and authority with which it enters the debate.

Internationally, "there is general acquiescence in a legal system which recognises as equals in law, states as disparate as the United States of America and Malta," says Professor Mackenzie.[9] Essentially, Switzerland is still a federation of states: the territory as well as the residual sovereignty of each Swiss canton is guaranteed by Article 5 of the Federal Constitution. As recently as the thirties of this century, there was a strong movement in Geneva for secession from Switzerland as an international free city: "a century's existence as a

Swiss canton ... had not been a sufficiently forceful
experience to wipe out memories of past self-sufficiency".[10]
Only in 1964, the canton of Aargau declined to send an
official delegation to the rather *avant-garde* Swiss National
Exhibition at Lausanne. Is the recent history of the movement to amalgamate the two half-cantons of Basel a pointer,
perhaps, to the future of constitutional reform in Switzerland?
In 1947, and again in 1960, these two half-cantons sought the
approval of the Federal legislature for their amalgamation, or
rather for their re-union, for it was only after the liberal
revolution of 1833 that the conservative city found its
interests to be incompatible with those of its liberal hinterland. In 1960, the Federal Parliament agreed to re-union and
representatives of the two half-cantons began to prepare a
draft constitution. It was well known that the procedures for
acceptance of the new unified constitution by each half-
canton and for the necessary amendment of the Federal
Constitution would be long drawn out. Only last year, however, the present author could write as if it was only a matter
of time before the two halves were re-united and the one
"county borough problem" in Switzerland was solved – by
request of each half and by general consent. He should have
known his Switzerland better. In the referendum held on
6th December, 1969, to ratify the draft constitution, Basel-
Landschaft opted to remain out by 48,183 votes to 32,222
in a 76% poll. Even in the city, one-third of those who voted
was against amalgamation. Now Basel is not Rutland, or even
the Isle of Wight. It is, perhaps, the banking capital of Europe,
while if the banks themselves are within the city, many of
those who work in them reside and vote in the other half-
canton. Indeed, with Solothurn, Basel-Landschaft is now the
most highly industrialised canton in Switzerland. Its population has been growing phenomenally, especially in the
commuter belt around the city: the increase between 1950
and 1960 was 40% (the fastest of any canton). Basel-Landschaft also has the highest proportion of students per head of
population of any canton without a university of its own,
though, up to 1963, it depended entirely upon the city for

"grammar school" education. Moreover, the movement for amalgamation is not new; it dates back to 1932 and there was agreement in principle on amalgamation between the two Governments as long ago as 1936, when the Landschaft was greatly attracted by the social security of the prosperous city. Yet, in the last resort, it was neither commuting or economic unity of interest which proved to be the key to the problem, but the old radical tradition of the Landschaft, which goes back to the Seventeenth Century and earlier. Liestal, the principal town of the Landschaft, was branded as *die rechte Wurzel der Rebellion* by the city authorities as long ago as 1653. It was in Liestal too that, after the French Revolution, the first tree of liberty in German Switzerland was planted. Again it was Basel-Landschaft which pioneered the movement to make Switzerland itself a referendum democracy in the 1860s: it was the referendum which saved its identity, as no other device could have done, in 1969![11]

Is it perhaps significant that it is at a time of growing prosperity for the Landschaft (even though the city remains more prosperous still) that the movement for amalgamation has come to an abrupt end. Only 8% of the citizens of the Landschaft now make a living from the soil: may it not be that the very sophistication of the prosperous suburban dweller makes him more susceptible to the appeal to tradition and identity and participation in government? It is not as if we were dealing with stubborn insularity: the two half-cantons have already established a joint body for the co-ordination of planning and one of the arguments against amalgamation was that co-operation was proving perfectly effective in dealing with the city's lack of space. The result of the Basel referendum may well be more of a pointer to the future than a hangover from the past.

In view of the repercussions on the balance of power within Switzerland as a whole, the only other major cantonal problem — the proposal for an entirely new canton consisting largely of the French-speaking part of the second largest canton, Bern — is a much more delicate issue. The emotions aroused and the language used — on both sides — makes the Bernese Jura "separatist movement" more akin to a movement for national independence than for local government reform within a unitary state: significantly, it was the *cantonal* government which sought, unsuccessfully, the extradition from France of Jean-Baptiste Hennin, a "Jurese extremist" convicted of arson, said to be the first Swiss to claim political asylum abroad. Fundamentally, decentralisation is more consistent than amalgamation with the political genius of Switzerland and the first report of the federal commission set up to give advice on this problem[12] provides for self-determination for the Jura and a series of referenda to determine both the extent of the autonomy which is desired and the extent of the area which desires it. The first stage in the process of putting the problem to the electorate of the Jurese communes has already been accepted by the electorate of Bern as a whole and it may be that, in the Jura, unlike Basel, it will be the reformers who eventually prevail. Again the tide seems to be running in favour of decentralisation rather than against it. The prosperous "separatists" of the Jura certainly regard cantonal status as something as tangible and worth fighting for as complete national independence and it was only by 15,000 votes to 16,000 that they failed to gain a majority (in the Jura itself) in the cantonal referendum of 1959. The creation of a new canton with a population of only 122,000 in one of the most sophisticated parts of a sophisticated country would really have given the Redcliffe-Maud Commission something to think about. For all the power of big business, national and international, it seems that the residual and delegated power, the status and the influence of a Swiss canton are advantages still worth fighting for.

II

Constitutional reform is unlikely to affect the boundaries of the Swiss cantons. Neither does there seem to be any determined movement for the general amalgamation of communes. For Graubünden, this point is best made by considering the views of critics of the present regime. A strong plea for amalgamating the administration and schools of two adjoining communes which already act jointly in church affairs and in forestry rather loses force when one realises that the populations of the two communes are, respectively, 193 and 103.[13] So do scathing attacks on the fragmentation of the canton, when the remedy proposed is the amalgamation of communes with "less than 100 inhabitants" with their neighbours "whenever this is geographically possible",[14] and bitter comments about the stagnation of a particular commune, when the apparent solution is a joint association of communes in a valley whose total population is some 1,700.[15] The cantonal government of Graubünden would certainly like to facilitate the amalgamation of the smallest communes, but appear to be well satisfied with communes as small as the smallest urban districts of Wales: they themselves revere the tradition of autonomy.[16]

More interesting still is the attitude of a Zürich editor who advocates greater co-operation in planning in the Upper Engadine. Pointing out that the communes there (eleven for 10,449 people) have jointly administered a hospital for half a century and have been jointly helping agriculture, promoting Romansch and improving the educational system, he appeals for more co-operation in preparing the infrastructure for a mounting population, and in preserving natural beauty and architectural style. In spite of all this he emphasises that, even in "this relatively homogeneous region", the requirements of the various villages vary so much that planning must remain, in law, a matter for each commune.[17] What is required is co-operation, especially along the boundaries.

Perhaps it is in Graubünden of all cantons that local autonomy dies hardest. If amalgamation becomes fashionable anywhere in Switzerland, this is most likely in Vaud, not only because of pressure on space but because of the less directly democratic (if not less liberal) political tradition. In 1964, twenty-four communes in the region of Lausanne (including the city itself, for there is no 'county borough problem' here), "confrontées quotidiennement aux problèmes posés par la rapide croissance de l'agglomération lausannoise", commissioned, together with the cantonal Department of Public Works, a study preliminary to the compilation of a regional plan. The style of the resulting document[18] is as contemporary as one would expect from a region whose university gave its name to a school of economic planning which emphasises the importance of the region and advocates the separation of politics and economics. Inevitably the authors list amongst the obstacles to good planning "la fragmentation du territoire en unités administrative locales"[19] (adding for good measure "le cloisonnement vertical entre les divers services qui retarde ou empêche une action coordonnée", a factor which deserves more attention in the United Kingdom). Equally inevitably to the student of Switzerland, they only mention in passing the possibility under Vaudois law of amalgamating communes. Instead they devote a chapter to the various forms of intercommunal association short of amalgamation.[20] They underline the advantages of an Association des Communes under Article 123 of the Vaudois Local Government Act of 1956, which, like an English joint board, can take decisions without the prior approval of the constituent bodies. They also bring out the ensuing restriction of autonomy and the difficulty of finding the right constitution where the communes vary in size. The study concludes by emphasising that different problems require different types of organisation and different groupings of communes to tackle them. It points out that a general co-ordinating body could be made up of a variety of local groups of varying legal standing. To advocate "une solution souple, qui tienne aussi bien compte des particularités locales que des besoins de l'ensemble" will seem an astonishingly untidy conclusion to the English public servant. Perhaps the key to it all is to be found in the section entitled "Information", where the authors stress the importance of keeping in touch with the people:

> "Pour avoir quelque chance d'aboutir, une politique
> d'aménagement du territoire doit pouvoir faire appel

à la participation des citoyens. Si l'on attend du citoyen son consentement vis-à-vis des contraintes, des charges inhérentes au phénomène de l'urbanisation, encore faut-il lui offrir les moyens d'en comprendre la nécessité."[21]

In advocating a general co-ordinating body made up of a variety of local groups, GERL hold out the practice in Zürich as an example, as well they might, not only because growth has presented a greater challenge to Zürich than to any other Swiss city but also because the City of Zürich was a pioneer of planning at the beginning of the century and can be assumed to be conscious of the vast amount of work done on regional planning in Germany. The remarkable fact is that, in spite of the choice of expanding the city boundary as the solution for Greater Zürich's problems in the inter-war period, further amalgamation now seems to be rejected — in the least particularistic, and most economically progressive, canton of all, the power-house of Swiss industrial and financial development.[22] The first amalgamation of communes with the city took place in 1893 and a further eight were added in 1934, after an eight-year debate between, on the one hand, the parties of the right and centre which did not want "Red Zürich" to become more powerful and, on the other, the social-democrats of Zürich and the councils of most of the communes Zürich proposed to take in — these actively sought amalgamation, irrespective of party, since, owing to the Depression, they lacked the resources to provide schools, roads and welfare services for the working-class families who had been moving out of the city. One commune, Oerlikon, had experienced a 323% increase in population between 1888 and 1920, while the average increase for the twelve communes first considered for amalgamation was 180%. A compromise was eventually reached whereby eight out of a possible twelve communes were amalgamated with the city and better provision was made for equalisation of resources within the canton.

It was under the leadership of Emile Klöti, soon to become one of the most distinguished of all Zürich's mayors, that the social-democrats had worked for the *Eingemeindung* of 1934;[23] it was Klöti indeed who, as early as 1914, as "Baudirektor" (head of the city building department) had arranged a competition for the future planning of Greater Zürich. Yet, after the Second World War, when the problem of controlling the expansion of Zürich arose once again, it was Klöti himself who put forward the view that a third *Eingemeindung* was out of the question: Zürich was already strong enough to be able to share the advantages of a great city with the whole region: further territorial expansion would only lead to the destruction of valuable local autonomy and the overflow of bureaucracy. The joint planning of land use and transportation in Greater Zürich was thus entrusted in 1958 to a joint association, with six regional groups. In the words of one of the planners involved, Hans Aregger, the aim of the association is "to integrate the various autonomous communes on a co-operative basis into an overall city region, so far as necessary to achieve balance in structure and design, without destroying the special features and character of individual places, and the preservation of their political autonomy is an essential part of this."[24] Once again, it appears that co-operation, far from being out-moded, may be coming into favour in societies which have already passed through the pressures for amalgamation now being experienced in England – societies sophisticated enough to appreciate the value of political autonomy and familiar enough with the planning process to be able to form joint associations without loss of face.

III

There are two main lines of argument which are put forward in justification of Swiss decentralisation. In the first place, it is argued positively that decentralisation, far from making it more difficult to achieve efficiency, actually helps to make local government more efficient in the most immediate sense. The very process of handing over sources of taxation, political power and additional functions to local authorities helps to strengthen those authorities. A small unit of government in Switzerland is a bigger concern than a unit of similar population in the United Kingdom. Not only is it free from any general doctrine of *ultra vires* but it has far greater potential financially. On the absence of *ultra vires,* one must agree with the Maud Committee that "even more important than the actual extension of power is the different atmosphere in which a local authority enjoying general competence operates. The members think in terms of the citizens' needs as a whole and regard themselves as responsible for local well-being ... the public think in terms of the responsibility of the local authority when in England they would turn to the central government".[25] As to finance, it should be noted that, in 1966, the total expenditure of Graubünden, SF315,859,684, was almost quadruple that of a somewhat larger Welsh County.[26] Again the fashionable winter resort of Klosters spent in that year SF3,318,369[27] as compared with the £101,927 spent by the prosperous summer resort of Tenby (population 4,520; product of penny rate £995)[28] — not a third as much, while almost half Tenby's expenditure was on housing, a factor which does not apply at Klosters.

Again, the Swiss distaste for bureaucracy and the strong lay element in government, which decentralisation makes possible, tends to blur the distinction between private and public life, much to the benefit of each. Switzerland is a welfare society rather than a welfare state. Communal projects receive more voluntary support than is the case in the United Kingdom, while the authorities in turn work through and help to support a variety of voluntary organisations and private practitioners. A few years ago, Basel announced that "in ten years fifty schools had been built by almost as many architects"[29] (mostly as a result of competitions open to every tax-paying architect). In Graubünden, it is the churches which run most of the homes for the elderly, while the evening institute at Chur was recently presented to the city by the chain-store co-operative, Migros: no less than 4,000 people

enrolled for courses on the first day, the most popular
course being, significantly, local history. Even in the work of
town and country planning, a voluntary association of cantons,
communes, architects and civil engineers, *the Vereinigung
für Landesplanung,* together with its regional groups, and the
Institute of Planning at the Technical University of Zürich
have hitherto had the main responsibility for providing
advice and co-ordination (as already mentioned, in a recent
referendum, the Federal Government succeeded in obtaining
power to lay down guide-lines in the field of planning)[30]. In
some cantons, the inspection of schools is undertaken, not
by officials, but by lay committees.[31] Indeed the small number of officers employed full-time in cantonal education
departments,[32] compared with county education departments
in the United Kingdom, is puzzling even if one allows for the
communes taking much of the weight. Have we perhaps too
many unnecessary middle-men between the central department (itself to some extent superfluous) and the schools?
Even Bern, with a population approaching one million, only
has fifteen full-time officers in its Ministry of Education.*
Aargau, with a population approaching 400,000, only has
three, including a typist, Schwyz only two, while in some of
the smallest cantons there are no officials who deal only with
education. The Secretary for Education of Zug is also Secretary of two other departments, while the Secretary for Education of Uri is a part-time officer who also has his own legal
practice! All this will appear disgracefully backward to Welsh
educationalists, but there is no reason to think that education
in the classroom suffers in Switzerland. And after all, there
are hundreds of independent schools in the United Kingdom
which are perfectly well able to flourish without the support
of a formal advisory structure: not all of these, by any
means, have the advantage of a superior staff. Moreover, in
Switzerland as a whole, it appears that the educational
administrator is essentially a co-ordinator and an adviser

---

* Inspectors are excluded from these figures: Bern has twelve *Bezirksinspektoren,*
Uri two general inspectors, two for domestic subjects and two for physical
training.

rather than a director whose word is law in the communes. For that matter, many schools have no headmaster and are controlled by the staff as a whole or by a committee of teachers.

The close liaison between private and public life, coupled with local autonomy, has also been a great advantage to the Swiss economy. It was not the federal government which took the initiative in saving the watch industry of the Jura during the inter-war depression but the cantonal government of Neuchatel.[33] Similarly, it was not even the Canton but the City of Zürich which saved the well-known turbine manufacturing concern of Escher Wyss from closure during the same period, and preserved the jobs of at least nine hundred people. The City actually acquired the works before letting it to a newly-formed company, which received the right to buy the City out after a certain period: in the meantime, Canton and City together guaranteed to meet any loss up to a certain sum.[34] An interesting feature of this transaction is that the City had undertaken responsibility for unemployment benefit, so that the saving in this field could be set off against the cost of acquiring the company.

The fact that each canton has its state bank has also been decisive in promoting development outside the big cities,[35] as has the way in which cantonal and communal governments can acquire an interest in what, on the face of it, is a private company. The cantonal government of Valais, for example, holds 51% of the capital of an important electricity company (55 communes also have shares) and is able to attract industry by charging lower tariffs than the rest of the country.[36] Another important factor is the power of a canton or commune to exempt a new undertaking wholly or partially from taxation — according to Bellwald, such factors as taxation and site costs are more important than transport costs in determining industrial location in Switzerland. In 1946, the mountain commune of St. Nicholas (population 1,200) succeeded in attracting a motor-car accessory firm employing 400, which it exempted from taxes for 10 years:[37] only a dozen of the workers came from outside the district. Bellwald, a far from romantic writer, ("(Die Bauer) wollen nicht in den unwirtschaftlichen, mühseligen Wirtschaftsformen verharren, um einige Touristen die gute alte Zeit erleben zu lassen")[38] is very concerned at the slow pace of development in the mountains and the widening of the gap in living standards between townsman and alpine small-holder. He nevertheless considers that the greater vitality and slower rate of de-population of the Swiss, as compared with the French Alps is due more to the communal autonomy of Switzerland than to the character of her people.[39] And though Bellwald argues a good case for national guide-lines in economic planning, one is bound to say that the less favoured areas of Switzerland appear to do better now, with the accent on local powers, than those of Wales, with the accent on central intervention. Fundamentally, it is political power which determines the content of a plan. Bellwald assumes that a national plan would impose a limit on the growth of cities for the sake of greater industrial development in the mountain villages and, in Switzerland, the federal system does ensure a certain balance of power at the national level, so that it might well be to the advantage of the cantons to support a broadly conceived national plan. Left to themselves, however, dominant conurbations are likely to wish to create immense, de-populated, national parks. Those who seek, by central planning, to promote the redistribution of wealth within one country must be careful not to condemn fragmentation out of hand. In considering the very question of central intervention, Henri Roh, Director of the cantonal association which has had conspicuous success in promoting economic development in the Valais, asks "do not the least favoured regions run the risk of being abandoned, under the pretext that the social costs of saving them would be too great? Is this not to some extent what certain mountain areas of France have experienced? In a similar situation, Switzerland has reacted entirely differently thanks to the vitality of her secondary bodies, the cantons and the communes, who possess broad powers to act and an independence unknown in a centralised state".[40]

To argue that every sparsely populated locality which, chooses to remain within a certain state should always have to accept what is in the interests of the thickly populated areas or the larger cities of that state, for better or for worse, is to court apathy at best and tyranny at worst. Efficiency has far more to fear from apathy and tyranny than from democracy: in the last resort, justice is the only safeguard against them and justice is beyond price. Switzerland can certainly provide concrete examples of some of the most obvious arguments for central control but not all of these are as simple as they appear. If, as we have seen, the absence of centrally imposed planning regulations has not, in general, prevented Switzerland from attaining higher standards than the United Kingdom, the fact also has to be faced that such a well-known resort as Puntraschigna (Pontresina), in such an outstanding region of natural beauty as the Upper Engadine, was without a planning act until 1964 and that the tiny commune of Segl (Sils) – in the middle of that "metaphysical" landscape which so inspired Nietzsche – provides in its development plan for an ultimate population of 30,000, a provision which has caused fury in Swiss mountaineering and preservationist circles. On the face of it, here is a classic case for centralisation in the name of high standards and the general good of humanity, but is this so in fact? This is not the first threat to the character of Segl. In 1946, in consideration of SF300,000 raised by public subscription by the amenity societies, Segl and the adjoining commune agreed to keep the incomparable Lej da Segl (Silsersee) inviolable for 99 years, at a time when they were being pressed to grant a concession to a hydro-electricity company bent on turning it into a reservoir.[41] It is being hinted that Segl is merely stepping up the price of remaining unspoilt and that this is what is making the amenity societies so indignant. Fundamentally, is not the debate between the centre and the localities in Switzerland, as elsewhere, about power and finance rather than about standards? The price of preserving the National Parks in Wales is now being paid, in part, by small farmers and un-employed or badly paid workmen denied the opportunity of raising their living standards by cashing in unhampered upon the prosperity of the English Midlands. The price of preserving Segl has been in the past, and may yet in the future, be shared by the thousands who enjoy its beauty. Not that the people of places like Segl are as unheeding of the beauty and the peace of the mountains as is sometimes assumed: throughout the twenties the great mountain guide Christian Klucker fought a successful fight as President of the Commune against the blandishments of the hydro-electricity concerns. It is, after all, because they wish to be able to make a living amongst their own people, in their own mountains, that the people of communes like Segl are sometimes tempted to develop them in incongruous ways. Their dilemma is a very real one, and made all the more acute by increasing pressure to conform with trends in the cities. It is better to resolve such dilemmas by genuine negotiation than by superior force.

Even in the country, the industrial city often plays the role of destroyer of natural beauty rather than of preservationist. Perhaps the best example of all of the respect which sophisticated urban Switzerland can display towards the smallest and most remote communes, is the way in which the village of Splügen was saved from drowning in the forties of this century.[42] Although the Swiss succeeded in avoiding attack by Hitler in 1940, their country was totally surrounded by the Axis powers and their allies and coal and oil were in very short supply. The electricity companies had to seek fresh sources of water power and one large consortium, representing most of the industrial areas of Switzerland, put forward a scheme which would have involved drowning Splügen and two other small villages on the Hinterrhein, with a total population of 430. It was the intention of the company to build a new village and also to offer land in'a much more fertile part of the canton to the seventeen families for whom there would be insufficient agricultural land left in their own valley. Two of the families concerned moved voluntarily and declared the greatest satisfaction with the arrangements made for them. In 1942, the communal assemblies of the three villages nevertheless finally refused the application of the consortium for their water rights. Another fifteen communes in the district would have profited greatly from the scheme without any loss of land and they were very much in favour of it: so was the Cantonal Government, and in a situation like this, even under Swiss law, it would have been possible to compel the minority to give in. The Cantonal Government, acting quasi-judicially, nevertheless held that the objecting communes had "sufficient grounds" for their resistance, while a further appeal to the Federal Tribunal was abandoned in order to give the President of the Federal Council himself the opportunity to discuss the matter with representatives of the three communes. Eventually, the main reservoir for the scheme was built in a remote valley over the border in Italy, with only a smaller reservoir on the Hinterrhein and no drowning of villages. Streams in the original area still had to be tapped, however, so that all eighteen communes involved both ate their cake and kept it: having escaped drowning, they nevertheless receive substantial royalties in exchange for their water rights.

On the face of it, one of the more disturbing features of education in Switzerland is the fact that, on the whole, it is highly selective, particularly in the country, where the length of the school year in some communes is so short that the teachers have to find other employment in the summer: in one commune the headmaster, who is also president and clerk of his commune, works in the fingerprint section of the cantonal police during the summer. Only in 1946 did the substantial communes of Poschiavo and Brusio vote to extend the school year from twenty-eight weeks to thirty-six.[43] There is also a good deal of variation in the number of years of compulsory schooling and in the availability of grants for further education.

Again, while the general standard of school building and equipment in Switzerland is extraordinarily high[44] and some schools, even in a mountain canton like Graubünden, are architectural gems, impossible of achievement within United Kingdom departmental cost limits, there are a few neither purpose-built nor possessed of a formal playground. All in all,

however, the concern with education in Switzerland is much
as one would expect in a very advanced country. It is not the
government at Bern but the economy that demands that Swiss
education should be good. If some farming communities
prefer to have their children home throughout the summer,
is this not more realistic in terms of the local economy and
also more idealistic in terms of local values? Not everyone
accepts that a short school year is a disadvantage and, at the
cantonal college at Chur, which provides "upper grammar
school" education for much of the canton, pupils from the
small schools have a reputation for being "less tired" than
their fellows: the villages of Graubünden have a reputation
for producing eminent men, including, at the moment, the
Rector of the University of Zürich and the President of the
Swiss Federal Tribunal. For that matter, not everyone in
Switzerland equates the good life with "getting on" in a large
town and it is a matter for reflection that it is precisely this
preoccupation of our society with "getting on," with the
"rat race," with "climbing the ladder," that so nauseates
some of the best students at American and European Universities, some of them to the point of wishing to contract out
of society altogether. The provision of equal opportunity
in education is usually presented as something which no
individual should be denied. Would it not be as truthful to
present it as something which modern technology demands or
as a way of pressurising the average into the careers which the
state requires? Here again it is so often the city which is tapping the pool of ability, and delineating the proper field for
ambition, at the expense of the country, and not only the city
as opposed to the country, but the capital at the expense of
the provinces. We must beware of reformers who profess to be
concerned with individual equality but who are primarily concerned with extending their own way of life and their own
domain.

IV

The real justification of autonomy is not that localities can be trusted to conform in their own interests to certain minimum standards, but that they are free to be different: free not only to pursue their own interests for their own sake without having the disadvantage of legal subordination added to any inherent weaknesses, but free in case it is they who are right and the central authority which is wrong. This is the second line of argument in justification of decentralisation in Switzerland. Yet one hears men of democratic conviction presenting the difficulties which have arisen between West German Länder and the Federal Government at Bonn as evidence against federalism. Would that such difficulties could have arisen under the Nazis!

To many Englishmen today, the object of local government is to provide efficient services, to give the ratepayer his money's-worth. At a recent international conference on Amalgamation and Co-operation, the Chief Whip of the Greater London Council said that the only yardstick that could be used was "the finest service at the cheapest possible price", whereupon a NALGO representative interposed that "as local government was big business, the methods of big business should be employed".[45] In Switzerland, fortunately for the human race, the principal object of local government is still to enable a locality to retain as much freedom as possible. How else can one explain the existence of a strong movement, independent of the state, to encourage wealthy lowland communes to help poor Alpine communes to provide better amenities without having to succumb to bureaucracy and lose their identity? *Der Schweizerischen Patenschaft für bedrängte Berggemeinden* was established in 1940. It helps to attract light industry to the mountains and provide "extras" like deep-freezes and launderettes in poor communes and it promotes direct aid of commune by commune. In 1965, for example, the *Vorstand* of Wetzikon, a town of 10,500 people in Kanton Zürich, put before their *Versammlung* a proposal to grant SF5,000 per annum for five years to Tschappina, a commune 6,000 feet up in the Heinzenberg (GR), the grant being to provide a water undertaking. This in itself is astonishing. What strains all belief is that the *Versammlung* not only accepted the proposal, but doubled the amount of the grant.[46] One is assured that the cantonal government never considered setting it off against the equalisation or any other grant.

The Swiss are unlikely to accept the doctrine that no possibility of discord between central and local authority should be allowed to delay the administrator, no boundary tolerated that cuts across the pattern of optimum economic efficiency. The very existence of their state bears witness to the opposite concept — that, in the essentials, the standards of Bern may be higher than those of Berlin, that Geneva is better cut off from its economic hinterland than included in the France which produced the Vichy regime, that it was better for the young people of Poschiavo to have to cross two seven-thousand-foot passes to their (largely German-speaking) cantonal college than to have their education provided by Mussolini just across the border in the same Italian-speaking valley. If these are extreme examples, this does not mean that, in drawing local government boundaries in the United Kingdom, we should not give weight to the less striking political disadvantages which can be set off against less striking economic advantages: the advantage to one small Welsh county, for example, of keeping out of the bitter party strife, characteristic of local government in the more prosperous neighbouring county, the advantage to Flintshire of being one of the most important and distinctive counties of Wales, rather than a peripheral district of a Merseyside economic region.

The Axis countries whose doctrines and conduct were so repugnant to the Swiss were neighbours who spoke the same languages. It was easy enough to identify them as enemies after 1940. In the late thirties, however, it was just as well that the city police of Social-democrat Zürich were free to watch the Nazis at a time when the federal and cantonal police were far more interested in Communists[47] and that, during the crisis of September 1938, some communes on the German border were able to mobilise on their own initiative without waiting for orders from Bern.[48] Today the threat of dictatorship is subtler: essentially it is a threat from within:

but it is against threats from within that a decentralised, ultra-democratic system of local government is the best defence.

Max Frisch and Friedrich Dürrenmatt, the two best-known contemporary Swiss authors, can be wonderfully eloquent about what they regard as the conservatism, the stagnation, the philistinism, of a neutral and federal Switzerland. One suspects, however, that they would wax even more indignant were they to be confronted with the centralist, aligned versions of these universal failings. The way in which such men are prepared to wound their own countrymen to the core, is itself evidence that Switzerland is as healthy a country as any in the essentials as well as in efficiency. For all his cynicism about the idealised versions of Swiss democracy purveyed by the Establishment — not least to tourists — it is to the democratic tradition of Switzerland that Frisch himself must appeal in the last resort:

"Machen Sie Gebrauch von der Freiheit, bevor sie verrostet ist. Machen Sie Gebrauch von der Freiheit, denn sie gehört zu den Dingen, die sehr rasch und rettungslos verrosten, wenn man sie nicht braucht. Mit einem Wort: Machen Sie Gebrauch von der Freiheit."[49] — "In one word: make use of your freedom."

Notes to Chapter 7

1. *Weltgeschichtliche Betrachtungen* (ed. Rudolf Marx, Stuttgart 1969), pp.34-35. "The small state exists so that there may be one spot on earth where the largest possible proportion of the inhabitants are citizens in the fullest sense of the word . . . the small state possesses nothing but real freedom, an ideal possession which fully balances the huge advantages of the big state; any lapse into despotism cuts the ground from under its feet."
2. Uberfremdung 2, in the collection *Öffentlichkeit als Partner*, Frankfurt 1967, p.125. ". . . the small state offers — the word freedom embarrasses me — the greatest possible latitude for private opinion, because the small state, weak as it is, cannot become an idol to which the individual has to be sacrificed."
3. See W. A. Johr and F. Kneschaurek, Study of the Efficiency of a Small Nation: Switzerland, in Robinson (ed.), *The Economic Consequences of the Size of Nations*, London 1960.
4. D. V. Donnison, *The Government of Housing*, London, 1967.
5. Jul Bachmann and Stanislaus von Moos, *New Directions in Swiss Architec-*

ture, (trans. C. Casparis), London 1969, p.14.

6. B. M. Biucchi, *The Industrial Revolution in Switzerland 1700-1914*, The Fontana Economic History of Europe, London 1969, p.12. The description quoted is Goethe's.

7. *L'Élu Local*, Janvier 1968, p.35.

8. For an account in English of the main issues see A. Baur in *The Swiss Observer* (London) 9 and 23 August and 13 September 1968. Cf. the views of student-staff study groups set up at the University of Zürich to consider questions posed by the president of the commission and reported at length in *Neue Zürcher Zeitung*, 7 April 1968, p.21.

9. W. J. M. Mackenzie, *Politics and Social Science*, London 1967, p.370.

10. Bozeman, *Regional Conflicts around Geneva*, Stanford 1949, p.403.

11. For much of the background and many of the facts on the Basel problem, I am indebted to F. R. Allemann's account in *25 mal Die Schweiz* esp. pp.217-221 and to "MM", Baselland and Baselstadt Remain Independent, *Swiss Observer*, 23 January 1969.

12. Max Petitpierre and others, Premier rapport de la Commission confédérée de bons offices pour le Jura du 13 mai 1969 (also in German); see also P.M.B., The Jura Problem in *The Swiss Observer*, 10 October 1969 and Allemann, Jura -Der Kanton, den es nicht gibt, in *25 mal Die Schweiz*.

13. A. Engi, Tschiertschen und Prada, TG 24, 1965, p.97.

14. Töndury, p.196.

15. D. Giovanoli, Soglio zwischen Planung und Wirklichkeit, TG 26, 1966, p.60.

16. Abschied des Grossen Rates, 1966.

17. C. Walther, Orts und Regionalplanung in Feriengebieten, TG 25, 1966, p.50.

18. Groupes d'études de la région lausannoise (GERL) — J. Barbier, P. Conne et L. Veuve -La Région Lausannoise de Lutry à Morges, Etude préalable à l'aménagement régional, Lausanne 1966.

19. GERL, p.128.

20. *Ibid.*, pp.129-130. The treatment is similar in GERL's latest volume (Sept. 1969).

21. *Ibid.*, p.128.

22. See Allemann p.89 et seq. for a general account of Zürich: Der metropolitane Kanton.

23. The account of this problem is based on P. Schmid-Ammann. *Emile Klöti, Stadtpräsident von Zürich, Ein Schweizerischer Staatsmann*, Zürich 1965 esp. pp.165-173 and pp.296-299.

24. *Ibid.*, p.299. Cf. Bellwald p.60.

25. Management of Local Government I, para.49.

26. Kanton Graubunden, Staatsrechnung 1966, p.246. The Welsh county, Carmarthenshire (pop.166,320) spent £8.8m. The figures require analysis in the light of comparative costs but so great a gap would take a good deal of explaining.

27. Gemeinde Klosters-Serneus, Rechnungsablage an die Landsgemeinde, 1966 (Verwaltungsrechnung only) p.10.

28. Tenby Borough Council, Abstract of Accounts for the year ended 31 March 1966 (Expenditure under General Rate Fund Revenue, Corporate Estate, Pier and Harbour and Housing Accounts).

29. Bachmann and von Moos, p.34.

30. *Ibid.*, p.33; Bellwald pp.90-92.

31. Kloss, p.75.

32. *Ibid.*, pp.58-59, from which all the details in the ensuing paragraph are taken.

33. Henri Roh, Fédéralisme politique et décentralisation économique et industriele, Sion 1960, pp.235-236.

34. Schmid-Ammann, pp.180-184.

35. Roh, p.269.

36. *Ibid.*, pp.320-325.

37. *Ibid.*, p.358.

38. Bellwald, p.38.
39. *Ibid.*, p.61.
40. Roh, p.382.
41. Töndury pp.128-129. In Wales, at least one National Park Committee take the view that developers in a National Park should be compensated when required to adopt higher standards than are expected outside the Parks.
42. Much of the following account is based on Töndury pp.291-295 and on the article by Mani cited in the previous chapter. For a fuller account see my article, Gwerthu Dwr yn y Grisons, *Barn*, Rhagfyr 1968 (in Welsh).
43. R. Tognina und R. Zala, *Das Puschlav*, Bern 1963, p.16. On selectivity, see also Töndury p.189 and Peter Newell, Gingerly Tapping The Pool of Ability, *Times Educational Supplement*, 20 June 1969.
44. See Bachmann and von Moos' section on school architecture, pp.86-103, and, on equipment, Jean-André Comte, Audio Visual Aids, *Times Educational Supplement*, 15 May 1970.
45. Report of Stockholm Conference, *IULA Newsletter*, Nov., 1967.
46. TG 24, 1965, pp.316-317.
47. Schmid-Ammann, pp.210-211.
48. Elizabeth Wiskemann, *Undeclared War*, 2nd ed., London 1967, p.302.
49. Festrede 1957, in *Öffentlichkeit als Partner*, p.14.

8. Outline of a Flexible Approach

"Beth yw trefnu teyrnas? Crefft
Sydd eto'n cropian."*
WALDO WILLIAMS

IN DRAWING up blueprints for the local government structure of the United Kingdom, it is necessary to escape from the
idea that reform is primarily a matter of the size and shape
of the unit. The revitalisation of local government depends
upon giving local authorities a general power to tax and a
general power to act, coupled with a recognition that, in
internal affairs, the role of central government is to co-
ordinate, advise and support, as opposed to supervising and
directing. It depends also on the readiness of local authorities
themselves to substitute powerful, identifiable, full-time, lay
leadership for the Chief Officer in Committee, and the formal,
prepared questioning of such leaders by back benchers for
that interminable turning over of pages in unison which is so
often a large committee's sole contribution to decision-
making. The substitution of a few ministers for a dozen or so
large executive committees would not only improve the speed,
quality and continuity of decision-making. Paradoxically, by
concentrating responsibility and enabling some laymen to
acquire the know-how to stand up to the professionals, it
would also make local government more sensitive to public
opinion. The revitalisation of local government depends above
all upon stimulating public interest. Nothing is more important

* Lit.—What is organising a state? A craft still crawling.

191

than the preparation of secondary school pupils for active citizenship by means of political studies proper, of intensive study of the local environment and of courses in the appreciation, on the one hand, of good landscape and good design and, on the other, of those human qualities which emerge in great literature.

The introduction of the referendum into local government is also worth considering, particularly if a less childish type of party politics evolves in a new, more responsible, type of local government unit. At present, it is customary amongst elected members and officers alike to condemn referenda as an abdication of responsibility on their part or as a sell-out to ignorance and emotion or as the negation of systematic decision-making. Few who dismiss the referendum out of hand have much idea of the referendum in practice, however. In Switzerland, a referendum is preceded by a long debate of the issues in the local press, with the parties and voluntary bodies of all kinds playing their part. A sober statement of the executive's viewpoint is sent to each elector with his voting-card. In the case of an initiative, the referendum is usually on a point of broad principle, the drafting of detailed legislation, should the initiative succeed, being left to the executive, the acceptance of that legislation to a second referendum. Neither should the use of the referendum be interpreted as a surrender to that crude idea of democracy as a system whereby any ninety-nine people may happily override the wishes of any ninety-eight. Democracy, according to the author's old Quaker history master, is "government by discussion and consent." In Switzerland, there is ample provision for discussion before a referendum while, at the national level, a majority of the cantons, as well as a majority of the people, have to consent to a proposal. Again, most executives are, at every level of government, multi-party colleges, so that the referendum itself is essentially a check that there is popular support for something already agreed between the parties, while the initiative ensures that the establishment does not become too complacent in the face of new issues.

In spite of all this, one must concede that it would be unwise to try to introduce a system as highly decentralised and democratic as that of the Swiss into the United Kingdom in the course of a few years. The fact must be faced that, over much of the United Kingdom, even outside the conurbations, the sense of locality is poorly developed and seldom respected: does not the very term "the locals" have a ring of mild contempt about it? How far we have to go to attain a rich local political life can be gauged by comparing the United Kingdom Press with that of Switzerland. With the English dailies facing such financial difficulties that, according to Lord Thomson, only four of the nine would survive under stress; with papers of such true quality, as well as prestige, as *The Times* and *The Guardian* losing over £1 million and £800,000 a year respectively, it is a mystery how Switzerland manages to support so many good dailies. Admittedly, the Swiss suffer little from restrictive practices by the printing unions, are technically ingenious, and are prepared to appoint young, inexperienced men to editorial posts; admittedly, Switzerland has no distribution difficulties compared with the United States or even with Wales, where there is still no satisfactory road or rail link between Cardiff and Bangor. These factors alone could not possibly account, however, for the fact that, in 1960, the Swiss readership of 1,486,000 could support no less than 120 dailies, only two of which had disappeared by 1968.[1] Including weeklies, there are no less than 400 newspapers in Switzerland, 138 of which are published in communes with less than 4,000 inhabitants and only 11 of which have circulations exceeding 50,000. No less than 93.5% of the Swiss papers have, in fact, circulations of less than 20,000 and some of these are papers of considerable repute: the *Journal de Genève,* for example, had a circulation of only 13,520 in 1967[2] (not surprising perhaps when it is capable of a front page banner headline such as "Masterly Interpretation of Beethoven's Third by Klemperer"). The *Journal* is only one of five dailies published in Geneva, all but one of which have a London correspondent: the *Journal* itself also has correspondents — not necessarily exclusive or full-time — in Paris, Bonn, Brussels, Vienna, Prague, Bern,

Basel, Zürich and Lausanne and at the United Nations. The *Tribune de Genève* (1967 circulation: 60,000) has correspondents in Moscow and in Washington, while *La Suisse* (53,000) sent two reporters to Cape Kennedy to witness the first rocket to the moon. The great *Neue Zürcher Zeitung* [3] has twenty highly-qualified, well-paid correspondents all over the world, on a circulation of only 90,000, 19% of which is abroad.

In spite of the sustained, intelligent interest of Swiss newspapers in foreign affairs, their basic strength is obviously the loyalty of local readers "as attached to them as to the plot of land visible from the bell-tower of the Parish Church" and, often, a local political party. Very few of these papers cross cantonal boundaries. They are a vital accompaniment of cantonal and communal autonomy and of direct democracy. If decentralisation is to succeed in the United Kingdom, we shall have somehow to expand, sober down, raise the standards and broaden the outlook of the local press. At the same time, there will have to be thorough-going decentralisation within the B.B.C., with regional news integrated with national and international news rather than tagged on to it in separate but minor programmes. The establishment of separate broadcasting corporations for Scotland and for Wales might be the beginning of this process, which could do so much to promote free debate generally as well as intelligent concern about regional and local issues.

Many consider that the low vitality of English localities means that local government can be written off with a clear conscience. Actually, it is a danger signal for the health of the nations of Britain at every level and all the more reason for trying to preserve what local feeling does exist and for trying to promote it elsewhere. But the attempt must be made circumspectly, seeking, in Macaulay's phrase, to "remove a vast amount of evil without shocking a vast amount of prejudice". The chronic lack of trust of local power characteristic of the Civil Service — essentially a view that some human beings have a divine right to rule others — is fundamentally evil but so is any suggestion that localities should be trusted shocking to the many people who accept any constitution as it stands.

One of the more acceptable methods of restoring power to local government does involve the restructuring of local government areas. Here an approach should be made from two directions. In the first place, there should be substantial decentralisation of central government power, including power of taxation, to Scotland, Wales, Cornwall and a dozen or so English provinces. From the point of view of local government, it is not of the utmost relevance whether such decentralisation amounts to a full-blown federal system or merely to a system whereby elected councils take over the strategic planning of their provinces, together with certain executive functions, but remain subject to a less rigorous form of central control. The essential factors are that provincial councils should be directly elected, should have their own paid, full-time ministers, should have their work highlighted on radio and television and in the regional press and should be free to determine the local government system proper according to the circumstances of their own province.*

By Swiss standards, there is no reason why power should not be devolved to units comparable in size with the present counties and county boroughs and it may be desirable to base some provinces on historic counties like Lancashire or Kent. At the same time, it has to be recognised that the English, if not the Scots and the Welsh, are used to a higher numerical scale than the Swiss and that devolution to provinces on the scale of the economic planning regions would make the English imagination boggle less than devolution to counties. Again the County Borough problem is most amicably solved

---

* This work is mainly concerned with local government within the United Kingdom and the author in no way seeks to imply that federal status within that Kingdom is the utmost to which Wales and Scotland should aspire: if, as has been reported, the European Economic Community proposes to allot to Ireland, Denmark and Norway ten members each of the European Parliament, as opposed to Britain's 36, and three votes each in the Council of Ministers, as opposed to Britain's ten, it is difficult to see how Scotland, which has almost twice the population of Ireland, and Wales, which has twice Ireland's Gross National Product, can reasonably be content with anything less than full membership of the Community in their own right — a proposition which carries no implication of "economic separation" (whatever that may mean) and ought, therefore, to receive wide support from outside Plaid Cymru and the Liberal Party.

within a unit which is too large either to be dominated by one city or to be identified with an existing county, while arrangements would, in any case, have to be made for strategic planning over wider areas than most of the present counties.

The imminence of some kind of European Federation might also be put forward as an argument for devolution to large provinces. One of the functions which is likely to be devolved upwards to a European institution is the allocation of resources for regional development and it will be in the interests of Wales, Scotland and the English provinces to develop a sense of economic and political identity with a view to direct lobbying at Brussels. Again, regionalism is more compatible with a genuine sense of Europe than is the confrontation within Europe of three or four huge, centralised states, each of which has a tradition of dominance and of empire: regionalism too would probably help to prevent a United Europe from becoming merely a larger, more dangerous, more uniform version of the type of state it supersedes. More unity at the continental and world level and more decentralisation at the regional and local level are complementary rather than conflicting ideals: each is necessary to make the other tolerable. It is a condition precedent for the survival of small nations, distinctive regions and historic cities that they should be prepared to co-operate and that the boundaries between them should be low; equally it is a condition precedent of a world or a European state that its internal divisions should be strong enough to ward off tyranny, to break up monotony, to secure buoyancy and to avert that condition which Senator Fulbright describes as "the arrogance of power." There may well be a place within the new Europe for local and regional units which neither seek to be exclusive nor feel that they can pass on the initial responsibility for their own area to the central government. In such a Europe, it is Whitehall, not local government, which is the more likely to become redundant.

The second approach to a new local government system is from below. First of all, an attempt should be made to identify the cells from which larger units could be built up.

To define the types of community which constitute the basic
cells of political life is difficult: ideally they should choose
themselves, subjectively, not objectively, and then, having
considered the resources available to them and the possible
uses to which these resources could be put, decide the extent
to which they should link up with neighbouring units, either
by giving up political status altogether or by federation. At all
levels of government it is probably the federal principle
which is most likely to promote a feeling of community and
self-help. This principle keeps asserting itself even in systems
which are formally unitary; the rural districts were designed
to be, essentially, federations of parishes, while Jeffrey
Stanyer has shown how "a striking feature of County Government is the fact that County Councillors tend to be also
District Councillors and Rural District Councillors tend to be
Parish Councillors":[4] in Devon, in 1964, 65% of all County
Council candidates were also District or Parish Councillors.
The percentage of Pembrokeshire County Councillors who are
also District Councillors is 36%: many Committee Chairmen
are exclusively "County Men" and tend to make a virtue of
this, but not a few members of influence openly hold themselves out as district men first and county men second.
Stanyer draws attention to M. J. C. Vile's view that some
states within the American Union themselves show a federal
structure and we have already noted Gasser's view that the
cantonal parliaments of Switzerland are essentially assemblies
of communal officials.

On the Continent, the federation of communes in associations with specific, as opposed to general, objects is a well
developed tradition, while, in the United Kingdom, the grouping of Parishes is sometimes undertaken under Section 45 of
the Local Government Act 1933. Joint committees and boards
are nevertheless unpopular in the United Kingdom, as is
delegation: according to the English Royal Commission "there
is a wide measure of agreement in local government that
delegation is an unsatisfactory arrangement".[5] The Commission nevertheless envisaged that their provincial councils
would set up committees "in conjunction with the authorities

concerned, to deal with those planning questions that require to be considered as a whole",[6] while the Labour Government's White Paper envisaged delegation by unitary authorities to district committees, upon which representatives of the common councils would sit as of right.[7] Joint committees proper do tend to be slow to execute their projects because their constituent authorities have different priorities and cannot always pull together. Joint boards, whose resolutions do not require ratification are, on the other hand, almost impervious to democratic control, and have little regard for the financial responsibility of their constituents. One should not exaggerate the defects of joint committees, however: the Welsh Joint Education Committee has a good deal of fruit to show for its efforts. "Politically", says P. J. Madgwick, "the committee is not able to develop leadership or drives to counter the local loyalties, pride and sensitivities of the authorities. Despite these formidable handicaps, the WJEC has created for itself over twenty years a position of considerable influence as a regional body ... It is a good example of the tying together of small local units to utilise the potential of the existing system. It has demonstrated that Wales is viable as a region".[8] And if the WJEC has so far failed, for example, to establish its proposed mountaineering and sailing centres, who is to say that the authorities which held back these projects were not, at a time of economic crisis, right to do so? It is in fact the loss of democratic control which is the major defect of joint bodies in the United Kingdom. Everywhere the experience is that, once an authority has appointed its members to, say, a water board or a police authority, it loses all influence over that body, while the members themselves complain that they are mere rubber stamps for decisions taken by the officers. Bodies with one purpose only are much more susceptible to domination by an officer than multi-purpose bodies in which a number of departmental officers have to fight for a share of the cake, often providing substance and professional advocacy for what is essentially a lay political view. Again, joint bodies often cover wide areas, which allows the members little opportunity to arrange beforehand to work together and discourages regular attendance by the old, who are often ailing, and the young, who are usually busy. Few authorities make any arrangements for their representatives on joint bodies to report back to them or make their re-election any more than a formality. It is not that joint bodies cannot be controlled, but that the constituent bodies act merely as formal electoral colleges instead of continuing to assume that they are still basically responsible to their own electors for the function in question. If there is a latent federalism at work within many County Councils, the tendency of *ad hoc* Joint Committees and Boards is to act as unitary bodies, with members identifying themselves with the service rather than with the citizen. The remedy is to amalgamate different services rather than different areas and to make it clear that, whatever arrangements an authority may make to execute a function jointly, the point of reference for the citizen is still the constituent authority.

We still have to identify the cells – the communes – from which main authorities should be composed. Each province should, of course, be free to evolve its own local government system. In order to make a start, however, it might be as well to accept existing County and Municipal Boroughs and Urban Districts as communes, leaving them to institute Ward Meetings, initially as advisory bodies only: there should be a right for, say, any one hundred electors to demand the convening of a Ward Meeting. Outside the towns and the few rural districts which do have an identity of their own, some parishes could be retained and others could come together on the basis of Primary School catchment areas. Between the commune and the province there might be, in some provinces, one tier of most-purpose authorities, many of them based on historic counties (and all of them known as "counties"), though the bigger communes might themselves become most-purpose authorities. The important factors are that the commune should play a major part in the process of delimiting areas and that there should be the utmost flexibility in the allocation of functions.

Basically, commune and county would both be omnicompetent and omni-responsible, subject to their actions not being repugnant to national, provincial, and in the case of communes, county law. The province, for its part, would assume the role of the central government in laying down minimum standards and fundamental policies – some of them, according to the degree of devolution, at the behest of the central government – in equalising resources and in ensuring the co-ordination of neighbouring authorities. The most-purpose authority would have a duty to see to the execution of major statutes and a sole right to execute them during a transitional period of, say, ten years. It would nevertheless be empowered to make arrangements with communes for the transfer of responsibility in whole or in part to them, with a corresponding financial adjustment. The province would have a duty to provide support by way of advice and arbitration and to set up such specialist institutions as were not provided by the counties jointly. Even in terms of the conventional wisdom, units of local government need not be nearly as big as the Royal Commissions suggested, if the province is available to provide the jam, and the special diets of widely scattered minorities, leaving local government proper to provide the bread and butter.

The system supported would differ from Redcliffe-Maud's in several respects. In the first place, the counties could vary greatly in size and be as small as their citizens wished: their functions would be made to measure and in some cases they would cover town areas only or country areas only. In the second place, the commune, even if not large or ambitious enough to become a county with major executive functions, would have power to decide, at first instance, all planning applications within its own area: the county and the province, as well as individuals, would have a right of appeal to an administrative court against any planning decision (positive or negative) but the grounds for appeal should be so defined as to discourage appeal on a mere matter of opinion. The commune would be obliged to comply with any firm strategic and structural plans issued by the province and the county but at the very least any design plan for a particular commune would require the ratification of that commune. The county would thus have every incentive to make planning positive, rather than negative, and to proceed by dialogue rather than by remote authority. In the third place, the communal council would become the managing or governing body of the schools, residential homes and other local institutions within their own areas, though there could well be provision for the co-option of parents, teachers, residents and others by the council when they were sitting in a particular capacity; the commune would also be expected to undertake minor, if not major, housing development in accordance with local demand and assist in the day-to-day management of housing estates in their locality. Fourthly, the commune would have a duty to act as the local agent of the county and the county as the local agent of the province; this would not affect the autonomy of commune and county within their own spheres but at the very least would enable a county to use each communal office as its own local office for obtaining and providing information: for this purpose, the county would be obliged to pay a good salary (full or part-time according to the size of the commune) to a Communal Clerk so that each commune would have at least one officer of calibre.

It is not for a Welshman to attempt to delineate the local government areas which might result in England or in Scotland from reform along the lines advocated in the preceding pages. This work is concerned more with emphasising certain values and trying to alter the direction of reform rather than with advocating an ideal system which could be achieved overnight. Of the systems which have been put forward by the Royal Commissions or by their critics, the one which does point in the right direction is that advocated by Professor Peter Hall, Mr. J. P. Mackintosh, M.P., Mr. K. P. Poole (an academic who has had the great advantage of serving in local government), Professor Robson and Professor Self, in a letter which appeared in *The Times* on 4th February, 1970 (see Appendix 2), and was supported in a long and well argued leader on the following day. This system accords closely with the views of Derek Senior, in particular with his "second-best alternative", where-

SCOTLAND

NORTHERN

YORKSHIRE
AND
HUMBERSIDE

NORTH
WEST

EAST
MIDLANDS

WEST
MIDLANDS

ANGLIA

WALES

SOUTH
CENTRAL

SOUTH
EAST

SOUTH WEST

PROPOSED ELEVEN REGIONS

Map 5. Mackintosh's Regions of England.

Map 6. A Europe of Regions.

by 12-15 provincial councils would take the place of his 35 first-choice top tier authorities, the number of second tier authorities remaining at 148. This solution seems to have been regarded by Senior as second-best in part because of his doubts about the readiness of the central government to devolve sufficient power to provincial councils to make it worthwhile to establish them.[9] In their evidence to the Crowther Commission, the Town and Country Planning Association also support "the establishment of twelve to fifteen elected regional councils in England and Wales," for the sake of strategic planning. They emphasise that Senior's "second-best alternative" is "not some sort of unhappy compromise but, in fact, the best possible solution".[10]

The authors of the letter to *The Times* accept that unitary authorities have many advantages but are convinced that the Redcliffe-Maud areas are too small for strategic land-use planning, transport and large scale development, and too large for the personal services. Their provinces would undertake "the structure/strategic plan, as opposed to local design planning," housing overspill, refuse disposal, water supply, the fire service, probably the police and a few other services which make less personal impact on the citizen; the provinces would also "stand ready to supply any of the highly specialised aspects of the social services which exceed the capacities of the districts". The hundred or so units within the provinces would remain most-purpose authorities. If the number of these units could be higher than that contemplated by the authors and certainly not tied to any magic figure like 250,000; and if the neighbourhood councils within them could be encouraged to develop at least along the lines advocated by the Open Group in their *Social Reform in the Centrifugal Society*[11] (they seek "to be firmer than Maud about certain minimum responsibilities the bottom tier of local councils should have" and advocate an element of syndicalism in housing, education and welfare) we should be moving in the right direction. In particular, the neighbourhood councils should have some planning powers for, as Jane Morton has pointed out, local communities as such are in fact more concerned about and affected by environmental than social services.[12]

From the top, it will certainly be argued that the system outlined above has too many tiers but it has fewer than society itself. To strike out a tier in an administrative structure does not make any corresponding natural unit disappear. It merely tempts the administrator to take so many short cuts that he loses in friction any time he may have gained in having fewer formal rungs to climb. As it happens, the difficulties of tiers are exaggerated today by the fact that each tier can deal directly with the central government, so that there is no semblance of a chain of authority and responsibility, with district supervising parish and county supervising district. To say that each subordinate unit must have a residue of sovereignty and a sphere in which it governs in its own right is not to suggest that, outside that sphere, each cannot be the subject of respectful control by the tier immediately above, rather than by a remote central government. Looked at as a whole, a system with many tiers and much autonomy will appear very complicated: with good management, however, the participants themselves will usually only be concerned with the tier immediately above and the tier immediately below.

Some will be appalled at the prospect of four tiers of government within England, not to mention a European tier and, in some fields, a world tier; others will find it hard to accept that a community council should have any decisive power in the field of planning. To many, the whole point of regional planning by elective provincial authorities is to ensure that the same body controls both the congested cities and the open spaces upon which new towns can be built. There can, of course, be no argument about the need for regional bodies responsible for considering the development both of city and metropolitan regions and of large provinces as a whole. The argument is about the nature of such bodies, the extent to which they should be, on the one hand, authoritarian and monolithic, or, on the other, federal and co-operative. The large unit as opposed to the small, the city, as opposed to the country, already have immense economic, political and cultural power. The natural tendency of cities is to exploit the weaker units within their sphere of influence and we should beware of accepting, in the name of good planning, the sort of relationship which is condemned as imperialism in the case of a great power and its satellites: in Switzerland, planning is only now beginning to shake off its former association with the Nazis.

Today, it is the vertical divisions between professions which make people short-sighted and intolerant, not the horizontal divisions between parishes. Where you were born is accidental. What profession trained you goes to the root of your self-respect. Doctors and social workers are like oil and water; accountants and solicitors are fighting a cold war in our municipal halls, while as Leopold Kohr puts it, "if a business man knows a sculptor, he is suspected of being a sex pervert. If an engineer knows a philosopher, he is suspected of being a spy." Mass-communication and mobility have, however, killed parochialism. The task today is to keep the parish alive, not to break down its isolationism. It is the small unit which requires the protection of the law so that it can bring some bargaining power into that dialogue which is the only civilised method of government.

Unless the small, comprehensible unit survives, unless children are taught to understand and appreciate their immediate community, the quality of regional planning itself will suffer. Regional planning must not surrender to mobility and population growth where it could provide the basis for a more satisfying, conservationist, culture altogether. It is aimless mobility and wasteful growth themselves which are the basic problems and it is by the cultivation of community in depth in small units that one begins to counteract these tendencies and create a world society which has some hope of living within the world's resources. For a small community is the world on such a scale that not one of us can escape his responsibility for replacing triviality with pride, humanity, humour and taste and for rooting out as much misery as we can within the human condition.

Notes to Chapter 8

1. For much of what follows I am indebted to two articles by P.M.B., "The Swiss Press Today" and "Further aspects of the Swiss Press" in the *Swiss Observer*, 10 April and 24 April 1970.
2. For details of the Geneva press, see Codding, *Veyrier*, p.35.
3. On the NZZ see Allemann. pp.124-26, who describes *The Times* in comparison with the NZZ as "provincial" in coverage but "avant-garde" in production.
4. *County Government in England and Wales,* London 1967, pp.45-46.
5. RCLGE I, para.70.
6. *Ibid.,* para.414.
7. Cmnd.4276, para.52.
8. The Welsh Joint Education Committee after 21 Years, *Local Government Chronicle,* 13 September 1969, pp.1703-4.
9. Senior, paras.503 and 504.
10. *Town and Country Planning,* Vol.8, No.6 (June 1970), pp.270-72.
11. *New Society* pamphlet, London, 1969.
12. *The Best Laid Schemes? A Cool Look at Local Government Reform,* London 1970, pp.87-8. Miss Morton's book is published as mine goes to press and I can do no more than say that it is well worth reading both for a summary of the issues raised by the Royal Commissions and for the author's own thoughts on the subject.

9. The Community of Communities: Wales

". . . cymdeithas o gymdeithasau yw cenedl rydd, a dyma'r awr i gymdeithasau bychain ymuno mewn cyfunderfn gydweithredol ac amrywiol er maentumio rhyddid. Canys peth lleol yw rhyddid . . ."

SAUNDERS LEWIS

(. . . a free nation is a community of communities, and the hour has come for small communities to join together in a co-operative and diversified system in order to maintain freedom. For freedom is a local thing . . .)

I

The last set of local government proposals to deal with England and Wales together were those of the ill-fated Local Government Boundary Commission of 1947, the Commission disbanded by Aneurin Bevan. Ever since, Wales has enjoyed separate treatment, with the Local Government Commission for Wales producing draft proposals in 1961, and final proposals in 1962, and with the Welsh Office, established in 1964, going it alone and producing its first White Paper well in advance of the reports of the Royal Commissions on England and on Scotland. If in form Wales has had separate treatment from England, however, the thinking behind the various proposals put forward for Wales has been essentially English. Dominated as Wales is by England, familiar as many Welshmen are with English conditions and fashions, it is a common fault of Welsh administrators, politicians and academics to refuse to accept Wales as she is.

The four basic faults of local government in England, as listed by the Redcliffe-Maud Commission,[1] can be summarised as follows:

209

1. Local Government areas no longer fit the pattern of life and work.
2. Town is divided from country by the County Borough system.
3. Services are divided between counties and county districts.
4. Many authorities are too small in size and revenue.

The first and second of these faults do not apply to Wales to anything like the extent to which they apply to England. We have only four County Boroughs, at least one of which, Merthyr, can hardly be said to divide town and country to a significant degree. Our basic problem, even in the industrial areas, is depopulation. The population of Merthyr dropped from 80,000 to 56,000 between 1921 and 1961 and is still dropping, while that of the Rhondda has diminished by 16,000 during the last 20 years. It is precisely the opposite state of affairs, a population explosion, which has destroyed old boundaries and made local government reform and regional planning so urgent a matter in England. Birmingham, for example, has to find sites for another 15,000 houses outside its own boundaries by 1975, while England as a whole has to find room for the equivalent of 40 new Bristols or 200 new Cambridges by the end of the century. Judging by current trends, Wales will be lucky if her population increases to any significant degree. Except for tourist traffic, most of which is generated over the border, it is just not true of a rural Welsh County Planning Authority that, "when making provisions for housing, employment, shopping, education, recreation and the consequent traffic," it is "often coping with demands and pressures existing not only in its own area, but also from areas outside its boundaries",[2] to quote the written evidence of the Ministry of Housing and Local Government to the English Royal Commission.

As for the fourth fault, while Welsh authorities are particularly small by English standards, this is related as much to drawbacks and defects in the geographical and economic structure of Wales as to any obsolescence on the part of the local government structure. No amount of amalgamation will, for example, provide Pembrokeshire with a polytechnic within easy reach. There is no branch of Marks and Spencers in Haverfordwest, immense though the area of activity of that firm must be: the necessary population is just not there. Demographically, Wales is predestined to doing things on a smaller scale than England. To insist that a rural Welsh county requires a population of 200,000 is almost like saying that an English County Borough cannot be an efficient unit for health and education without including in its boundaries at least one mountain rising to 2,000 feet and at least 1,500 yards of safe bathing beach.

If most of the area of Wales is sparsely populated and if our older industrial areas are losing their population, Wales nevertheless enjoys those social advantages which are usually associated with mountains and with mining valleys – a pronounced sense of family and community, plenty of practice in democracy, the remnants, at least, of a common culture and an appreciation of education that cuts across class, even where its eye is on the main chance. In some areas, these virtues have been dissipated by the emigration of young people or by failure to assimilate new forces. Elsewhere, however, the Welsh tradition is capable, not only of survival, but of adaptation and development. For decades, the young people of rural Wales have accepted their pop music from America and their politics from England. Now they have developed, not merely a pop idiom but a pop industry of their own, to such effect that groups from the industrial south-east are learning to sing in Welsh for the sake of their pockets as well as of their popularity. Both idiom and industry have strong political overtones: the world of Welsh pop is only one end of a spectrum at the other end of which may be found the young technocrats and academics who produced such a comprehensive economic plan for Wales for the Plaid Cymru Research Group, a plan which recently drew praise from Lord Crowther.

The significance of all this is, not only that Welsh communities are more likely to resist the coming of large units – or, if not to resist them, to resent their coming, which is even more debilitating — the passing of the small unit is, in Wales, more likely to involve a loss and less likely to involve a gain. There is much less point in enabling communities to appoint more official organisers of this and that if they themselves need less organising. The voluntary principle runs deep into Welsh life. Before the conquest of 1282, few of our leaders had achieved much success in building up a unitary Welsh state: in England, "the primary unit was England . . . In Wales the primary unit was the commote, an area which might on occasion be no larger than a single parish, and whose name is the basis of the Welsh word for neighbour."[3] Between 1282 and the Act of Union of 1536, the March remained an area of free lordships. And no sooner had the Tudors accustomed Wales to central authority than the rise of non-conformity began to fragment Welsh life once again in the sphere which really mattered. It has been suggested that, when non-conformity was dominant and government still remote from ordinary life, Wales virtually had self-government: by the same token, the localities of Wales were also largely autonomous during the last century.

Organised religion carries comparatively little weight in Wales today, but the political ethos of non-conformity still colours social attitudes over much of the country. People who have seen for themselves that ministers of religion subject to little, if any, central supervision and control are in no way inferior to those of the hierarchical churches are likely to be sceptical about the difference which more administrators and advisers can make to the quality of teaching in schools or to the work of social workers in the field.* People who have been used to taking a vote on every question from the selection of

---

* Of all the religious denominations, the most unauthoritarian and, indeed, anarchic of all — the Congregationalist — probably has not only the best educated ministry but the ministry most receptive to new ideas. Each Congregational congregation is completely autonomous and directly democratic, while the Welsh Congregational Union itself is a voluntary organisation which anyone can join as a voting member, and which has only persuasive powers over the affiliated churches. Autonomy does not mean isolation, however, and one wonders whether social workers and teachers would not be happier and more efficient as independent contractors (individually or in partnership) than under the direct supervision of Directors, a point not without relevance to the question of local authority areas.

visiting preachers to the cost of a new organ — and to discussing abstract questions like "Are there degrees of sin?" without expert guidance — are not likely to welcome large units in which their votes count for nothing. For better or for worse, democracy is the Welsh way of life. Attitudes rooted in non-conformity — or in the free principalities and lordships of the Middle Ages — still crop up in the Trade Union, the Flower Show and the Swimming Pool Association. As the authors of *The Miners' Next Step* put it, "the men who work in the mine are surely as competent to elect (officials) as shareholders who may never have seen a colliery. To have a vote in determining who shall be your fireman, manager, inspector etc. is to have a vote in determining the conditions which shall rule your working life ... To vote for a man to represent you in Parliament, to make rules for, and assist in appointing officials to rule you, is a different proposition altogether".[4]

In the course of a plea for the retention of small units, Wynne Samuel admits that "the bane of local government in the past has been magnified and dangerously narrow parochialism".[5] It is quite possible, however, that this trait has only been kept alive during the past twenty-five years by fear of amalgamation. The spirit of co-operation for which Samuel pleads — in order to save small authorities — has been a feature of social life in both rural and industrial Wales. It was the Liberal Tom Ellis who claimed in 1892 that, though Wales was then largely individualist, one could not but feel that it had been "the land of *Cyf*raith, *Cyf*ar, *Cyf*nawdd, *Cym*orthau and *Cym*anfaoedd,* the land of social co-operation, of associative effort" and that it was "significant that the initiator in Britain of the movement for collective and municipal activity in the common effort for the common good was Robert Owen, who embodied ... the spirit of the old Welsh social economy".[6]

---

* The Welsh prefix *Cyf* or *Cym* means 'together'.

II

If Wales has taken little advantage of separate treatment and has failed to insist on a local government system adapted to her own geography and her own ways of thought, this is probably because Welsh administrative autonomy is a comparatively new concept and because only in recent years has the University of Wales constituted departments of political science and government. On the whole, such political thought as has been generated in Wales has been concerned with devolution from Westminster as opposed to local government within Wales. Indeed, the assumption is often made that the first step to the solution of any specifically Welsh problem is a Welsh Parliament: even a question like the status of the Welsh language was neglected for generations, tacitly on this ground.

The first White Paper on Local Government issued by the Welsh Office (Cmnd. 3340) had a familiar ring, both to those acquainted with conventional English thought on the subject and to those who had studied previous proposals for Wales. It proposed the reduction of the number of counties from thirteen to five, the inclusion of the County Borough of Merthyr in the County of Glamorgan and the reduction of the number of county districts from 163 to 36. It also proposed a nominated Council for Wales – "an evolution of the Welsh Economic Council and certain other organisations peculiar to Wales" – to encourage co-operation between local authorities. Three of the five counties were to be created by amalgamation, the five northern counties becoming the County of Gwynedd, Montgomeryshire, Breconshire and Radnorshire becoming the County of Powys and the three south-western counties forming the County of Dyfed; Glamorgan and Monmouthshire were to be subjected only to minor boundaries changes; later the Labour Government accepted that the five counties of North Wales should form two new counties rather than one. The Local Government Boundary Commission of 1947 had put forward tentative plans for grouping the rural counties on lines broadly similar to those

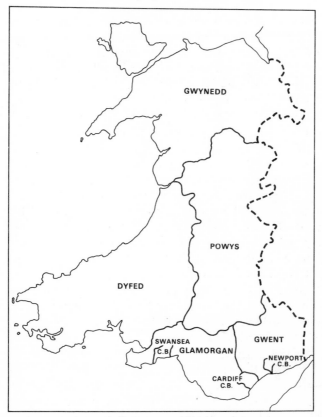

Map 7. Welsh Office Wales

of the White Paper. In 1961, again, the Local Government Commission for Wales had advocated five counties in their draft proposals, with Radnor and Brecon going in with Monmouthshire, and Montgomeryshire joining Denbigh and Flint to form a second county in the north. The final proposals of that Commission, published in December, 1962, provided for seven counties, however – by leaving well alone in Anglesey (which was well represented on the Commission) and by carving out a brand new county across the centre of Wales. The constant theme behind all these proposals is the need for larger counties: that so many different permutations were considered feasible suggests, however, that large coun-

ties were advocated more as an act of faith than as a practical
solution for actual difficulties.

The first White Paper was blatantly unsatisfactory in several
ways.[7] It hardly touched the question of South-East Wales –
about the only part of Wales where the pattern of life and
work *had* changed substantially – and it came as no surprise
when, after the Redcliffe-Maud Report, the Welsh Office
published a second White Paper (Cmnd.4310) amending the
first. This dealt only with Glamorgan and Monmouthshire and
proposed their division into three Redcliffe-Maud type unitary
authorities based on Swansea, Cardiff and Newport respectively. The position remained unsatisfactory, however, even
from the point of view of conventional reformers. For one
thing, if the city region principle was to prevail, parts of
Carmarthenshire and Breconshire should have been considered
along with Glamorgan and Monmouthshire; for another it was
odd of the Labour Government to propose the retention of
district councils, with very limited powers, in the remainder
of Wales, and in the remainder of Wales alone. This in itself
suggests that Wales should have had – and should now have –
a Royal Commission of her own.

Another unsatisfactory feature of the first White Paper was
its reliance on the case put forward by the Local Government
Commission for Wales in 1962, a case already out of date
(most of the specific defects listed in it had already been
remedied) and never tested at public inquiries as had been
intended, and a case which Sir Keith Joseph, on behalf of the
Government of the day, had declared to be unconvincing.
Had not the Local Government Commission themselves
admitted that, within the limits imposed upon them, the job
of reorganisation could not be done properly?[8] Again we
come up against the fatal flaw in all recent reports on reorganisation: that they deal principally with areas, whereas
the basic problems are in the realm of functions and, still
more, finance.

Mainly by a process of assertion and rarely by pin-pointing
defects of substance, the Local Government Commission did,
nevertheless, create a general impression that local govern-

ment in Wales was, as they put it, incapable of "more than mere maintenance of a standard of service barely sufficient to stave off adverse criticism from the public, from the press and from the overseeing government department".[9] Now there is certainly a good deal wrong with government in Wales, but its defects are not confined to local, as opposed to central, government or to small, as opposed to large, authorities. In Pembrokeshire, for example, the County Council Homes for the Elderly are all in superlative condition, while Withybush Hospital, the responsibility of a central department, actually has holes in the floor. Again, the road system for which the County Council is responsible is the subject of general admiration, while the railway system, centrally controlled, is not only worse than it was in the thirties but is not even kept clean and tidy.[10] If a county is too small to have a council of its own, there is little doubt that the unit which takes over will find providing it with a full service to be "uneconomic".

Local Government in Wales was prepared in secrecy by a working party, consisting of Professor Ivor Gowan (a former civil servant as well as a former councillor) and senior officers from six Ministries, which consulted "a number of people whose names were suggested by the Local Authority Associations for their knowledge and experience of local government"[11] but whose names have never been disclosed. The Welsh Office were thus able to play down discussion of an alternative solution which, according to the White Paper itself, was favoured by a substantial minority of their informal advisers; had the working party been a Royal Commission, Wales might have produced her own Derek Senior! The working party did construct two hypothetical models.[12] The rejected model provided for a single tier of most-purpose authorities, but it was only about two years after the publication of the White Paper that Rhys David of the *Western Mail* managed to obtain a map of these authorities, many of which were based on the existing counties.[13] Only eighteen months before the publication of the White Paper, Professor Gowan himself had expressed support for a similar solution in his inaugural lecture. In this lecture, the Professor

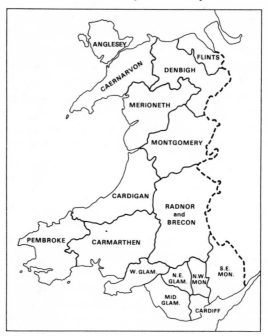

Map 8. Wales: the Organic Alternative. The administrative map of Wales as it would appear divided into 16 "most-purpose" authorities.

SUGGESTED MOST-PURPOSE AUTHORITIES

	Population in 1964	Area	Ratable Value at 1/4/65
Anglesey	53,650	176,964	1,254,741
Caernarvonshire	119,820	364,108	3,351,592
Merioneth	38,870	422,372	977,729
Denbighshire (including the present detached parts of Flintshire)	182,502	458,377	5,542,155
Flintshire (remainder)	149,758	133,308	6,926,193
Montgomeryshire	43,720	510,110	829,329
Breconshire and Radnorshire	72,620	770,446	1,823,224
Cardiganshire	53,250	443,189	1,190,929
Carmarthenshire	167,120	592,577	4,408,843
Pembrokeshire	95,350	393,007	3,040,597
West Glamorgan	309,570	161,514	11,530,879
Cardiff	319,718	35,200	13,990,004
North-East Glamorgan	274,522	83,817	4,580,913
Mid-Glamorgan	272,264	201,905	10,770,285
North West Monmouthshire	246,042	95,526	5,728,447
South East Monmouthshire	270,047	254,176	9,840,174

listed a number of functions, including "training colleges, technical colleges, certain types of special school, water supply, police, fire, civil defence, most aspects of town and country planning, national parks and provision for the arts," which "could be done much better and more efficiently for an administrative unit of the size of Wales than on a county basis".[14] He therefore suggested an elected council for Wales, together with most-purpose authorities for most of the present counties, "discharging a great deal of the work which the present County Councils do, as well as most of the work now carried out by the County Districts, notably housing and health".

The essential feature of Gowan's plan was that an elected Council for Wales would take the weight off the weaker counties as well as dealing with the strategic planning of Wales as a whole. According to the political correspondents of the Welsh Press, there was, however, both opposition in the Labour Cabinet to a really radical reform of government in Wales in advance of England and opposition amongst a group of Welsh Members of Parliament to an elected council for Wales capable of becoming a focus for nationalism: no doubt it was the same group which had managed to keep Glamorgan and Monmouthshire almost intact in the first White Paper. As for the local authorities concerned, they were consulted only in the most formal sense, mostly through the local authority associations for England and Wales.[15] As for the people of Wales, they seemed to count for nothing. One cannot close a branch railway line to passenger services without a public inquiry, but counties, several of which have existed since the Thirteenth Century, can apparently be destroyed overnight by the unilateral action of the central government. Again, while the electors of Wales have had the opportunity of voting, county by county, on a question as trivial (at a time when the television service is open almost all day) as the opening of public houses on Sunday, there has not even been the most superficial kind of social survey to try to determine whether they wish to retain their county, town and district councils.

The great merit of the alternative solution in the first White

Paper is that it preserves the sense of community of counties with generally accessible county towns and at the same time provides, at the Welsh level, an authority which can compete with the largest English authorities in population and power — a Lancashire or a Birmingham as opposed to a Devon or Shropshire. The proposed new counties are too small to be outstanding large authorities as well as too large to develop a compensatory sense of community. There is little point in amalgamating the present counties merely to provide counties which in no case will have a greater population than Shropshire and which in one case, Powys, will be much weaker than several of the counties due for amalgamation. There is, on the other hand, every reason for resisting amalgamation for the sake of democracy. The proposed counties of Gwynedd, Dyfed, Powys and Clwyd have no common focus and their internal railway systems are on the point of vanishing. Their constituent counties have much less in common than, say, Huntingdonshire and Cambridgeshire, of which the (pre-Redcliffe-Maud) Local Government Commission for England stated, "the character and limitation of the area, the hostility to large units and the lack of genuine leadership in favour of it made the likelihood of good county government very uncertain if a single county were to be created." In fact, most of the rural counties of Wales are natural centres of administration and recognised as such by such bodies as building societies, insurance companies and the Press.[16]

Mr. T. L. Jones, the Chairman of the Pembrokeshire County Council Finance and General Purposes Committee, who practices as an accountant some nine miles from the county town, stated in the course of a debate on reorganisation (on 17 February 1970), "the only authority I would be interested in serving is one responsible for more or less all the local government services in its area, that area being a distinctive area, well known to me, and one within which I can travel to meetings without spending an undue amount of time and expense." In practice, this means areas of more or less the size of the present counties, not only for the sake of travelling to meetings and local knowledge, but also for the sake of constituencies in which an amateur can keep in touch with the electors. Such areas in Wales are more than mere convenient areas. They are communities with a wealth of history and considerable human potential. At one time the "county families" which thought in terms of a county as a whole, rather than of their own locality, were very limited in number. Now it is sportsmen, *eisteddfodwyr,* pop groups, farmers, members of Women's Institutes, naturalists, schoolchildren, who think in terms of their county. Most Welsh people interviewed on television seem to give their origin by reference to their county: few Welsh people have any awareness of the ancient principalities of Gwynedd, Dyfed and Powys: Wales today divides into thirteen counties almost as naturally as the year divides into twelve months. A time when people can so easily lose their roots and sense of identity is not the right time to try to create new loyalties from scratch; neither is it honest to argue that voluntary associations can continue to act on a county basis under the new regime, that it is only county councils, not counties, that are really being amalgamated: the County Council in the County Town is the focus of power and without it a different pattern will emerge. How many county voluntary associations will survive the loss of at least seven county towns of which county government is one of the few growth industries?

It would be vain to draw up firm proposals for the local government structure of Wales until a decision has been taken on the question of an elected Welsh Council. The survival of some of the smaller counties depends upon the institution of such a council, but an elected council is also worth having in its own right. On the one hand, it would have the advantage of that massive Welsh emotional support which now has to be directed into sport. On the other, it would, even according to the conventional wisdom, be big enough to levy a local income tax, to pay full-time Ministers, to attract outstanding practitioners of the new management techniques, and to provide a career structure for a graduate administrative class. It would be wrong for any Government to act on the Welsh Office White Papers when so much academic, political and public opinion across the whole party spectrum in Wales now appears to favour an elected council capable both of providing supportive services for local government and of taking over services from the Welsh Office and other departments of state. In 1963, one of the most incisive thinkers in the Labour Party, Mr. Gwilym Prys Davies, now Chairman of the Welsh Hospital Board, published a pamphlet with a foreword — admittedly non-commital — by the Rt. Hon. James Griffiths, advocating an elected council for Wales,[17] while, according to J. P. Mackintosh, "it is not hard to imagine that such a convinced democrat as Cledwyn Hughes (the Secretary of State at the time) would have preferred (the nominated Council for Wales) to have been elected, perhaps on the basis of two members for each Parliamentary Constituency".[18] Then there is Professor Gowan's inaugural lecture of 1966, the Professor being a member of the Conservative Party's Panel on Welsh Affairs and a former Conservative County Councillor. Plaid Cymru naturally favour an elected council as better than nothing, while Professor Keith-Lucas, on behalf of the Liberals, suggested much the same solution as Professor Gowan as early as 1962 and Professor Robson regards this solution as "bolder and more imaginative" than that of the Local Government Commission.[19] Two successive Commissions have reported that it is impossible to reform local government in Wales without a review of functions and finance as well as of boundaries, while Mr. James Griffiths succeeded in keeping Wales out of the purview of the Redcliffe-Maud Commission on the grounds that the Welsh Office themselves intended to consider functions and finance. How, therefore, can anyone accept White Papers which hardly touch upon finance and functions? However mercilessly the first White Paper may have dealt with tender concepts like local loyalty and democracy, which take so long to cultivate, on the more technical side of local government, it was completely conservative.

III

An elected council for Wales helping to support and supplement the work of most-purpose authorities mostly based on the existing rural counties could, even within the limits of the conventional wisdom, provide Wales with a more democratic and organic form of local government than the system advocated in the White Paper. At the same time, provision should also be made for those smaller cells with which people are even more ready to identify themselves. There is little point in striving to retain the type of district council advocated in the White Paper, however. There is no prospect at all of any delegation of functions to them and even if – against all the odds – they retain their two remaining functions of substance, sewerage and housing, they will be under increasing pressure to become central agents in these. As Wynne Samuel puts it, "if the White Paper proposals, with the important addenda published since by the Secretary of State for Wales, are embodied in a Parliamentary Bill, it does mean that, whatever may be said for the new County Council Administrative Units, the proposed new District Councils will be ineffective, stripped of almost all the powers and functions which are now vested in Borough and District Councils".[20] Even today, the functions of a district council are hardly worth having in themselves. Sewerage is essentially technical, immensely expensive, potentially dangerous and largely dependent on Welsh Office loan sanction: it is essentially a function for an authority concerned with pollution over a large area.[21] Housing should be the affair primarily of the tenants themselves, insofar as they are ordinary families, and of a Social Services Department, insofar as they are families in need of special help. In any case, it is not functions such as these which make county district councils important today, but the fact that they provide their districts with a general intelligence and executive service capable of bringing pressure upon other authorities. The type of commune suggested in the previous chapter will do this work just as well as the present county district. One thus suggests that even the smallest borough and urban district councils should remain in being as communes with a general power to raise taxes, and a general power to act, but no specific duty other than planning decisions, providing the higher authorities with information about their own area and providing the public with information about government services at all levels. They would also have the right to act as school governors and managers of old peoples' homes and other county institutions in their own area, and the right to raise extra revenue (on or off the rates) to effect improvements at these institutions. The areas of rural district councils would, in consultation with their electors, be divided into communes with similar functions, possibly on the basis of primary school catchment areas. In some areas, the parishes surrounding a town might wish to join it, while some home-geneous rural districts like Llŷn in Caernarvonshire might be retained. Each commune would have a clerk paid out of the county fund. Which local services they should take over would be a matter for negotiation with the county: initially, they should all, perhaps, be vested in the county.

IV

There remains the difficult question of how exactly to divide up South-East Wales. In his inaugural lecture, Professor Gowan states that Radnorshire is too small to be a most-purpose authority and that Glamorgan and Monmouthshire are too large. The solution for Radnorshire is relatively simple: to join Breconshire, with which it forms a single parliamentary constituency, or alternatively, to rely rather more than the other counties upon a Council for Wales. Glamorgan and Monmouthshire present some difficulty. On the one hand, one does not wish to detract from the autonomy of Swansea, Newport and Merthyr, let alone from that of the capital city of Cardiff. Neither does one wish to destroy administrative counties which have a good record in many fields and which have not been slow to co-operate with the rest of Wales. Of the unitary authorities proposed in the

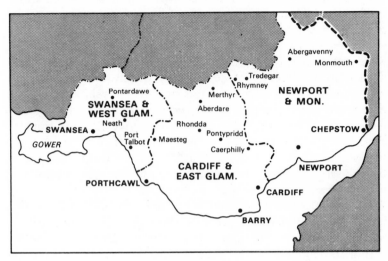

Map 9. South-East Wales

second Welsh Office White Paper, one – Cardiff and East Glamorgan – would have an even greater population (919,000) than the present administrative county of Glamorgan (742,000). Such authorities would deprive of their political identity both the proud valleys which pioneered socialism and some of the few units in Wales where a Conservative can breath freely. As Rhys David puts it, "the new Cardiff authority will contain ten former borough or urban councils with a population of between 20,000 and 40,000, two of between 60,000 and 100,000, as well as Cardiff itself with 300,000. Each of these areas has been used to considerable autonomy and will feel particularly strongly the loss of civic powers. Barry, Merthyr, Pontypridd, Aberdare, Maesteg, Bridgend and Caerphilly, all well established urban centres, will be expected to adjust to having scarcely more powers than are now held by parish councils."[22] No wonder that the Lord Mayor of Cardiff, Alderman Lincoln Hallinan, should have protested against the prospect of Cardiff being "swamped and degraded" by the new proposals and said that he was "sad at seeing the City in danger of being reduced after its past greatness and capital status to a mere community council whose views are requested on local opinions". As Alwyn D. Rees put it in an editorial in *Barn*,[23] there are two ways of destroying the feeling of community of any unit: one is to join units between which there is no existing relationship so that it will take generations for the new unit to create a new feeling of community; the other is to divide the traditional units; the proposals in the second Welsh Office White Paper succeed both in destroying Cardiff, Swansea and Newport by the first method and in paralysing Glamorgan and Monmouthshire by the second.

   Could one then leave well alone and rely upon a Council for Wales to undertake, possibly through the medium of a special committee or committees upon which the local authorities concerned were represented, the strategic planning of the city regions or of industrial South Wales as a whole? The main objection to this is the fact that Glamorgan is so strong numerically in relation to the other units of Wales: with almost one-third of the population, it could, especially in combination with a Monmouthshire of like political complexion, dominate a Council for Wales to the point where Cardiff, as well as particular valleys within the county itself, felt that the Council was merely a rubber stamp for Glamorgan. Again, as we have seen, district councils on the present – or any likely future – pattern do not have sufficient functions of substance to be worthwhile: it is surprising to find Professor Gowan arguing that the solution is to retain the areas of the proposed new unitary authorities, but to divide them into districts like the proposed new counties.[24] A Redcliffe-Maud metropolitan solution would have been preferable to this, but again a metropolitan region either for the whole of industrial South Wales or for East Glamorgan would be too large in relation to the rest of Wales. The best solution for South-East Wales is probably to retain Cardiff, Swansea and Newport, divide Glamorgan and Monmouthshire into several new most-purpose counties and institute a committee for the

strategic planning of industrial South Wales as a whole —
preferably as a committee of the Council for Wales. Exactly
how many new authorities this would involve would be a
matter for argument: Plaid Cymru suggest six, while even the
magic figure of 250,000 would allow us to split administrative
Glamorgan into three: there could even be as many most-
purpose authorities as the districts proposed in the White
Paper — fifteen, none of which would be as small as Cardiganshire and many of which would have a population of 100,000.
The principle might even be extended to Carmarthenshire,
with a separate authority for the Llanelli region, and to Den-
bighshire, with an authority for the Wrexham region. It is
with regret that one would break up some Glamorgan departments, though the Council for Wales would probably inherit
the expertise and the special institutions which they have
built up. Paradoxically, the division of Glamorgan would also
enable a broader view to be taken of industrial South Wales
as a whole.[25] For all the arguments in the White Paper for
regarding Cardiff, Swansea and Newport as the foci of distinct
regions, the problems of the valleys, the coastal strip and the
intervening areas of South Wales are linked latitudinally as
well as longtitudinally. The strategy requires a broader view
than that of the proposed unitary authorities — one need only
think of the link between Newport and Cardiff: the detail
requires very much narrower views. Again, the basic question
is not, how big the unit should be but, what sort of unit — an
authoritarian unit imposed from outside, or a federal unit
built up from below, a unit of command or a unit of co-
ordination, and there can be no argument as to which a
Welshman prefers and within which he is at his best. "The
image and prestige of such a U-class as we possess are in-
sufficiently powerful to compel social emulation," says Glyn
Jones ". . . the Welshman is (not) fundamentally less snobbish
than the Englishman, but he lives in a society whose climate
gives the exercise of snobbery less opportunity."[26]

V

Wales has more to gain than most countries from putting her system of local government right and more to lose than most countries from not doing so. That the doyen of the Welsh nationalist movement, Saunders Lewis, should have placed so much emphasis on the nation as a society of societies, or a community of communities,[27] suggests that the Welsh concept of nationality itself is less artificial, less illusory, less inimical to local reality than such concepts have sometimes proved to be. That a man like Raymond Williams from the Border Country of Monmouthshire is so preoccupied with the development of a "common culture" and communities which govern themselves, and are not governed by Them,[28] suggests that the emphasis on government by community is something which unifies Wales across all those divisions of language, background and philosophy which make Welshness, in all its variety, at once so well worth preserving and so difficult to preserve.

There can hardly be a country in the world — not even Switzerland — whose literature is so suffused with regional and local feeling as that of Wales. "The people of Llanuwchllyn, the land of Llanuwchllyn, the history of Llanuwchllyn" — to Owen Edwards, who had such influence upon Welsh-medium education, this was Wales; and if Llanuwchllyn was essentially "a collection of homes," so was Wales, her history "not the history of kings . . . but the history of the counsellors and leaders of the people".[29] Llanuwchllyn proper was only the first of many Llanuwchllyns in recent Welsh literature: Llanddeiniolen, for example, where, as a child, Edwards' biographer, W. J. Gruffydd, "could describe the mantelpiece of almost every home in the district, could recognise the particular scent of each hearth, know in which home there was a framed portrait of Garibaldi, in which a copy of the *Gwyddionadur*, who owned a yellow cat called Sam, and where there was a glass rolling-pin on the wall;"[30] or D. J. Williams' Llansawel — less political and literary than Llanddeiniolen — "one of the most committee-less districts in the whole of

Wales" no less — and less fanciful and contrived than Dylan Thomas' Laugharne for all its complement of wits and characters; and then, at the other extreme, Iorwerth Peate's Llanbrynmair — more than a landscape for his poetry, more than the material culture which made Peate the founder of the Welsh Folk Museum at St. Fagans, mainly indeed a religious and political attitude of uncompromising individualism, rationality and pacifism.

Parry-Williams' Rhyd-ddu, Llwyd o'r Bryn's Sarnau, T. Rowland Hughes' Llanberis, Kate Roberts' Rhosgadfan, Hugh Evans' Cwm Eithin, Islwyn Williams' Ystalyfera, Myfyr Wyn's Sirhywi, J. Glyn Davies' Llŷn, Caradog Prichard's Bethesda, I. D. Hooson's Rhos, Glanffrwd's Llanwynno, Marion Eames' Dolgellau: the list is interminable but each contribution added utterly distinctive. In Anglesey, according to Emyr Humphreys, "roadmen . . . write splendid books which ostensibly are about their experiences in the Great War or working on paddle steamers on the Mississippi but are in fact paeans of unrestrained praise to the island of their birth."[31] And is not "Sir Gaerfyrddin" (Carmarthenshire) one of the recurring images of the greatest of our recent poets?

In Glamorgan and Monmouthshire, the tradition continues in English, somewhat distorted at times by playing to the international gallery but still recognisable in Jack Jones' Merthyr and Gwyn Thomas' Rhondda, in the "Passionate People" of Gwyn Jones' Monmouthshire, in Idris Davies' Rhymni and in Dylan Thomas' Swansea. Of all the regional writing of Wales it is, however, the poetry of Waldo Williams which is at once the most profound and the most political, with the co-operative ways of the farming community on the southern slopes of the Preseli transformed into a vision of society, and their long tradition of independence of mind steeling the poet to defend this vision at all costs:

> "Hon oedd fy ffenestr, y cynaeafu a'r cneifio
> Mi welais drefn yn fy mhalas draw.
> Mae rhu, mae rhaib drwy'r fforest ddiffenestr
> Cadwn y mur rhag y bwystfil, cadwn y
>   ffynnon rhag y baw"[32]

However symbolic the land itself may be in this literature of locality, however pervasive the history, it celebrates people above all, and celebrates them with that Welsh gift for lionising outwardly very ordinary men and women for what they are, not for where they have reached: Rhobet Wiliam y Wern Ddu, Dafydd Ifans y Siop, Catrin Cadwaladr, Cymdeithas y Porfeydd Gwelltog, Gruffydd Jones y Deryn Mawr.

In English, Glyn Jones has summed it up admirably in a long poem to Merthyr:

> "Lord, when they kill me, let the job be thorough
> And carried out *inside* that county borough
> Known as Merthyr, in Glamorganshire . . .
> Not sheep and birds about me, but lively men,
> And dead men's memories,
> O Lord. Amen."[33] (*his* italics)

Few enough Welsh people are aware of the wealth of their own localities; few try to harness local feeling to local government; even the ablest of the few cannot put the humanity of it all into adequate words; the curriculum of many of our schools tends to be narrow and British rather than human and parochial. But the potential, the propensity, is still there for developing that intelligent love of one's own locality upon which any revival of local government and of general democracy must be based. And there are undoubtedly some outstanding Welshmen in politics and in government today principally for the love of that collection of localities, Wales.

Notes on Chapter 9

1. RCLGE I, para.6.
2. RCLGE, Written Evidence of the Ministry of Housing and Local Government, H.M.S.O. 1967, para.41.
3. Dafydd Jenkins, Law and Government in Wales before the Act of Union, *Welsh Studies in Public Law,* Cardiff 1970, p.7.
4. Unofficial Reform Committee of the South Wales Miners Federation, *The Miners' Next Step,* 1912, extract in Pelling (ed.), *The Challenge of Socialism,* London 1954, pp.214-5.
5. Local Government Reorganisation, *Ymchwil* (Plaid Cymru Research Group) No.16. Mr. Samuel is Town Clerk of Tenby and a member of the Local Government Reform Panel of the Assembly of European Municipalities.
6. *Addresses and Speeches,* p.22.
7. For a review of the White Paper, see my article, Local Government in Wales, 131 *Justice of the Peace and Local Government Review,* 546-8.

8. Report and Proposals paras.17 and 18.

9. *Ibid.*, para.357.

10. Pembrokeshire County Council, *A Unitary Authority for Pembrokeshire*, Haverfordwest, 1970, p.9. The reader is referred to this report for a detailed application to Pembrokeshire of many of the points made generally in the present work. See also the Memoranda of the Anglesey and Cardiganshire County Councils on the White Paper and the Isle of Wight County Council's two-volume "miniature Maud".

11. Cmnd.3340, para.4.

12. *Ibid.*, paras.4 and 12.

13. Rhys David Reveals the Shadow Plan, *Western Mail,*

14. *Government in Wales*, Cardiff 1966. Professor Gowan subsequently supported the White Paper proposals in the press.

15. See my article in *Barn*, Ionawr 1968.

16. See Harold Carter, *The Towns of Wales, A Study in Urban Geography*, Cardiff 1966, pp.118-19 (esp. Fig.18) and p.351.

17. *Cyngor Canol i Gymru*, Aberystwyth 1963.

18. Scottish Nationalism, *Political Quarterly*, Vol.38 No.4 (Oct.-Dec.1967), p.402.

19. Bryan Keith-Lucas, *A Plan for Wales*, London 1962. Robson, *Local Government in Crisis* (2nd ed. 1968) p.132. Professor Robson has a brief chapter on the Situation in Wales, in which he takes Mr. Gwynfor Evans to task for "the extreme conservatism of a Welsh radical." Judging by the Official Report of the Welsh Grand Committee (11 December 1968), however, Mr. Evans appears to support much the same solution as Keith-Lucas and the reason why the Government's proposals should be dropped is "to allow a Welsh Parliament to examine the matter and to legislate on it." (Second Sitting, Col.54) This is certainly the position of Plaid Cymru (Press Statement issued with *An Economic Plan for Wales*, Cardiff, 1970).

20. *Ymchwil*, No.16.

21. The Departmental Working Party on Sewage Disposal recommend that there should be integration of sewage and water conservation functions, which clearly points to larger authorities (Taken for Granted, H.M.S.O. 1970, para.430), though one member, Mr. Ian Percival Q.C. has reservations on the need for integration as opposed to co-ordination and says, "I should have thought that there were quite enough inefficient monsters at work." (p.55).

22. A Case for Compromise, *Western Mail*, 13 May 1970.

23. Mai, 1970.

24. Two-tier Government is Essential in South Wales, *Local Government Chronicle*, 4 April 1970. Tightening Up the Welsh Plan, *Western Mail*, 20 March, 1970.

25. For the present lack of overall thinking and conflicting strategies, see Comment by "Pragma" in *Journal of the Town Planning Institute*, Vol.56, No.1, January 1970 and J. B. Hilling, What Future For The Valleys, *Western Mail*, 4 March 1970.

26. *The Dragon Has Two Tongues, Essays on Anglo-Welsh Writers and Writing,* London, 1968, p.15. This beautifully written book is a far more general introduction to Welsh society than its title might suggest: it must be one of the most important books about Wales ever written.

27. Saunders Lewis, *Cymru Wedi'r Rhyfel*, 2nd ed., Aberystwyth 1942, pp.22-23. D. Myrddin Lloyd, Syniadau Gwleidyddol Saunders Lewis in Pennar Davies (Ed.) *Saunders Lewis, Ei Feddwl a'i Waith*, Denbigh 1950, pp.47-50.

28. See the last chapter of *Culture and Society*, and also Williams's essay in *Conviction* (Ed. Mackenzie) 1958 and his novel, *Border Country*.

29.   W. J. Gruffydd, *Cofiant Owen Morgan Edwards I,* Aberystwyth 1937, pp.1 and 2.
30.   *Hen Atgofion,* 3rd ed., Aberystwyth 1956, p.11.
31.   In Love With An Island, *The Spectator,* 22 August 1970.
32.   From Preseli, *Dail Pren,* Aberystwyth 1956. Waldo Williams has been declared bankrupt, had his goods seized and been imprisoned for refusing to pay income tax while military conscription was in force in Wales. He was nevertheless invited by the Pembrokeshire County Council to open the new school at Llandysilio, where he was brought up. A Quaker, he has written in praise of the Welsh Catholic martyrs of the Counter Reformation. A mystic, he has also written some of the wittiest light verse in Welsh.
33.   For the poem in full, see Gerald Morgan (ed.), *This World of Wales, An Anthology of Anglo-Welsh Poetry,* Cardiff 1968, pp.115-118, or J. S. Williams and Meic Stephens, *The Lilting House, An anthology of Anglo-Welsh Poetry 1916-67,* London and Llandybie 1969, pp.50-53.

Appendix

I

From *Barn,* July 1970, by kind permission of the Editor.

The Editor,
The Times,
Printing House Square,
London, E.C.4.

9th June, 1970.

Sir,

The changing fortunes of political parties are of less importance than the maintenance of confidence in the procedures whereby such changes are determined, and it is this confidence that will be sadly shaken in Wales during the forthcoming election. Inasmuch as television has been allowed to become a major electioneering medium, the decision to deny Plaid Cymru more than a fleeting moment to present its case to the Welsh people strikes at the very foundations of democracy.

Like the Conservative and Labour Parties (and unlike the Liberal Party), Plaid Cymru will have a candidate in every one of the thirty-six Welsh constituencies. Since its policy is designed for Wales and not for Britain, it can hardly be expected to contest seats in England. Before 1964, no political party was allowed any broadcasting time unless it contested a minimum of fifty seats — fourteen more than there are in Wales. The injustice of this was recognised in 1964, but the subsequent decision to allow the Scottish

233

Nationalist Party and Plaid Cymru only five minutes each per annum on radio and television within their own territories bore no relation to any principle. Recently, the leaders of the three major British parties decided to share out two and a quarter hours of pre-election party-political television on Welsh channels as follows:

Labour Party (36 candidates): 5 ten minute programmes = 50 minutes.

Conservative Party (36 candidates): 5 ten minute programmes = 50 minutes.

Liberal Party (about 16 candidates): 3 ten minute programmes = 30 minutes.

Plaid Cymru (36 candidates): ½ a ten minute programme = 5 minutes.

The impression given is that, in British parliamentary democracy, possession is nine-tenths of the law, and this impression cannot be removed by a further minor concession to justice. The Welsh and Scottish parties are in any case at a disadvantage because their potential voters receive their main news programmes from London and these programmes naturally give most of their attention to the parties which dominate the scene in England. Given the present system, this in-built bias is largely inevitable, but there can be no legitimate reason for not dividing television time in Wales itself according to the number of candidates which each party has in Welsh constituencies.

We have been deeply disturbed during recent years by the growing number of gifted and morally upright young people in Wales who have resorted in exasperation to infringements of the law and have suffered imprisonment in support of a Welsh cause about the justice of which there can be no dispute. Until now, it was possible to argue with some degree of conviction that their failure to secure justice through constitutional channels was due to bureaucratic inertia rather than to a deliberate abuse of power. If the forthcoming 'election by television' is conducted as described, we shall have no arguments left. No one can defend such a travesty of democracy or the legitimacy of a Parliament elected by such methods. Unless the iniquity of what they are about can be brought home to Mr. Wilson, Mr. Heath and Mr. Thorpe before it is too late, much more than the result of an election will be at stake in Wales during the next few weeks.

Yours faithfully,

(Rt. Rev.) G. O. WILLIAMS, Bishop of Bangor.

(Rev.) J. E. MEREDITH, Moderator Elect of the Presbyterian Church of Wales.

(Prof.) STEPHEN J. WILLIAMS, President of the Welsh Congregational Union.

(Rev.) D. ENOC DAVIES, President of the Welsh Assembly of the Methodist Church.

(Mr.) DIC HUGHES, President of the Welsh Baptist Union.

(Rev.) D. JACOB DAVIES, Chairman of the Welsh Department of Unitarian and Free Christian Churches.

(Rev.) GWILYM R. TILSLEY, Archdruid of Wales and Ex-President of the Welsh Assembly of the Methodist Church.

[N.B. According to *Barn,* the letter was submitted to *The Guardian* when it became clear that *The Times* did not intend to print it but *The Guardian* did not print it either.]

II

From *The Times,* 4 February 1970, by kind permission
of the authors

TWO TIERS OR ONE?

From Professor Peter Hall and Others

Sir,

Fundamental changes in the local government system are
not likely, and indeed ought not, to occur more than about
once in a century, and we are alarmed therefore at the unhappy polarization of views about the way in which the
system should be recast. On the one hand it is urged that the
Redcliffe-Maud recommendations should broadly be adopted,
subject to the addition of two or three metropolitan areas to
those proposed for Merseyside, "Selnec" and the West Midlands; on the other there are proposals for refurbishing the
existing two-tier system of local government, with district
authorities of 100,000 or so population carrying out minor
functions and top-tier authorities of about half a million
responsible for major ones.

In our view neither of these alternatives will do. The
Redcliffe-Maud recommendations, because of their over-
emphasis of the very real advantages of unitary authorities,
involve the creation of areas too large for responsive administration, of personal services, and too small for functions
such as land use regulation, transport and large-scale development which need to be planned or carried out, at least in part,
over wide areas.

The proposed provinces with their exiguous powers, and
local councils promising the worst kind of administrative
confusion, add little if anything to the strength of the
proposals. For example, Sheffield, a candidate for inclusion
in an additional metropolitan area, might move from all-

purpose county borough local government to the bottom of three — possibly four — tiers: local council, metropolitan district council, metropolitan area council and provincial council. So much for a new stream-lined and comprehensible local government system.

The alternative proposition retains many of the worst features of the present system: district councils still inadequate in resources to possess worthwhile powers; and top-tier authorities covering too small an area for planning and large-scale operational purposes.

We have all independently, and now wish jointly, to urge a different proposition: one hundred or more district authorities, their lines drawn to meet socio-geographic considerations (Redcliffe-Maud found 130 to 140, Senior 148, coherent units) to carry out most functions in whole or part; twelve or so large regions, to carry out those functions which call for a wider area — the structure/strategic plan, as opposed to local design planning, housing overspill (but not housing management), refuse disposal (but not refuse collection), water supply, the fire-service, the police (probably) and a few more which demand a larger than district but smaller than provincial area, and many of which make less personal impact upon the citizen. Additionally, the regional authority would stand ready to supply any of the highly specialised aspects of the social services which exceed the capacities of the districts.

Here is a workable system — call it two-tier or not as you prefer — which recognises the virtues of all-purpose authorities and retains them where they are most significant, but by admitting distinctions which the Royal Commission deny or compromise upon, goes further, we submit, than other alternatives towards meeting the twin canons in their terms of reference — effectiveness and local democracy.

Yours faithfully,

PETER HALL, Professor of Geography, University of Reading.

JOHN P. MACKINTOSH, Labour M.P. for Berwick and East Lothian.

K. P. POOLE, Senior Lecturer in Local Government, University of Kent at Canterbury.

W. A. ROBSON, Professor Emeritus of Public Administration, University of London.

P. J. O. SELF, Professor of Public Administration, London School of Economics.

Index

239

242 *Index*